Scepticism

The Problems of Philosophy: Their Past and Present

General Editor: Ted Honderich
Grote Professor of the Philosophy of Mind and Logic
University College London

Each book in this series brings into clear view and deals with a great, persistent, or significant problem of philosophy. The first part of each book presents the history of the problem. The second part, of an analytical kind, develops and defends the author's preferred solution.

Private Ownership
James O. Grunebaum

Religious Belief and the Will
Louis P. Pojman

Rationality
Harold I. Brown

The Rational Foundations of Ethics
T. L. S. Sprigge

Moral Knowledge
Alan H. Goldman

Personal Identity
Harold W. Noonan

Practical Reasoning
Robert Audi

Mind–body Identity Theories
Cynthia Macdonald

If P then Q, the Foundations of
Logic and Argument
David H. Sanford

The Infinite
A. W. Moore

Thought and Language
J. M. Moravcsik

Human Consciousness
Alastair Hannay

Explaining Explanation
David Hillel-Ruben

Scepticism

Christopher Hookway

London and New York

First published 1990 by Routledge
11 New Fetter Lane, London EC4P 4EE

Simultaneously published in the USA and Canada
by Routledge
a division of Routledge, Chapman and Hall, Inc.
29 West 35th Street, New York, NY 10001

Typeset by LaserScript Limited, Mitcham, Surrey
Printed in Great Britain by T.J. Press (Padstow) Ltd, Padstow, Cornwall

British Library Cataloguing in Publication Data
Hookway, Christopher
Scepticism – (The problems of philosophy).
1. Scepticism
I. Title II. Series
121.5

Library of Congress Cataloging in Publication Data
Hookway, Christopher.
Scepticism / Christopher Hookway.
p. cm. — (The Problems of philosophy)
Includes bibliographical references.
1. Skepticism. I. Title. II. Series:
Problems of philosophy
(Routledge (Firm))
B837.H64   1990
149'73—dc20   90–32318

ISBN 0–415–03396–9

Contents

Contents

Contents

Preface

This book is concerned with a collection of arguments which has been growing for two thousand years, and which appears to deny all of our cognitive achievements. We cannot know whether there is a world of independent objects outside our own minds, we cannot be justified in beliefs about the contents of other people's minds, we have no grounds for taking the discoveries of scientists and historians at face value, and so on. We can know nothing – not even that we can know nothing: none of our beliefs is justified. In this book, I am not concerned with particular forms of scepticism – scepticism about other minds, or about historical knowledge, etc. Instead, I examine the general structure of the arguments belonging to this sceptical canon; and I try to decide whether those arguments can in fact threaten our common sense view of the world and our most certain opinions.

'The problem of scepticism' has an odd position in modern philosophy. Students new to the subject respond readily to the suggestion that we cannot establish that our 'waking' experience is not all a dream. The role of Descartes' writings in the way we characterize 'modern philosophy' and in our strategies for introducing it to students suggest that epistemological questions are the core of the subject and that answering scepticism is fundamental to that core. Yet we commonly encounter the charge that attaching importance to the need to refute scepticism is a sign of a distorted philosophical perspective, one that has turned us aside from real problems to deal with puzzles that have no bearing on anything of importance. The first problem of scepticism is thus not to defend or refute it, but rather to explain why we should care about responding to these familiar sceptical arguments.

One reason for this scepticism about the interest of scepticism is that we do not experience the suggestion that all may be a dream as any sort of threat. None of us recognizes it as a real possibility: no serious doubts in our ordinary beliefs result from thinking about it. It is impossible to be a sceptic, we are told, and the attempt to prove what nobody doubts prevents our addressing a range of questions about our ways of investigating the world which genuinely arise from difficulties facing our inquiries. If we are to take scepticism seriously, we must pay proper attention to explaining why doing so matters.

The first six chapters of this book take up four themes in the history of philosophers' engagement with scepticism, focusing throughout on the wider intellectual projects which motivate philosophers' concern with scepticism. The ancient Greek Pyrrhonists bequeathed a large battery of sceptical arguments to later philosophers, but, unlike more recent discussions, their scepticism had a positive ethical dimension. As the writings of the second century Pyrrhonist Sextus Empiricus show, recognizing the force of sceptical challenges was supposed to enable us to suspend belief on all things and, rather surprisingly, to achieve a way of life that was tranquil and fulfilling. René Descartes (1596–1650) enlarged the canon of sceptical arguments, seeking the strongest possible sceptical challenges, defeat of which would establish the credentials of a new science which criticized both common sense and established scientific traditions in order to reveal the mechanisms of nature. David Hume (1711–76) reached a subtle form of scepticism by a different route: rather than relying upon the established canon of challenges to opinions, he sought a natural science of mind, and it appeared to be a consequence of his theory that our epistemic achievements could not be taken at face value. Discussion of these figures enables us to survey the range of sceptical arguments in the philosophical literature, but it also forces us to examine the special philosophical opinions and motivations which led these thinkers to take scepticism seriously.

The fourth historical theme, introduced in chapter II but discussed more fully in chapter VI, is the common sense tradition which denies the relevance of arguments from the sceptical canon to the assessment of our beliefs and methods of inquiry. Exploiting the observation that our confidence in our opinions is never shaken by these sceptical arguments, it offered a variety of explanations of why trusting our common sense certainties is legitimate. As well as examining the writings of the most famous member of this school, Thomas Reid (1710–96), we consider a number of thinkers who, while they are not normally thought of as 'common sense philosophers', can be understood as adopting a similar style of response to scepticism. As well as Reid's near contemporary, Immanuel Kant (1724–1804), these include twentieth century philosophers such as W. V. O. Quine and Ludwig Wittgenstein.

Since so many philosophers have discussed scepticism, a discussion of the history of the 'problem' can avoid superficiality only by being very selective. While I am conscious that a different perspective on this history might have emerged had I chosen to examine the contributions of other philosophers, I hope that the choices I have made allow the most important sceptical themes to emerge. There is little explicit discussion of the pragmatist tradition, but that should not disguise the extent to which my way of thinking about these issues has been shaped by my reading of Charles Peirce (see Hookway 1985). The positive response to scepticism advanced in chapters VII–XI belongs to the tradition described in my fourth historical theme – the common sense tradition. But it could be described as pragmatist in spirit.

This positive response takes seriously the idea that scepticism raises a philosophical problem only if it presents a genuine threat to our cognitive achievements, and chapter VII is devoted to a discussion of how we should understand the 'target' of scepticism. After dismissing some common views of what is threatened – the suggestion that sceptical arguments challenge the possibility of knowledge or certainty – it is argued that sceptical arguments question our ability to participate in the activities involved in inquiry without feeling that our ability to take responsibility for our actions is compromised. Subsequent chapters clarify this perspective, using it to discuss other philosophers' views of scepticism and to explain the importance of concepts like 'knowledge' and 'justified belief' before offering a way of avoiding the impact of sceptical challenges in the final chapter.

I am indebted to my colleagues in Birmingham, several of whom have commented on drafts of portions of the book and with whom I have discussed my views on many occasions. I have benefited also from presenting work in progress as lectures and papers at other universities. From an ancestor of chapter X, which was presented to a graduate seminar in the mid-1970s, to a draft of chapter XI to the department of History and Philosophy of Science in 1989, by way of two papers to the Moral Science Club, Cambridge University has been exposed to a lot of this material and its response to it has led to many improvements. Other institutions which have provided stimulating discussions include the Universities of Keele, Liverpool, Sheffield, Newcastle, Leicester and Lancaster, University College London, and the London School of

Economics. Material from the second half of the book formed the basis of a rewarding and enjoyable series of seminars at the University of Valencia. I am grateful to everybody who contributed to these discussions.

Some of this material has previously appeared in print. I am grateful to Alastair Hannay, editor of *Inquiry*, for agreeing to the appearance of a few sentences from 'The Epicurean argument: determinism and scepticism' in chapter VIII. This appeared in *Inquiry*, volume 32, pp. 79–94. And a slightly different version of chapter VII appeared as 'Scepticism and autonomy' in *Proceedings of the Aristotelian Society* volume XC, 1989–90, pp. 103–18. Passages common to the two versions are © The Aristotelian Society 1990, and are reprinted by courtesy of the editor.

Notes on references

Works cited in the text are listed in the bibliography and are normally referred to by author/date. There are some exceptions to this practice, where standard systems of reference are employed.

References to Kant's *Critique of Pure Reason* provide page references to the first edition ('A') and the second edition ('B'), using N. Kemp Smith's translation (London, Macmillan, 1961).

In referring to the works of Sextus Empiricus, 'PH' indicates *Outlines of Pyrrhonism* and 'M' indicates *Against the Mathematicians*. References give book and standard page numbers. Translations are taken from R. G. Bury (Sextus Empiricus 1933–49) and from Annas and Barnes (1985).

When discussing Peirce's writings, I refer to the *Collected Papers* (Pierce 1931–58) as 'CP', giving volume and numbered paragraph, and to *The Writings of Charles S. Peirce* (1982–) as 'W', giving volume and page.

CHAPTER I

Pyrrhonism: the Life without Belief

1. Introduction

Sceptical arguments were discussed by the earliest Greek philosophers, and both Plato and Aristotle considered fairly extreme sceptical positions in the course of developing their positive views. However, for our purposes, the most important form of Greek scepticism dates from the Hellenistic period. In the early part of the third century BC, Arcesilaus became leader of Plato's Academy; through his influence – and that of Carneades a century later – the Academy became associated with a subtle form of scepticism. The Pyrrhonist movement was founded by Aenesidemus when he broke away from the Academy during the first century. He too defended scepticism and took the movement's name from an earlier philosopher, Pyrrho of Elis, who was reputed to have secured happiness through translating his scepticism into practice. As we shall see, Pyrrhonists stressed this practical dimension of their scepticism, claiming to defend a more consistent scepticism than their Academic predecessors.

There are several reasons for concentrating upon the Pyrrhonist school. First, extensive writings by Sextus Empiricus, a late member of the school, have survived. His *Outlines of Pyrrhonism* and *Against the Mathematicians* provide a handbook of Pyrrhonism. Writing in the first century AD, Sextus was probably not an original thinker. However he compiled a compendium of the accumulated wisdom of several centuries of Pyrrhonist thought. Second, these texts are fundamental for understanding the impact of ancient scepticism upon modern philosophy. They began to be studied in the fifteenth and sixteenth centuries, and were translated into Latin in the 1560s. The concern with epistemology and scepticism which characterized much modern

1

philosophy partly reflected the impact of Sextus' writings upon early modern thinkers. We must understand Pyrrhonism if we are to make sense of their responses to scepticism.

A third reason for studying these writings is that ancient scepticism differs from modern versions. Where twentieth-century philosophers interpret scepticism as the doctrine that none of our beliefs are justified, or that none of them count as knowledge, ancient scepticism seems more radical. The Pyrrhonist attacks the possibility of belief: his argument is directed towards persuading us to suspend judgment on all things. The practical dimension of ancient scepticism is that a true Pyrrhonist has no beliefs at all. For the most part, modern philosophers perceive scepticism as a threat. Sceptical arguments challenge our sense that we have reliable information about our surroundings, and force us to reflect upon justification and truth hoping to restore our assurance that we do have knowledge. In contrast to this, Pyrrhonists come to question the desirability of knowledge: the life of one who holds no beliefs turns out to be tranquil and fulfilling. Other philosophers had seen the pursuit of truth as a means to achieving a happy life; Pyrrhonists alleged that happiness was secured by abandoning this pursuit.

There is a further difference. Since the seventeenth century, a major focus of discussions of scepticism within epistemology has been the problem of the external world. A concern with how subjective data can provide information about an objective world joins discussions of scepticism to examinations of the nature of perception. How can what is given to us through perception justify the view that there is a world of external objects? The ancient sceptical texts do not formulate the problem of the external world in the modern style. Their scepticism is directed much more broadly and is not linked to specific theories of perception. This is related to the moral dimension of ancient scepticism, and raises some interesting issues: why was there this change in the nature of philosophers' concern with scepticism?; and did the broader practical orientation of the ancient variety represent philosophical insights which have been lost to modern philosophy?

Before examining the details of Pyrrhonism, it will be useful to acknowledge some *prima facie* difficulties that it faces. If we hold in mind a number of 'obvious objections' to the position just described, we shall appreciate the subtlety of the Pyrrhonist response to them. First, if Pyrrhonism is a philosophical position, then a Pyrrhonist must hold certain philosophical beliefs. This seems to conflict with his willingness to suspend judgment on all things. It is inconsistent to judge that one

2

must suspend judgment on all things – just as it is inconsistent to claim to *know* that nothing can be known. There is a structural problem here about how a sceptic can reconcile the philosophical conclusion that knowledge or belief is impossible with his claim that this is a conclusion which he believes or knows to be true.

Second, there is a tension between two features of Pyrrhonism. We cannot act in the world unless, as well as having desires, we have beliefs about how those desires can be satisfied. Somebody who lived wholly without beliefs would be unable to act, having no opinions to guide his pursuit of his ends. Moreover, having no beliefs about his surroundings, he would be unable to foresee impending danger and take precautions. That such a life would be fulfilling and tranquil is highly dubious. Not only might the agent be reduced to torpor, unable to pursue the ends which are constitutive of his happiness, but he would be assailed by unpleasant surprises which he was unable to anticipate. Although he does not believe that jumping from the window is a hazardous way to leave a high building, and has no opinion that hitting the ground from a great height would be painful, there is little chance that he would endure such a fall without disturbing his tranquillity. These reflections suggest a third difficulty. In most such cases, suspension of belief is psychologically impossible: it is absurd that a philosophical argument could genuinely produce agnosticism about the objects of the great majority of everyday beliefs. Although we have not yet considered the arguments that are designed to produce suspension of belief, we can feel confident that no such argument could achieve its desired object. It is in the spirit of these objections that Hume complained:

> The great subverter of *Pyrrhonism* or the excessive principles of scepticism is action, and employment, and the occupations of common life. These principles may flourish and triumph in the schools; where it is, indeed, difficult, if not impossible, to refute them. But as soon as they leave the shade, and by the presence of the real objects, which actuate our passions and sentiments, are put in opposition to the more powerful principles of our nature, they vanish like smoke, and leave the most determined sceptic in the same condition as other mortals.
>
> (1748 p.126)

and Thomas Reid observed that 'the great Pyrrho himself forgot his principles on some occasions', being said to have been in 'such a passion with his cook, who probably had not roasted his dinner to his

3

mind, that with the spit in his hand and the meat upon it, he pursued him even into the market place' (1764 p.102).

Sextus Empiricus was familiar with such arguments. The objection that the claim to know that nothing can be known involved an inconsistent 'negative dogmatism' was employed by the Pyrrhonists themselves against the 'Academic Scepticism' of Arcesilaus and his followers. Pyrrhonists sought consistency: to be a Pyrrhonist did not involve holding philosophical beliefs, and, even without beliefs, they claimed that there was a satisfactory basis for action. The most distinctive characteristics of Pyrrhonism involve its sophisticated response to these *prima facie* difficulties.

2. *Pyrrhonism: the elements*

In his *Outlines of Pyrrhonism*, Sextus provides a definition of scepticism:

> Scepticism is an ability, or mental attitude, which opposes appearances to judgments in any way whatsoever, with the result that, owing to the equipollence of the objects and reasons thus opposed, we are brought firstly to a state of mental suspense and next to a state of 'unperturbedness' or quietude.

(PH1 8)

The characterization of scepticism as an 'ability' rather than a 'doctrine' is the key to his response to some of the objections mentioned above. However, we shall understand this most clearly if we first examine the 'main basic principle' of Sextus' scepticism, which is 'opposing to every proposition an equal proposition: for we believe that as a consequence of this we shall end by ceasing to dogmatize' (PH1 12).

If 'a dogmatist' defends a proposition as true, a sceptic will present considerations which count against it, forcing the dogmatist to admit that considerations on either side of the matter are equally balanced and hence to suspend judgment on the matter. In chapter XII of *Outlines of Pyrrhonism*, this practice is illustrated. The sceptic will oppose appearances: for example, someone who affirms that a tower is square is reminded that it only appears so from close up and appears round from a distance. One inference can be opposed by another: meeting someone 'who argues the existence of Providence from the order of the heavenly bodies', the Pyrrhonist will argue to a contrary conclusion from the fact that 'often the good fare ill and the bad fare well'. Or the claims of currently unrefuted theories can be challenged by citing cases where theories which seemed irrefutable were subsequently disproved. Such examples may not be wholly convincing, but they illustrate sceptical practice. If a dogmatist insists upon maintaining his own view in the face of these opposing considerations, he can be asked the principle or criterion he relies upon in so doing. When such a rule is presented, this too can be subjected to sceptical attack. The upshot is that he must own that the matter is, at present, unresolved.

Book I of *Outlines of Pyrrhonism* is largely a handbook of techniques to be employed in thus opposing appearances. Myriad considerations are introduced, divided into ten classes – the tropes or modes of scepticism. Mastery of these enables the sceptic to juxtapose considerations so that we must admit that they are 'equipollent' – equally balanced on each side of a question. The consequence of this is 'epochē': suspension of judgment. It does not lead to the negative dogmatism of asserting that the question has no answer or even of claiming that the truth is forever hidden. The Pyrrhonist continues to inquire, admitting only that the question is still open and that we do not yet know how to answer it.

This brings us to the move from 'mental suspense' (*epochē*) to 'unperturbedness' (*ataraxia*). The connection between knowledge and fulfilment is a common theme in Greek philosophy: knowledge was held to be necessary for virtue and for happiness; the growth of knowledge would enhance human happiness. For the Pyrrhonist's Stoic contemporaries, the good life was one of tranquillity or unperturbedness: *ataraxia* was part of the good. Pyrrhonists threatened this link between knowledge and the good life in two ways: they questioned the possibility of knowledge, and they challenged its desirability. Faced with the appearance that all questions remained open, they turned away from the project of inquiry and found the tranquillity which, it had been supposed, could only be obtained through inquiry. It was not offered as a philosophical conclusion that happiness was to be obtained in this fashion, and no theoretical reasons were offered for expecting it to occur. Rather, that tranquillity results from questioning the desirability of knowledge is a contingent matter. In a famous passage, Sextus alludes to the painter Appelles: despairing of ever being able to paint a horse's foam, he threw his sponge at his canvas, only for it to produce the precise effect that he sought (PH1 28). In the same way, happiness is achieved through abandoning the pursuit of truth.

5

Once the pursuit of the truth is abandoned, the individual lives without 'belief' (dogma). This life, while probably quiet and conservative, avoids the inertia or torpor predicted by Hume. If he avoids 'belief', the Pyrrhonist 'acquiesces in appearances': he is guided by sensory appearances and by bodily needs and natural desires; he conforms to the prevailing customs and standards of his society; and he acquires the skills of a trade or craft. Like Sextus himself, he may live as a doctor. He has no opinions about the non-evident natures of things. So if the Pyrrhonist position is to escape the charge of inconsistency, its interpretation of 'belief' (dogma) must differ from our familiar concept of belief or opinion. As is suggested by the role of the concept in pre-Pyrrhonist Greek moral philosophy, belief has a narrower application than our initial response to Pyrrhonism supposed. Consequently, we must pay close attention to this distinction between belief (dogma) and appearance; if it is internal to the development of Greek philosophy, and is not echoed in our own framework of concepts, then there may be few insights to be gained from Pyrrhonian scepticism.

How should we respond to the challenge that if Pyrrhonism is a philosophical position, then it must involve holding (philosophical) beliefs? Pyrrhonism is a philosophical outlook because it is a response to philosophical claims; it presents a body of techniques for challenging philosophical doctrines. But its positive character involves turning away from philosophy. Pyrrhonists question the desirability of philosophical knowledge, claiming to find what philosophy had sought through abandoning philosophical aspirations. If holding a philosophical position involves defending philosophical *doctrines*, then Pyrrhonism is an *anti-philosophical* stance. The sceptic does not deny that knowledge or justification is possible; nor does he defend as a dogma that knowledge is undesirable. Rather, he concedes that it *appears* that the aims of inquiry are not achievable; and he adds that the truth does not *seem* as desirable as had once been thought.

So understood, Pyrrhonism resembles a method of philosophical therapy rather than a set of doctrines. As we shall see, this raises some difficult issues about how we can engage with Pyrrhonist writings: it is not obvious that they should be seen as presenting rational arguments to be evaluated according to logical standards. Moreover, just what is the role of the achievement of *ataraxia* in the 'defence' of the position. If the benefits of Pyrrhonist lifestyle can be displayed in practice, then arguments that do no more than raise *prima facie* difficulties for the pursuit of truth may suffice to win converts to the sceptical outlook. If

6

there were no such benefits, a dogmatist may discern only a cause for further philosophical inquiry. The anti-philosophical character of the position means that what is at issue is *conversion* rather than rational persuasion.

3. The modes

Book 1 of *Outlines of Pyrrhonism* is largely devoted to the ten modes (or tropes) of Aenesidemus, a traditional collection of techniques to be employed in securing suspension of belief. A Pyrrhonist who has mastered these techniques can use them to challenge assertions made by dogmatists or to combat his own dispositions to judge propositions to be true. With the possible exception of the mode of relation (the eighth mode), these modes exhibit a common pattern. Appearance is relative: how something appears depends upon the cognitive constitution of the subject of appearance; it depends upon the context of the object of appearance; and it depends upon relations between the two, for example the distance between them. If somebody accepts an appearance as a true account of reality, he can be reminded that it appears differently to different observers, or to the same observer standing in different circumstances. Unless he can explain why the appearance he wishes to accept possesses some special authority, it seems that he should withdraw his endorsement of it, claiming only that its object appears this way to such an observer standing in such a relation to the object.

This can be illustrated through the first mode or trope, which 'shows that the same impressions are not produced by the same objects owing to the differences in animals' (PH1 40). Describing a wide variety of 'facts' and observations about animal sensory experience, Sextus attempts to shake our confidence that the sensory impressions produced by objects are the same for all animals. Stressing differences in origins (some come from eggs, others are live born, etc.) and casual observations of the structure of the sensory apparatus of other animals, he argues that different animals have very different physical constitutions. Since we are well aware that how things appear to us depends upon the physical state of our perceptual apparatus, we naturally suspect that creatures with different physical constitutions should receive different impressions (PH1 43). Exploiting the philosophical myth that things look yellow to people with jaundice and red to those whose eyes are bloodshot, he conjectures that things look red to animals whose eyes are in general bloodshot. Experience of trick mirrors suggests that animals

7

whose eyes are concave or convex should receive impressions unlike ours (PH1 48). Creatures covered with scales or feathers may be expected to have different tactile impressions; those with rough dry tongues will find that things taste different; and those 'which have the pupil of the eye slanting and elongated' (PH1 47) will have different visual impressions. Moreover, since our preferences reflect the impressions that things make upon us, we can take the fact that animals have radically different likes and dislikes as showing that they receive different impressions from the same objects (PH1 55–8).

The pattern of argument is as follows:

1 x appears F to animals of kind K
2 x appears F^* to animals of kind K^*
3 It is impossible to decide whether the appearances of K or K^* have authority
4 so we suspend judgment as to whether x is really F or F^*.

(Annas and Barnes 1985 p.39, Striker 1983)

The modes catalogue facts and anecdotes to be used in employing this sort of argument against a dogmatist. Notice, however, that (1) and (2) are consistent: that the sun looks yellow to humans and grey to cows can be part of a single coherent story of the world. It is only against the background of an inquiry concerned with how things *are* in contrast to how they *appear* that the different appearances can be said to *conflict*. The sun cannot, it seems, both be yellow 'in its nature' and grey 'in its nature'. Hence, it is best to see these sceptical challenges as directed against the possibility of various special intellectual projects of this kind. (For further discussion of the philosophical significance of conflicting appearances, see Burnyeat 1979.)

The second trope or mode similarly exploits differences in the physical constitutions and tastes of people. Due to a difference in the 'predominant humours', 'the body of an Indian differs in shape from that of a Scythian' (PH1 80): moreover, 'Indians enjoy some things, our people other things, and the enjoyment of different things is an indication that we receive varying impressions from the underlying objects' (PH1 80–1). The third and fourth modes provide more information about how appearances are relative to the condition of the observer. The third claims that objects make different impressions upon different senses: sweet oil, it appears, 'pleases the sense of smell but displeases the taste' (PH1 92). And the fourth stresses that how things appear to us can depend upon whether we are drunk or sober, angry or calm, hungry or sated, old or young. These first four modes work in the same way: an enormous variety of observations is introduced intended to persuade us that the impressions things make upon us depend not only upon the character of the things themselves but also upon our own constitutions and dispositions. If we claim that human impressions have authority over those of animals, the Pyrrhonist still has the second, third and fourth modes at his disposal; and someone's stubborn insistence that his own appearances are decisive may still be challenged using the third and fourth modes.

What does Sextus do with these observations? Towards the end of his discussion of the first mode, he concludes:

> But if the same things appear different owing to the variety in animals, we shall, indeed, be able to state our own impressions of the real object, but as to its essential nature we shall suspend judgment.

> (PH1 59)

We can make relational judgments about how things appear to us, but we have no basis for saying how things actually are. We obviously cannot employ our own impressions on the grounds that they appear right to us; we require an objective basis for relying upon them. And a proof that our impressions were reliable would not help either: unless the proof appeared sound to us, we should not be justified in relying upon it; but it would be circular to ground our confidence in how things appear to us in the fact that a proof appears good to us (PH1 61 cf. 115–16).

These remarks introduce a fundamental aspect of Sextus' argumentation. Given the conflicts among appearances, we require a rule which will determine which appearances provide us with knowledge of reality. Sceptical probing can then always question why we should think that this rule or criterion is an adequate one. If we merely say that it appears to be adequate, we are guilty of circularity; if we appeal to a further rule or criterion to validate the first one, then we take the first step towards an infinite regress (see PH2 20). This difficulty – the problem of the criterion – is brought to bear by the four modes which, in their different ways, show the relativity of the impressions to the state of the perceiver. This inevitably raises the question of why we should regard them as a reliable source of information about reality, rather than as reflections of subjective illusion. This question can only be answered by providing a rule or criterion.

Most of the other modes proceed in the same vein, pointing to respects in which an object's appearance depends upon features of its context and thus raising the question which appearances are veridical. A ship looks small from a distance, large from close up (PH1 118); the light from a lamp is dim in the sun but bright in the shade (PH1 119); an oar appears bent in water, but straight when out of the water (PH1 119). This forces us to suspend judgment whenever an appearance is of something at a particular distance or location, for 'anyone wishing to give preference to some of these impressions over others will be attempting the impossible' (PH1 121–2). Silver filings appear black when by themselves, white when combined: we cannot say whether they are really white or black (PH1 129–30). And so on: Sextus notes that a substance appears precious because of its rarity, so its value need not reflect its nature; and he responds to those who affirm the correctness of their moral standards, customs and religious practices by pointing to the diversity of such standards and practices in different societies.

These ten modes are not the only sceptical arguments discussed by Sextus: for example, he considers modes challenging our ability to arrive at causal explanations of phenomena (see Barnes 1983). Important, too, are the five modes of Agrippa (PH1 196–9). A dogmatist's claim to have discovered the truth can be challenged by showing that the proposition in question is a matter of 'undecidable dissension ... both in ordinary life and among philosophers'. Second, 'in the mode deriving from infinite regress, we say that what is brought forward as a warrant for the matter in question needs another warrant, which itself needs another, and so *ad infinitum*, so that we have no point from which to begin to establish anything, and suspension of judgment follows'. The third mode is relativity: how something appears is always relative to the subject judging and context, and 'we suspend judgment on what it is like in its nature'. The mode from hypothesis accuses the dogmatist of blocking the infinite regress of justification with something 'assume[d] simply and without proof in virtue of a concession'. Finally, the reciprocal mode accuses the dogmatist of circularity: his justification of his judgment rests ultimately upon propositions whose warrant depends upon the judgment at issue.

This concern with justification, infinite regress and circularity is far closer to modern styles of philosophical discussion than the more famous ten modes. And the abstract epistemological formulations seem more appropriate to a philosophical discussion, a feature they share with the general discussion of the problem of the criterion alluded to earlier.

It may seem surprising that the modes of Agrippa did not supersede the other ten modes. In fact, the two sets of modes have distinct, complementary functions. The modes of Aenesidemus, by enabling the sceptic to provide an appearance which challenges the one which the dogmatist takes to be veridical, place the burden of argument upon the dogmatist to explain the authority of the appearance which he judges to be true. They force him to confront epistemological issues. The Agrippan modes then come into play in order to block any criterion the dogmatist may adopt for grounding the authority of this appearance. Although he does not explicitly state this, Sextus generally employs these modes in establishing step 3 of the Pyrrhonist demonstration described above (for a general discussion of this see Annas and Barnes pp. 88–92, 140–5).

The third Agrippan mode (relativity) functions slightly differently from the others. As Sextus notes, the ten modes all bring out ways in which appearance is relative; and the other Agrippan modes challenge uses of argument to establish the authority of one of these appearances over the others. One might suppose that this leads to an *anti-sceptical* conclusion – relativism. Thus, we *can* make judgments; but they all concern how things appear to creatures of particular kinds in particular contexts. The third mode is relevant to this response: we suspend judgment concerning *what things are like in their nature*. The relativist position just described seems close to Pyrrhonism rather than opposed to it. This brings us back to an issue we have discussed before: what are the beliefs, *dogmata*, or judgments which the Pyrrhonist forswears? If we take seriously the suggestion that accepting these relational propositions involves 'acquiescing in appearances' rather than making judgments, we must gain a better understanding of this apparently crucial distinction.

4. *Dogma and appearance*

What, then, is the difference between, on the one hand, having beliefs, making judgments, holding dogmata, and, on the other, acquiescing in appearances? What sort of distinction is it? Belief and judgment can be viewed as propositional attitudes; the statement that John believes that the distant tower is round has the form:

x *F* that *p*.

It is a familiar point that psychological states can differ in their propositional objects (the substituends for *p*) and in the attitude that is taken towards that proposition (the substituend for *F*). John can believe many different propositions; and he can believe, doubt, suppose, or hope that the distant tower is round.

This helps us to contrast two distinct ways of drawing our distinction. One approach would concede that a single concept of assent or acceptance is involved, and trace the distinction to different classes of propositions that can be accepted. The sceptic limits his assent to propositions with a very restricted subject matter. For example, we could imagine someone suspending judgment on all philosophical or scientific questions while happily assenting to claims about his immediate sensory experience. There are passages which suggest that this is what Sextus has in mind, and this has led some commentators to hold that the Pyrrhonist outlook rests upon a distinctive theory of perception, one which identifies appearances with the objects of immediate sensory experience (e.g. Stough 1969). Sextus' claim that the sceptic 'uses "dogma" in the sense of "assent to one of the non-evident objects of scientific inquiry" while the Pyrrhonian philosopher assents to nothing that is non-evident' (PH1 13–14), suggests that objects of inquiry can be divided into the evident and the non-evident, the sceptic assenting to the former but not the latter. Other passages support the view that it is the content of immediate sensory experience which is evident. For example:

we do not overthrow the affective sense-impressions which induce our assent involuntarily; and these impressions are 'the appearances'. And when we question whether the underlying object is such as it appears, we grant the fact that it appears, and our doubt does not concern the appearance itself but the account given of that appearance.

(PH1 19)

However, such interpretations are unsatisfactory. A Pyrrhonist who relied upon a distinctive philosophical theory about the nature of perception would inconsistently hold dogmata of his own: accepting such a theory would itself involve beliefs about what is non-evident. Moreover, although some appearances concern sensory information, many do not. Sextus' examples suggest that acquiescence in appearance can cover our reliance upon moral standards, our being convinced by arguments or proofs, and so on.

It is best to look for another interpretation, one which denies that appearances are a distinct ontological category. This second way of drawing the distinction contrasts two kinds of assent or acceptance: two modes of approval of propositions. Assertions made by sceptics and dogmatists may differ in force without differing in propositional content, acquiescing in the appearance that *p* and judging that *p* being two distinct mental attitudes towards a common proposition. This talk of force, propositional content and mental attitude itself looks like a fragment of philosophical theory, and we must be careful of committing the Pyrrhonist to a distinctive view about the structure of mental states. However, if we take care, this perspective can provide illumination.

A detour through the Stoic theory of judgment will be helpful (see Frede 1987 ch.9). The Stoics retained a Platonic view of knowledge. A wise man, they held, did not risk holding any false beliefs at all, but he did not purchase this immunity from error by widespread agnosticism. Rather, among our perceptual experiences are some which could not be misleading or erroneous, and wisdom confers an ability to identify which these are. Through our sensory encounters with the world (and perhaps in other ways), objects make impressions upon us. These impressions provide the material for judgment; the will can choose to accept some of these impressions as veridical. There is a distinction between the *passive* receipt of impressions, and the *activity* of accepting, rejecting or suspending judgment on them. Wisdom requires that we have a rule for acceptance which will prevent our making any judgments which are not true. Since all we have to go on in making a judgment is the impression that we are judging, we must rely upon some mark possessed by certain impressions (cognitive or 'cataleptic' impressions) which guarantees their truth.

As this suggests, the Stoics did not view impressions as non-conceptual sensory states, or as a non-propositional given. While the impressions of animals may have this character, we receive 'rational impressions' which have a propositional, subject–predicate, form. The view that impressions are passive is compatible with their having a conceptual structure; it denies only that they depend upon the will. Much sceptical writing had Stoic philosophy in its sights, so this provides a useful background for understanding Pyrrhonism. Moreover, the features of Stoic thought I wish to make use of reflect more pervasive features of the philosophical tradition. The most important points are: judgment is an operation of the will carried out upon impressions which have a propositional structure; and wisdom involves the possession of methods enabling us to tell which rational impressions are true. It is natural to read the sceptical modes as suggesting that there can be no such methods – there are no cataleptic impressions. In the light of the Stoic insistence that judgment is a voluntary activity involving the will, Sextus' linking of the evident with the involuntary is placed in a clearer perspective.

I find myself accepting certain propositions; either they are wholly irresistible or I find it natural to accept them. The phrase 'I find myself accepting' here is supposed to convey the idea that I am the passive recipient of these propositions. As an active reasoning agent, I can question my disposition to accept these things. Since I desire to believe things only if they are true, I can attempt to establish whether these 'beliefs' are acquired in ways that lead to true beliefs. I try to see if they can be defended against critical challenges; and I aspire to hold beliefs only if they can resist such challenges. If my disposition to accept a proposition cannot defeat critical challenges, then there are two possibilities: I may become agnostic about the proposition which, earlier, I found it natural to believe; or if doubting the proposition is psychologically impossible for me, I may still feel alienated from it, viewing it as a belief which I am constrained to believe but which I cannot rationally endorse. Behind this description is a certain conception of reason: we aspire to a sort of autonomous self-control in our cognitive activities. The power of reason is manifested in our ability to assent to things only when we can endorse them as true; and our alienation from those dispositions to assent which we cannot endorse or drive out is an indication of the limits of our rational autonomy. The same active critical involvement with our cognitive activities underlies the practice of assertion. We normally take it that when someone asserts a proposition they take responsibility for its truth: they commit themselves to its truth, and endorse it as true.

The dogmatist seeks propositions which he can actively endorse and responsibly commit himself to. Pyrrhonists abandon this active critical cognitive activity; a responsible inquirer finds there is nothing that he can responsibly endorse or commit himself to. Rather, he allows his life to be guided by the propositions that are naturally impressed upon him, while taking no responsibility for their truth or rationality. He is a ship buffeted by the impressions that come naturally, and does not aspire to autonomous rational self-control. Surprise at discovering *ataraxia* through this passive life enables a sceptic to turn his back upon reason. Whether we should describe this position as distinguishing two kinds of

14

assent, or as employing a unitary notion of assent within two distinct contexts of inquiry, is a question we can safely ignore: any answer to it rests upon a dogmatic philosophical theory of a sort that Pyrrhonists abjure.

At first glance, Jonathan Barnes' recent study of the use of 'dogma' in Greek supports the view that Sextus' scepticism was restricted by subject matter. Although the Greek word's central meaning was just 'belief', he argues, its customary use reflected more restrictive connotations: a dogma is a weighty belief, perhaps with political, ethical or philosophical importance. This suggests that Sceptics suspended judgment only about weighty scientific and philosophical matters and political or ethical principles. As Barnes notes, this explains the usage of Galen when he describes the different medical schools of the day. The empiricists, rejecting the rationalist reliance upon theories in treatment and diagnosis, base their diagnoses solely upon experiential generalizations. By consistently refusing to describe these observational beliefs as 'dogmata', Galen shows 'that a man may reject all dogmata and yet retain innumerable beliefs' (Barnes 1982 p.7).

However, as Barnes insists, even if everyday beliefs are not dogmata, Pyrrhonist scepticism will extend beyond weighty matters to mundane concerns. The sceptic will suspend judgment upon whether his bathwater is really warm or whether his present location is really in Athens. Various arguments can be used to support this view, but the simplest builds upon our remarks about the active character of dogmatic assent. Since judgment is dependent upon the will, our rational acceptance of a proposition can be distinguished from its appearing plausible to us. Barnes argues that, since the will relies upon proofs or criteria in rationally determining some impression to be true, scepticism about proof or about whether there is a criterion of truth prevents our actively endorsing any appearance, whatever its subject matter. Without a basis for choice, the will is impotent. Criteria of truth or validity would be dogmata (weighty matters of philosophical or scientific importance), so someone who is agnostic about all dogma has no basis for judging even undogmatic beliefs to be true. So scepticism about dogmata will infect the judgment in all its activities: the sceptic cannot judge propositions about the warmth of water or location to be true. Although he will, of course, find himself accepting many such claims.

5. *Assertion and action*

The question we now have to consider concerns what is involved in 'acquiescing' in an appearance that is not endorsed by the will. Unless we can make sense of this, we shall not know what it was like to be a Pyrrhonist, and we shall not be able to decide whether Pyrrhonism remains a real option for us or whether it rests upon an untenable philosophy of mind. I shall discuss this issue in two stages. A Pyrrhonist is not mute: he makes many utterances about how things appear, reporting his experiences and reasonings. If he is constantly making 'assertions', it is hard to see how he can fail to believe or judge what he asserts to be so. One commits oneself to something equally by asserting it and judging it: both seem to involve the will. Thus our first task is to explain what is supposed to be going on when a Pyrrhonist makes 'assertions'. The second task is to explain how what is announced in these 'assertions' can determine the sceptic's behaviour without being believed.

Diogenes describes the sceptic's utterances as 'confessions', and Sextus calls them 'avowals', stressing that they 'show' or 'reveal' a Pyrrhonist's mental state. Such avowals are apparently distinguished from full-blooded statements or assertions – they involve a different speech act. We do not use them to assert that we are in particular states, but rather to manifest the states we find ourselves in. As Barnes notes, Sextus might have welcomed Wittgenstein's claim that 'to call the avowal of a feeling a statement is misleading' (*Zettel* 549). In chapter XIX of book 1 of *Outlines of Pyrrhonism*, we read that many of the utterances of a Pyrrhonist (for example when he says that the evidence is equally balanced for and against a dogma) have a misleading surface form: they resemble affirmations or assertions but do not really function in this way. They are better seen as questions – who can find better evidence for one side or the other? – or admissions of ignorance. Thus Sextus seems to view the utterances of the sceptic as expressive, as avowals in, perhaps, Wittgenstein's sense, and not as statements which express propositions to which the will has attached itself in judgment: not every utterance of an indicative sentence is a statement which articulates the speaker's beliefs.

We now turn to the second task: how can appearances guide behaviour without being assented to by the will? How, as Sextus frequently avers that we can (e.g. PH2 246), can we live on the basis of experience and appearances without holding any beliefs or dogmata?

We shall approach this through an example. Suppose it appears to me that the water in my bath is boiling. However, my will does not commit itself to this proposition, I do not judge it to be actually true. In addition, I do not want to get into the bath if the water is boiling: it seems to me that that would be a bad thing, although I do not actually judge that this is so. What happens? Do I have any basis for actually getting into the bath or not? Will I be stuck immobile on the bathmat? Will I foolishly plunge in? Or will I sensibly allow the appearances to guide me in refusing to get in before cold water has been added?

If rational self-control – the deliberate exercise of reason and judg-ment – is essentially involved in action, then I am stuck. If only reason and judgment can mediate between experience and behaviour, then, it seems, I have no basis for acting in one way rather than another. How-ever, there is no reason to think that this mediating role must be filled by self-controlled deliberation or reasoning. Impressions guide the conduct of animals and children although they lack the capacity for deliberation and judgment. In the case above, I may just find myself not wanting to get in the bath – it will appear to me to be a bad idea. And in that case, I may just find myself not getting in the bath, looking for more cold water, and so on. There are natural processes whereby appearances yield fur-ther appearances through 'inference', appearances prompt desires, and appearances and desires lead to action. Rational deliberation involving judgment can interfere with this natural movement, inhibiting or con-trolling its operation. But it has a natural psychological momentum in the absence of this self-control. I simply find myself acting in accord-ance with appearances. The Pyrrhonist standpoint, in that case, involves a disengagement of reason and the will from the practice of utterance – from the choice of what is avowed – and from the determination of conduct. Acquiescence in appearances involves the practical decision not to inhibit this natural momentum through the operations of a faculty of reason which has become crippled through sceptical doubt. If there is no problem about how passive impressions can have a causal impact upon other appearances and upon behaviour, even when unaided by deliberation and the will, then there should be no difficulty about how a Pyrrhonist acts in response to desires and experiences.

We can now return to the material employed by a Pyrrhonist for the 'regulation of life'. It has four components:

one part of it lies in the guidance of nature, another in the constraint of the passions, another in the tradition of laws and customs, another in the instruction of the arts. Nature's guidance is that by which we are naturally capable of sensation and thought; constraint of the passions is that whereby hunger drives us to food as thirst to drink; tradition of customs and laws, that whereby we regard piety in the conduct of life as good, but impiety as evil; instruction of the arts, that whereby we are not inactive in such arts as we adopt.

(PH1 17)

It would be hard to argue that this does not allow the Pyrrhonist to participate in a wide range of activities, but it is a very *conservative* outlook: the appearances he relies upon are salient for him because of their conventional role. He is not guided by any demonstration that such a life will lead to happiness; nor does he believe that he is tracking the truth or the good in living by these appearances. Rather, since this conventional life *does* provide happiness or fulfilment, the Pyrrhonist can turn aside from the attempt to evaluate his beliefs critically and can rest content with the customary standards of his society. He has no need to make real assertions; the search for critical rational self-control has little to recommend it. Although it would be misleading to say that his Pyrrhonist outlook is *justified*, it is (in a sense) vindicated by its success. But – and this is a topic to be returned to below – its success seems all too fragile or contingent. How far does it depend upon the special conditions of Hellenistic society? How would a Pyrrhonist fare in the modern world?

6. Conclusion: Pyrrhonism and philosophy

There are a number of grounds for discontent with the position I have described. Many of the 'facts' used to induce suspension of belief are not facts at all; and even those that can be accepted seem too weak to induce any real doubt. I shall discuss this more fully in the following chapter, but two comments can be made now. First, we may agree that these 'facts' do not seriously challenge our ordinary disposition to 'accept' the propositions in question, while questioning how far our ordinary or natural inferential practices embody the ideal of rational self-control which informed the aspirations of Greek philosophers and was the target of the Pyrrhonists. What has been said so far leaves it open whether our everyday or common sense conception of the self is dogmatist or Pyrrhonist – or whether it corresponds to neither because both of these forms of self-consciousness are products of philosophical reflection.

Second, Pyrrhonist practice has an *ad hominem* character: for the therapy to work, all that is required is that the 'facts' introduced should be accepted by the sceptic's adversary. Since most of the questionable phenomena alluded to in Sextus' exposition of the tropes are drawn from zoological or biological writings of the day, and since most were probably accepted by Stoics and other dogmatists, they serve their purpose even if incorrect. The sceptic need not insist that they are true: they are a means of disrupting the dogmatist's activities from the inside (Annas and Barnes 1985 ch.2). In the closing section of *Outlines of Pyrrhonism*, entitled 'Why the sceptic sometimes purposely propounds arguments which are lacking in power of persuasion', Sextus is quite explicit about this. The Pyrrhonist is presented as 'a lover of his kind' who desires to 'cure by speech, as best he can, the self-conceit and rashness of the Dogmatists' (PH3 280). Developing the analogy with medical treatment, he insists that he chooses mild or strong arguments according to his view of what is required to 'restore to health' the rash dogmatists:

> the adherent of Sceptic principles does not scruple to propound at
> one time arguments that are weighty in their persuasiveness, and at
> another time such as appear less impressive, – and he does so on
> purpose, as the latter are frequently sufficent to enable him to
> effect his purpose.

> (PH3 281)

In a famous passage, Sextus compares sceptical arguments to a ladder which, once climbed, can be discarded (M8 481):

> Just as it is not impossible for the man who has ascended to a high
> place by a ladder to overturn the ladder with his foot after his
> ascent, so also it is not unlikely that the Sceptic after he has arrived
> at the demonstration of his thesis by means of the argument
> proving the non-existence of proof, as it were by a step-ladder,
> should then abolish this very argument.

Scepticism is not dogmatically committed to a body of arguments; it is vindicated finally, not by the arguments which persuade someone to suspend judgment, but by the *ataraxia* which is obtained in consequence of this suspension.

This *ad hominem* character explains another disturbing feature of Pyrrhonist argument. The interpretation I have offered may suggest that Sextus employs a particular philosophical theory of mind, one that distinguishes the passive receipt of impressions from the active judging of them as true, and employs a distinctive conception of reason. If this were correct, then scepticism would rest upon dogmatic philosophy. Fortunately it is not correct. In combating a particular dogmatist, a Pyrrhonist may work within that dogmatist's picture of mind – again, disrupting the philosophical outlook from the inside. This is likely to be particularly effective when the components of the theory of mind in question are presupposed by the dogmatist's conception of the nature of (philosophical) inquiry. Perhaps some variant of the picture of mind sketched above is involved in any philosophical pursuit of the truth: the target of Pyrrhonism would then be a tradition of inquiry which aspires to methods of investigation which will effectively distinguish true from false appearances. Unless involved in combating dogmatists, the Pyrrhonist who turns his back on the pursuit of truth simply has no need for a theoretical vocabulary in which to formulate a 'doctrine'.

CHAPTER II

The Legacy of Pyrrhonism

1. Introduction: how to resist Pyrrhonism

Pyrrhonist writings, rediscovered during the sixteenth century, influenced debates about epistemology and the foundations of science at the beginnings of modern philosophy. Towards the end of the chapter, we shall examine their impact, and look at some of the responses to them. Before doing so, we must look further at Pyrrhonism itself, beginning with a consideration of how it is possible to resist scepticism: what sorts of factors could enable someone to reject the sceptical outlook? This requires further examination of the context of Greek scepticism: we discuss how the Pyrrhonist lifestyle is supposed to provide *ataraxia*; and we examine the traditions of Greek medical inquiry in order to see how far Pyrrhonism would affect the practical affairs of life.

Since Pyrrhonists do not defend recognizable philosophical *positions*, and since they do not dogmatically insist upon the validity of their arguments, it is not immediately obvious how we should respond to their challenge. What styles of philosophical criticism can appropriately be directed against the sort of therapeutic philosophical practice we have been describing? Or better, how can a dogmatist defensibly *resist* the therapy? Since he and his Pyrrhonist opponent are not involved in a co-operative project of inquiry, it is not required that he be able to persuade the Pyrrhonist that his dogmatist outlook can be sustained; all that is necessary is that he be able to sustain it without succumbing to self-deception. Towards the end of this section, we shall introduce some responses that the Greek sceptics did encounter; but, first, it will be useful to consider this issue in more general terms.

21

Before doing so, let me redescribe some elements of the sceptical stance. We are concerned with:

1. A variety of projects of inquiry (or research programmes) which promise advances in knowledge leading to benefits of several kinds: practical benefits derived from new technology; increased happiness or fulfilment; the development of wisdom.
2. An ideal of rational self-control involving the idea of our being actively in control of our cognitive activities and able to take responsibility for their success or failure.

The mastery of sceptical practice supposedly enables a Pyrrhonist to frustrate the execution of the projects described in (1). It does this by exploiting limitations to the rational self-control (2) that has been achieved by dogmatic inquirers. Presumably the picture is as follows: our ordinary practice of challenging and defending beliefs – our common sense conception of taking responsibility for one's beliefs – implicitly prescribes standards or requirements which cannot be satisfied when we conduct these inquiries. Hence the Pyrrhonist approach can be seen as undermining these research programmes from the inside; they cannot be carried out in full self-consciousness of what one is doing and why. As we have seen, this destructive practice is crucially accompanied by the observation that abandoning these projects, and turning aside from this ideal of rational self-control, are not the disastrous moves they might appear. Doing so provides tranquillity and fulfilment.

Ideally, a dogmatist would try to meet the sceptical challenges. If he can show that there are cognitive impressions which cannot be juxtaposed with conflicting impressions of comparable strength, then the Pyrrhonist's spoiling tactics fail. If the problem of the criterion can be solved, then, once again, the dogmatist can brush off the challenges and continue with inquiry into non-evident matters. But this is not the only ploy open to a dogmatist. If he finds the Pyrrhonist's conservative lifestyle unattractive, and is unconvinced that it is desirable to turn away from the pursuit of knowledge, then he might reasonably continue with his inquiries hoping eventually to find a response to the sceptical challenges. Furthermore he can point to the successes of his research programmes: if the contingent fact of 'success' can vindicate the Pyrrhonist's proposals, then, surely, it can also vindicate our continuing with serious inquiry and philosophy. If scientific research, or philosophical criticism of moral and political matters, are making recognizable *progress*, then we are unlikely to abandon them in the face of sceptical challenges; a suitable criterion for life might then be not to adopt the Pyrrhonist's conservative retiring style of existence, but simply to avoid sceptics.

David Hiley has stressed that an important component of the enlightenment response to scepticism was an assurance that the search for knowledge leads to progress and to human happiness (1988 ch.2). To someone impressed by the apparent success of the dogmatic search for truth, sceptical challenges will seem empty. Our evident ability to make such cognitive progress reveals (it will be said) that we do have a satisfactory basis for discriminating between appearances: our success shows that we are close to getting it right, even if we cannot explain the basis upon which we do so. An appeal to Providence to explain this ability may not be ultimately satisfactory, but will certainly be sufficient to justify ignoring Pyrrhonist challenges. Moreover, once this direction is taken, a new significance attaches to the implausibility of many of Sextus' modes. If a tower looks round from a distance and square from close up, none of us seriously doubts that it is really square. The observation that animals have differently shaped eyes does not lead us to question ordinary perceptual claims. To use an anachronistic terminology: if a project of investigation presents a progressive research programme – problems are solved, fruitful new problems arise, practical benefits are forthcoming – the sceptic's challenges will be seen as providing irritating anomalies which do not touch our confidence in the value of the activity as a whole.

Another response to sceptical challenges notes that Pyrrhonist arguments tend to be directed at projects of inquiry with a definite kind of goal: knowledge of the non-evident real natures of things. They exploit the thought that *such* inquiries must be pursued with the kind of self-conscious rational self-control which calls for a basis of absolute certainty and a solution to the problem of the criterion. If we are to resist this Pyrrhonist route, then, instead of treating sceptical challenges as embarrassing anomalies or meeting them head on, we can argue that the ideal of rational self-control being employed is inappropriate to the kinds of inquiry at issue. This third strategy, which accuses sceptics of employing excessively strict conceptions of knowledge, justification or rationality is important for modern epistemology. In section 6 we shall introduce some early developments of this theme.

We have so far said little about how the Pyrrhonist life actually leads to tranquillity. We have noted that it is, in some way, a contingent matter that it does so, and in consequence we have expressed concern that it may do so only in the context provided by Hellenistic culture. As we saw, Hume's challenge to Pyrrhonism fails to take into account Sextus' account of the considerations which guide Pyrrhonists in planning their lives. But we have not considered a related question: just how rich and varied can a Pyrrhonist's life be? The previous paragraphs have rather taken for granted that Pyrrhonists forswear activities that can be interpreted as adding to our store of knowledge – they cannot participate in ordered *inquiry*, but ground their lives in everyday certainties and the practical techniques which ground their trades. Bearing in mind that Sextus, for example, worked as a physician, we may wonder whether this is so. Surely medical practice relies upon a growing corpus of information about disease, symptoms and methods of treatment: what attitude should a Pyrrhonist doctor take towards medical research?

2. *Rationalism and the good life*

Understanding the character of the Pyrrhonist's life requires an examination of the intellectual context of Greek scepticism; it is helpful to interpret it as a reaction to the tradition in Greek thought which can be described as *rationalist*. Rationalists hold that sensory appearance is unreliable as a source of stable knowledge, and turn to reason to provide accounts of how things really are; as Plato's cave analogy reveals, appearance may provide at best the fleeting shadows of a non-evident reality which sharply contrasts with everyday experience. Reason has the power to penetrate behind appearance to provide true knowledge. In this section and the next, we discuss two manifestations of Greek rationalism: its impact upon ethical thought; and the practice of the rationalist school of medicine which held that diagnosis and treatment must rest upon a theoretical understanding of the underlying causes of disease.

The idea that there are connections between virtue, fulfilment and the possession of knowledge recurs, in different forms, in Greek philosophy. The Socratic view that knowledge of Good and Evil is sufficient for virtue is one manifestation of the idea. Someone who is virtuous cannot act wrongly; wicked or negligent action is always to be understood as due to ignorance. This is sometimes accompanied by the thought that one who possesses ethical knowledge and thus acts rightly cannot be harmed; the assurance that one is acting rightly provides a confidence in one's virtue which cannot be disturbed. The Platonic view that the self receives its fullest realization in the life of theoretical understanding, reason being the essential or naturally ruling attribute of the soul, is a rather different manifestation of the view that virtue, fulfilment and possession of knowledge are closely linked. Stoic ethical thought also reflects this rationalist picture of reason and virtue.

The suggestion that epistemological difficulties threaten these rationalist ideals is already present in Plato's own works. In the earlier dialogues, Socrates does not advance any claims to knowledge; rather he challenges the dogmatic assertions of others in ways that resemble Pyrrhonist strategy, and claims that his own wisdom consists in an awareness of how little he knows. It is unsurprising, then, that the earliest systematic development of scepticism was within the Platonic academy. The early sceptics could see themselves as deploying Socratic aporetic practice against the dogmatic excess which Plato had increasingly used Socrates' name to champion. One way to read Pyrrhonist texts, then, is as a repudiation of the outlook described in the previous paragraph: reason does not seem to deliver what Plato promises for it; and rather than providing a means to fulfilment, the search for knowledge prevents our obtaining it. Siding with 'life', and abandoning dogmatic inquiry provides tranquillity and enables us to avoid harm and frustration. Where the Stoics presented their epistemology as a means to knowledge which could survive Socratic questioning, the Pyrrhonists celebrated the power of Socrates' critical resources. But the Pyrrhonists went further: to them, knowledge did not only seem impossible; it also seemed unnecessary for a fulfilling life.

Can anything be said to support the view that the Pyrrhonist's life will achieve the tranquillity that is missed by the dogmatist? Presumably there can be no guarantee that it will. The Pyrrhonist may have an optimistic trust or ungrounded hope that it will, and he can admit that experience suggests that it *appears* to do so. But, of course, he has no dogmatic grounds for assurance. However, we can recognize various perturbations which the sceptic – unlike his dogmatic rival – does not risk. When he forms conditional plans, these will take the form:

If it appears that P, do A in the hope that Q will result.

Of course, he may be disappointed: he may perform the action and Q not result, but his frustrations are of a different order from those that face the dogmatist. Suppose that the latter forms a conditional intention:

If P is the case, do A knowing that Q will then result.

25

First, he may fail to act on his plan, in spite of his best intention to do so, because his judgment that P is the case is in error: no corresponding problem faces our sceptic. If this occurs, he faces the additional frustration of realizing that he lacks the dogmatic knowledge on which he relied for *ataraxia*. If the agent succesfully does A but Q does not result, a sceptic can resignedly acknowledge the frailty of human hopes. A dogmatist, on the other hand, must once again admit that he has failed to achieve the dogmatic certainty that he sought. In each case, the dogmatist risks encountering a failure in his deepest projects – and this is a risk which the Sceptic does not face.

Of course, if the dogmatist has an effective method of obtaining certain knowledge of reality, he does not risk these perturbations. But to the sceptic – reflecting on the tropes and the general problem of the criterion – it appears that this is not available. The dogmatist risks failure in just that self-controlled pursuit of knowledge which was to ensure that he would always act well. The sceptical arguments show that the dogmatist lacks both an effective criterion to be employed in judgment and a clear conception of the reality against which his judgments are to be measured.

Interestingly, however, Sextus stresses other considerations when he describes the perturbations that the dogmatist faces. He stresses the 'disquiet' that faces anyone who believes that 'anything is by nature good or bad'. When he lacks what he deems good 'he believes himself to be tormented by things naturally bad' and seeks the good: but, once the good has been obtained, he is disquieted by 'irrational and immoderate elation' and driven to action by 'his dread of a change of fortune'. The sceptic, suspending judgment about what is naturally good, 'neither shuns nor pursues anything eagerly; and, in consequence, he is unperturbed' (PH1 27–8). The sceptic, unlike the dogmatist, takes things as they come and views none of his projects as essential to his well being or tranquillity.

This point seems less fundamental than those discussed above. If the dogmatist believes that knowledge is sufficient for virtue and tranquillity, and he believes that he has a criterion of truth, then he has no reason to fear such disappointment or frustration. Indeed, when it is argued that a virtuous person can genuinely be happy on the rack, the benefits claimed for the dogmatic life include the avoidance of just those insecurities which, according to Sextus, it inevitably involves. The passage is instructive in that it suggests that the Pyrrhonist secures his happiness by living rather unadventurously. It is only because nothing is very important to him that he copes with 'disappointment' and 'frustration' so well. The Pyrrhonist conservatively conforms to the prevailing standards, accepts such pleasures and pains as his life shall involve, performs his professional duties, but is untainted by any overarching aims or ambitions. He does not direct his life according to any general projects or goals but allows his identity and character to be determined by the contingencies of his situation – by the appearances which he receives and by his social and professional position.

This enables us to raise another issue which will concern us at the end of this chapter. Sextus Empiricus presents Pyrrhonists as champions of 'life': they defend the ordinary practices of common life against the critical pretensions of those champions of dogmatic reason who would ground fulfilment in knowledge of the non-evident. Although these claims suggest that a Pyrrhonist could have as full and varied a life as any ordinary person, there are other passages which lead us to suppose that Pyrrhonists have a most unadventurous and quiet existence. And we may feel uneasy about this tendency in their thought. In order to understand it, we must notice the enormous difference between the outlook of an 'ordinary person' and a Pyrrhonist. Although the latter lacks theoretical beliefs, it remains true, as Williams has remarked, that the sceptical standpoint is an essentially *intellectual* one. The uneducated person for whom the dogmatic life has never even been a serious *option* has not obtained *ataraxia*. The sceptical standpoint involves a decision to rest with appearances given that judgment always proves so unstable. It is the standpoint of someone for whom the dogmatist's search for self-control has existed as an option, and has been left behind. According to Williams, 'The Pyrrhonist had, in relation to the rest of society, the role of a sage – a very quiet one.' (Williams 1981 p.240): it is essential to his role that he has turned away from dogmatic life. The practice of such a 'born again' champion of life cannot but be quieter than that of someone for whom the question of how to live has never been formulated as a fundamental issue.

3. Rationalism and medicine

When describing how a Pyrrhonist would live, Sextus mentions that he would adopt a skill, such as that of a doctor; and it is well known that medicine was Sextus' own profession. Medical knowledge presumably grows, and we shall gain insight into the richness of a Pyrrhonist's life by considering how such a practitioner can develop his understanding of diagnosis and treatment of disease. As mentioned above, this is valuable because epistemological debates internal to the development of medicine were importantly involved in the growth of sceptical thought (Frede 1987 ch. 12–14 is an invaluable guide to these matters).

Rationalist doctors held that reason could provide information about the nature of disease and its causes, and they believed that a theoretical grasp of these matters would enable us to discover how the disease should be treated. Hence a responsible doctor should have an anatomical theory of the constitution of the human body which would enable him to distinguish its normal and abnormal states and explain the origins of abnormalities (Frede 1987 p.245). Rationalists held that:

> professional medical practice had to be based on scientific theory and that a scientific theory had to account for the phenomena in terms of the underlying reality, and that this reality included hidden natures, causes and actions, not open to observation, but only accessible to reason, e.g., atoms, invisible pores, functions of organs, or essences. Thus the rational method involves the knowledge of truths about unobservable items which can be obtained only by reason.
>
> (Frede 1987 pp.261–2)

Pyrrhonist doctors evidently repudiate this conception of medical practice – and there is some evidence that dismay at the variety of such anatomical theories defended by different theorists was a major stimulus to the emergence of systematic scepticism.

The other two schools of medical practice are closer to the Pyrrhonist outlook. Many Pyrrhonists were medical *empiricists*, and there is more than his name to suggest that Sextus belonged to this school. However in *Outlines of Pyrrhonism* Sextus distinguishes empiricism from Pyrrhonism and suggests (without actually claiming) that a Pyrrhonist should be a *Methodist*. Empiricists repudiated rationalist theory: it was inevitably speculative and, in view of the endless dispute and lack of consensus about medical theory, there was no reason to suppose it to be true. All that could ground a practice of diagnosis and treatment, they held, is experience: doctors rely upon their own experience of success and failure in treating ailments, and upon the testimony of others. Although they may find rationalist proposals useful, it is only their practical success which justifies their use. Methodism is a later development. It agrees with the empiricist critique of rationalism but rejects its refusal to admit that there is a certain basis for diagnosis and treatment. A relatively short period of training could apparently equip a Methodist doctor to perceive 'manifest generalities': just as some moral philosophers claim that our moral training enables us to apply moral concepts immediately in our experience, so the doctor is trained to classify ailments into three exceedingly general kinds. The general kind in question indicates to the trained physician the appropriate treatment. For example, it is immediately evident to the trained eye that someone is suffering from a contraction; and this indicates that dilation is the appropriate treatment. The Methodist outlook promises medical knowledge that is much more certain than anything available to a member of one of the other schools. It also promises this knowledge to anyone prepared to undergo a fairly short period of training.

The expectation of other ancient writers was that Pyrrhonism and medical empiricism went together; the empiricist doctor was guided by appearances while Methodists made unsceptical appeals to the need for certainty to ground their medical practice. What, then, were Sextus' reasons for allying Pyrrhonism with Methodism and distinguishing it from empiricism? He accused empiricists of being negative dogmatists; they positively affirm that nothing non-evident can be known whereas a sceptic should suspend judgment on that matter (PH1 236). And he gave two reasons why a Pyrrhonist could 'more easily' affirm Methodism. First

> just as the sceptic, in virtue of the compulsion of the affections, is
> guided by thirst to drink and by hunger to food, ... in the same way
> the Methodical physician is guided by the pathological affections
> to the corresponding remedies – by contraction to dilation, as when
> one seeks refuge in heat from the contraction due to the application
> of cold ... It is plain, too, that conditions which are naturally alien
> compel us to take measures for their removal, seeing that even the
> dog when it is pricked by a thorn proceeds to remove it.
>
> (PH1 238-9)

Second, although Methodists use theoretical notions like 'generality' and 'indication' they resemble sceptics in using them in an 'undogmatic and indeterminate sense' (PH1 239–40). 'Indication' is not used as a technical notion from the theory of signs but undogmatically to allude to 'guidance derived from the apparent affections, or symptoms ... for the discovery of the seemingly appropriate remedies' (PH1 240).

Frede contends that in spite of these comments, Pyrrhonism was associated with an undogmatic kind of empiricism. Sextus' target was 'traditional' empiricism which merited his complaints – and he supports this by noting that Sextus himself wrote a text on 'Empirical medicine', and was noted for his contributions to empiricist doctrine. This is an important issue for it is only if we can link Pyrrhonism with an undogmatic empiricism that we can see how Pyrrhonists can benefit from a growing body of medical lore and allow for a Pyrrhonist version of inquiry. Methodism fits with our conception of a Pyrrhonist's unadventurous life: acquiring the skills of a doctor involves mastering a limited technique which will not develop and grow over time. Rather than attempt to settle just what Sextus' position was and why he wrote as he did of Empiricism and Methodism, we shall just consider in a hypothetical fashion how a form of undogmatic empiricism *could* be compatible with the Pyrrhonist outlook. We shall then offer a conjecture about the link between Pyrrhonism and Methodism.

There is plainly no obstacle to collecting medical information in the empiricist manner while agnostic about whether reason could eventually arrive at theoretical underpinnings for diagnosis and treatment. The fundamental issue concerns whether doing so would involve a Pyrrhonist in dogmatic commitments of a positive kind. If, as seems undeniable, we have a natural propensity to form habits of expectation on the basis of apparent regularities, then we can see how experience can lead us, undogmatically, to accept generalizations which fit our experience. Presumably, we have a similar habit of acccepting the testimony of others unless it conflicts with other appearances to which we assent. Suppose then that our medical practice simply exploits this everyday practice; doctors are taught to put themselves in a position where habits of expectation will grow. The practice is vindicated by its success; it is salient for us, and we would abandon it if it began to frustrate our activities, but we provide it with no dogmatic or philosophical justification. Indeed, if a rationalist theory seemed attractive to a Pyrrhonist, he could use it undogmatically, continuing to do so until it was disappointed by experience. The sceptic's attitude towards theory may resemble that of an engineer who is trained to rely upon Newtonian mechanics for his practical purposes while sceptical as to whether it is really true; and his attitude towards empiricist methodology may be exactly the same. (For further discussion, see Frede 1987 ch.13.)

Frede goes further than this, claiming that sceptics can rely upon positive epistemological 'theories'. These could not be defended dogmatically, nor could they be critical or revisionary of our ordinary practices of inquiry. But since, as we have admitted, we do naturally arrive at generalizations, the Pyrrhonist could provide a description of apparent patterns in our natural practice of assenting to appearances. He would not endorse or criticize this practice or insist that we will not deviate from it in future, but such a description of our ways of coping with appearances does not conflict with Pyrrhonist tenets. Indeed, some parts of *Outlines of Pyrrhonism* fit that pattern. However in accepting such observations we must not lose sight of some fundamental aspects of Pyrrhonist practice. Sextus' discussions stress that Pyrrhonists assent (undogmatically) only to what is *evident* – to what they find themselves assured of. Once the notion of undogmatic assent is used so that we assent to theories through finding them useful while agnostic about the propriety of dogmatic assent to them, then Pyrrhonism moves closer to a kind of pragmatism which allows for a wide range of cognitive and other activities pursued in a rather uncommitted fashion. It is an interesting question whether a modern 'Pyrrhonist' could move in that direction. Such a view does not seem to be present in Sextus.

These remarks may help with understanding why Sextus mentions Methodical medicine approvingly. Even if Pyrrhonist practice resembles empiricist practice in forming expectations on the basis of experienced regularities rather than hunting for a few 'manifest generalities', a difference might emerge at the meta-theoretical level. There could well be a conflict between the Pyrrhonist stress upon the *evident* and empiricist discussions of 'hypotheses' which were admitted to be conjectural or hypothetical. Empiricists developed views about how inquiries *ought* to be organized, and employed normative theories of justification which, presumably, should guide the will in deciding which propositions to accept. This would not be acceptable to a Pyrrhonist. For the latter, empiricist techniques might induce expectations which are experienced as immediately evident or certain. Inductive testing causes (rather than justifies) expectations. Experience of instances of an empirical generalization could produce in a Pyrrhonist a state where perception of the symptoms of a disease would bring to his mind a particular course of treatment. Just as thirst prompts us to drink, so the symptom prompts a distinctive treatment. Even if Pyrrhonists abandon the traditional Methodist emphasis on the simple pattern of manifest generalities, and develop new styles of treatment under the prompting of experience, their relation to these empiricist techniques would reflect the relation of a Methodist to manifest generalities. They *find themselves favouring* a particular treatment as a natural result of the disease *appearing* to have a particular character. That this disposition results from natural tendencies to form empirical generalizations should not disguise the similarity with Methodism: both Pyrrhonists and Methodists allow themselves to be guided by natural tendencies to favour treatments rather then seeking rational self-control over their practice in the name of a normative epistemology.

4. Scepticism, common sense and life

This section continues our discussion of ancient scepticism by emphasizing those of its features which are most relevant to understanding its relations to later developments. The first of these involves Sextus' description of how a Pyrrhonist would regulate his life. As we have seen, sceptics are to be guided by appearances that are immediately evident to them. Sensory appearance, bodily appetites, and the customs of one's society are things one assents to undogmatically, things one finds *evident*; one finds oneself assenting to them. This assent, or acquiescence is untouched by sceptical challenges. Careful use of the modes may help to ensure that we do not slip and assent to them in a dogmatic manner. Sextus talks of championing *life* in allowing conduct to be determined in this way; he also claims that these dispositions to assent are *natural* – they flow from our nature. It accords with one use of an expression which philosophers have adapted for many purposes to claim that Sextus is a champion of *common sense*. We acquiesce in common sense certainties and refuse to trust reason when it attempts to criticize them or justify them.

That sceptical challenges do not touch such common sense beliefs, and that those patterns of assent which flow from our nature are more powerful than philosophical arguments which appear to discredit them, are pervasive themes in philosophical discussions of scepticism. However they are more often used to support the rejection of scepticism than to show how a life compatible with scepticism is possible. This brings out a respect in which ancient scepticism is less radical than the sceptical doctrines discussed by more recent philosophers: it does not seem to threaten 'life' and our ordinary patterns of assent. By exploiting the distinction between dogmatic assent and acquiescence in appearance, and stressing that sceptical challenges attack the former, we are left with resources for ordinary affairs of life. Modern philosophers view the strength of common sense or natural beliefs as showing that we do not really take sceptical arguments seriously: our common sense certainties reveal that we have no tendency to accept their conclusions. If sceptical arguments were to be effective, these natural certainties, it is supposed, would be undermined.

However the fact that sceptical challenges do not touch these natural certainties also reveals a respect in which ancient scepticism is more radical than some recent versions. Many modern discussions of justification and knowledge consider sceptical challenges to be *insulated* from our ordinary practice of assent. They are tools for elucidating concepts like justification and truth, or they pose challenges which must be met; but there is no admission that 'being a sceptic' is an option for us or that it can be seen as other than a threat. In so far as the strength of our common sense beliefs is not seen as refuting scepticism, it is still seen as conflicting with them. Although we have come to appreciate that the adoption of Pyrrhonism affects one's resources for living much less than might have been supposed, still scepticism for Sextus is a moral position. It changes one's life, leading to the abandonment of projects previously thought of as flowing naturally from the demands of our rationality. For some Greek philosophers, the good life demanded the successful completion of kinds of inquiry which Pyrrhonists abandon. A congeries of views about our reason being our essence, and the achievement of rational self-control our aim, were put in question. Since scepticism does not touch natural certainties, it can change our lives while those certainties remain intact. Scepticism has a definite phenomenology: sceptics live differently and have constantly to keep at bay an urge to dogmatism.

Finally, we should stress some other differences between ancient sceptical challenges and those that are characteristic of more recent philosophy. As we have mentioned before, it is striking that Sextus seems not to have discussed the problem of the external world. Defence of scepticism does not involve any consideration of solipsism and sceptical challenges linked to questions about the mechanisms of perception. The importance of this is hard to overestimate since, for modern philosophy, a concern with perception and the external world is central to most epistemology which takes scepticism seriously. A philosopher like Russell seems to treat 'scepticism' and 'solipsism' as synonyms (1948). Where Greek sceptics are concerned with whether we can say which appearances should be assented to, a post-Cartesian philosopher questions whether they may not *all* be illusory. This is reflected in the arguments employed to support scepticism. We cannot suggest that *all* might be an illusion without appealing to *hypothetical* explanations of our experience which would render all of our beliefs false. Our actual experience does not support this possibility. If our concern is only with how we can decide which appearances can be accepted, it may be enough to focus on actual conflicts that emerge between our experiences. It is striking that Sextus' defence of Pyrrhonism relies entirely upon actual conflicts: different animals, people, and senses experience things in different ways; how are we to choose between them? We should anticipate that the move to a concern with the solipsistic possibility that all might be illusion will call for an extension of the canon of sceptical arguments. The next chapter begins to examine these new sceptical arguments.

5. *The rediscovery of Pyrrhonism*

How far is Pyrrhonism an option for us now? Can it still be defended? According to David Hiley, its 'deep challenge' consists in raising the question of how criticism of the institutions, practices or traditions of the prevailing social order can be other than *ad hoc* (Hiley 1988 pp.3–4, 37), but he asks whether it can avoid becoming merely 'an apology for the existing order' (p.12). Are we enjoined simply to conform, undogmatically, to the standards and practices which we have inherited? Related problems for the Pyrrhonist route to fulfilment have been noted by Bernard Williams: 'There is ... no serious point of view, or at least none which can be publicly sustained, by which wars, calamities and social upheaval can be quite so distantly regarded as Scepticism suggested they should be' (1981 p.241). Moreover, as Williams also insists, both the legacy of Romanticism and much modern psychology holds 'a more sceptical view of *ataraxia* itself ' and 'a deeper view of the emotions' than Pyrrhonism allows. These criticisms are important because, as we have seen, if we cannot endorse the moral benefits of Pyrrhonism, we shall be forced to return to a closer examination of its epistemological strategies.

The suggestion that the Pyrrhonist approach to life is satisfactory only in particular circumstances gains support from an examination of the rediscovery of scepticism in sixteenth century Europe. Schmitt (1983) and Popkin (1979 ch.1–3) have described the process by which ancient sceptical writings became available and grew in influence during this period. Estienne's Latin translation of *Outlines of Pyrrhonism* in 1562 stimulated discussion of sceptical matters, but it was itself the symptom of a century of concern with scepticism.

Early Christian thinkers appear to have perceived scepticism as a threat: within the Byzantine church, in about 379, Gregory Nazianzen accused Pyrrhonism of entering the church 'as some sort of fearful and malignant disease' (Schmitt ibid p.234); and Augustine found it necessary to refute (Academic) scepticism in order to support his faith when he was converted around 386 (Kirwan 1983 pp.205–6). However from the fifteenth century we find theologians embracing sceptical arguments as a tool to defend their faith. During his debate with Luther, Erasmus both endorsed the critical force of sceptical argument and exploited the conservative character of the Pyrrhonist rules for the regulation of life. As well as challenging the capacity of reason to settle abstract theological questions, he can be interpreted as recommending believers to fall in with the traditional practices of the church without exciting themselves about doctrinal issues. This resembles Sextus' recommendation: 'although following the ordinary view, we affirm undogmatically that gods exist and reverence gods and ascribe to them foreknowledge, we argue against dogmatist religious claims' (PH3 2). Sextus concludes that 'we cannot apprehend whether God exists', observing that to claim knowledge of his existence may involve impiety: for if we judge him omniscient we must hold him responsible for evil, and if we deny that he is omniscient, we are forced to judge him 'either malignant or weak' (PH3 12). A different use of Pyrrhonist arguments was made by Gianfrancesco Pico della Mirandola who, around 1516, attacked the pretensions of Aristotelian science, claiming that truth and certainty could only be found in scripture (Schmitt 1983 p.236).

It was only eighteen years after the translation of Sextus' work that Montaigne published his influential *Apology for Raimond Sebond*, an elegant compendium of sceptical arguments, stressing the problem of the criterion, which contained little that would be unfamiliar to a reader of Sextus. As Penelhum points out, Montaigne draws two potentially inconsistent morals from his Pyrrhonism. He undertakes to 'take the choice of other men and keep myself in the station in which God has placed me': like Sextus, he simply conforms to prevailing customs. However after endorsing the sceptical view that man cannot 'rise above himself and humanity; for he cannot see but with his eyes nor take hold but with his own hand', he suggests that '[he] will rise if God will extraordinarily lend him a hand' (Montaigne II p.269, Penelhum 1983 p.296, and see Popkin 1979 ch.III). This was taken to suggest that the evident experience of the individual can provide a guide to salvation. It is easy to see that these recommendations can conflict: they are consistent only if receipt of Grace coincides with respecting local tradition (see Penelhum p.296). In a changing world, the different components of the Pyrrhonist guide to life can offer conflicting recommendations. They need not provide tranquillity.

While Sextus' recommendations may be workable in a small stable society, characterized by consensus on ethical and religious matters, where religion is largely constituted by a set of practices and norms of behaviour, they were not workable in sixteenth century Europe. 'Undogmatic assent' suggests a kind of tepid conformity incompatible with Christian faith. Luther famously responded to Erasmus' desire to abjure 'assertion': 'it is not the mark of a Christian mind to take no delight in assertions; on the contrary, a man must delight in assertions or he will be no Christian. And by assertion ... I mean a constant adhering, affirming, confessing, maintaining, and an invincible persevering ...' (Penelhum p.294). Christianity demanded a firm commitment which is not available to a Pyrrhonist. Penelhum plausibly argues that thinkers of the time mistakenly identified the Pyrrhonist's 'undogmatic assent' and the faith required by Christianity because both were normally described in contrast to rationally justified dogmatic assent (pp.296–301). It is unsurprising that subsequent defenders of a Pyrrhonist attitude towards religion (for example, Bayle and Hume) were generally perceived as closer to agnosticism than to belief.

The use of sceptical arguments in this period was generally aggressive: scepticism was still not insulated from the concerns of life, and Pyrrhonist arguments were generally used to attack the possibility of particular theological or scientific inquiries. It is difficult to contain the impact of such criticism. Both science and religion were found wanting in the light of considerations which many exponents of each had used to attack other inquiries but not their own. As well as failing to provide the kind of faith required for religion, the Pyrrhonist recommendation for the conduct of life is ineffective in conditions of intellectual turmoil. It becomes unclear what the customary standards of a society are. Appearances can be evident for an individual which conflict with the customary requirements of his society. Regular exposure to others whose beliefs and practices differ from ours can weaken the evidence of appearances upon which we might otherwise rely. Religious schism together with rapid growth in science can shake the appearance that the Pyrrhonist style of life answers to our needs.

The use of Pyrrhonist arguments for limited religious and scientific purposes had revealed 'an abyss of doubts ... , undercutting not only the grounds of religious knowledge, but of all natural knowledge as well' (Popkin 1979 p.108). Sceptical philosophers 'confronted the new, optimistic age in which they lived and prospered with a complete *crise pyrrhonienne*' (ibid.). The new science had overthrown Aristotelian science, showing it to be groundless; but it too lacked foundations because no criterion of truth was available. Hence by the early seventeenth century, the success of sceptical arguments seemed to constitute a problem. There were no longer the conditions, if there ever were, where a Pyrrhonist critique of all claims to rational knowledge could clear the ground for a tranquil and fulfilling life.

6. *Constructive scepticism*

Before turning in the following chapter to Descartes' role in the discussion of these issues, we shall introduce one theme in seventeenth century philosophy of science, both in Britain and on the Continent: this is the position often referred to as 'constructive' or 'mitigated' scepticism (see Popkin 1979 ch.7; Ferreira 1986 pp.12–31). This distinctive development in the discussion of sceptical arguments is neither an acquiescence in Pyrrhonist suspension of belief nor an attempt to refute scepticism by providing new secure grounds for dogmatic assent. Major figures in this search for a middle way between Pyrrhonism and dogmatism were the French thinkers Mersenne and Gassendi, and those, like John Wilkins, who were involved in the development of the Royal Society in London.

These philosophers agreed that Sextus' sceptical modes destroyed the pretensions of both dogmatic metaphysics and those scientific systems (such as those of the Aristotelians and Galileo) which purported to uncover the real natures of things. Wilkin's insistence on the Aristotelian principle that 'things of several kinds may admit and require several sorts of proofs, all of which may be good in their kind' (Wilkins 1675 p.20, cited by Ferreira 1986) is typical of thinkers in this tradition. Systems of *dogmatic* science or metaphysics must meet standards which are inappropriate to the new science or to ordinary religious belief. Consequently the impact of sceptical challenges can be contained.

Gassendi and Mersenne pointed out that even the Pyrrhonists allowed knowledge of appearances and granted the practical value of such knowledge. Developing laws describing regularities in appearance enables us, as Mersenne stressed, to uncover systematic relations between appearances and appreciate that they do not really 'conflict'. Many of these beliefs are certain, unshaken by sceptical challenges, even if we are unsure about the foundations of this certainty. The success of science in advancing understanding and providing practical benefits vindicates the practice of science, although it does not refute the sceptical charge that science does not reveal the real natures of things.

Gassendi went further, defending an atomistic theory which explained observable regularities by appeal to unobservable particles. But it was accepted only as providing the best explanation of appearances: science is a body of truths about appearances, not about 'reality'. Appearances suggest hypotheses to us, which appeal to our reason. We can accept these in a fallibilistic spirit, admitting that they may be mistaken. They are tested solely by reference to their ability to predict further experiences, and we do not view them as describing the underlying real nature of things. Reason leads us from what is experienced to what cannot be experienced, but ultimately it is experience which tests the theories. Guided by what seems agreeable to reason, testing this against experience, we arrive at hypotheses which are fruitful and predictively successful. We want no more. (For further discussion, see Popkin 1979 pp.141–6, Woolhouse 1988 ch.4, Walker 1983).

This constructive scepticism suggests an empiricist or pragmatist view of science, and it may not be sufficient to vindicate religious belief against sceptical attack. Religious belief would appear too tentative or hypothetical. However, Wilkins and other English thinkers in particular stressed the importance of kinds of *certainty* falling short of the absolute certainty assailed by the sceptics. Some principles are certain because any suggestion that could be used to challenge them would be so much less certain than they are themselves. Wilkins describes others as possessing moral certainty: to doubt them is possible but unreasonable. His examples: the fidelity and ability of witnesses to events; that there was such a man as Henry VIII; that there are such places as America and China; that we now see and are awake, etc. (Wilkins 1675 p.19). According to John Tillotson: 'It is possible all the People of France may die this night ... It is possible the sun may not rise to Morrow morning; and yet, for all this, I suppose that no Man hath the least Doubt but that it will' (1728 p.559). There are standards of rationality to which we all unhesitatingly assent; questioning shows that they reflect our nature rather than prejudice or training. It is unreasonable to disregard these common sense standards; so sceptical doubts are unreasonable.

Constructive scepticism influences discussion of these topics in several ways. First, as is clear, it begins to insulate discussions of scepticism from our day-to-day practices. Pyrrhonist arguments may be used to guide our understanding of what science is, of how it works, but it is now admitted that the successes of the new science simply cannot be put at risk by exercise of the Pyrrhonist modes. Since different things require different sorts of proof, 'nothing can be more irrational than for a man to doubt of, or deny the truth of any thing, because it cannot be made out by such kinds of proofs of which the nature of such a thing is not capable' (Wilkins 1675 p.20). Pyrrhonists apply excessive standards where they are inappropriate: '*Doubt* is a kind of *fear*... and 'tis the same kind of Madness for a Man to *doubt* of any thing, as to *hope for* or *fear* it, upon a mere possibility' (Wilkins 1675 p.25–6). Sceptical doubt is unreasonable.

This second feature, then, is a growing insistence on the variety of kinds of investigation: different kinds of inquiry have different aims, and are to be guided by different standards. It is illustrated by Pascal's remark that Pyrrhonism draws its strength from those who profess dogmatic knowledge 'of where reason and justice lie'. If there is no need to combat dogmatism, Pyrrhonism becomes ridiculous: if all were sceptics, 'they would be wrong' (*Pensées* 374, and see 434, and Popkin 1979 p.140). Third, there is a growing naturalism. Wilkins appeals to 'the common judgment of mankind' to establish whether 'the Human Nature be not so framed, as to acquiesce in such a Moral Certainty, as the nature of things is capable of ' (1675 p.25): 'The Universal Consent of Nations in all Places and Times ... must needs render any thing highly credible to all such as will but allow the Humane Nature to be rational, and to be naturally endowed with a Capacity of distinguishing betwixt Truth and Falsehood' (p.36).

As Popkin remarks, although the theoretical development of these themes occurred during the early seventeenth century, 'a new dogmatism had to develop and be demolished before this new solution to the *crise pyrrhonienne* could be accepted' (Popkin 1979 p.129). We see here anticipations of views later popularized by Hume and Reid; and critical discussion should be postponed until we consider their more sophisticated or considered positions. They are stressed here both because they illustrate some of the themes about resisting Pyrrhonism developed in earlier parts of this chapter, and because they provide background to our discussion of Descartes. Although these thinkers were influential in their time, constructive scepticism occupied a minor role while attempts were made, by Descartes and others, to meet sceptical challenges directly and provide foundations for dogmatic inquiry.

CHAPTER III

Descartes: the Deepest Scepticism

1. Making scepticism give birth to philosophical certainty

Before Descartes, there had been Sceptics, but who were only
Sceptics. Descartes taught his age the art of making Scepticism
give birth to philosophical Certainty.
(L'Abbé François Para du Phanjas, 1779, cited in Popkin 1979 p.172)

The dominant characteristic of Descartes' philosophy is a strategic one.
Both in the *Discourse on the Method* (1637) and in the *Meditations*
(1641) he provides radical sceptical arguments seeming stronger than
those employed by Sextus, Montaigne and Gassendi. But he is wholly
unsympathetic to scepticism, for the role of these arguments is to 'give
birth to philosophical certainty'. Pyrrhonists believed that they could
suspend judgment on all things, but this was only because they did not
push their scepticism far enough. And earlier critics of scepticism were
equally half-hearted in relying upon common sense to dismiss sceptical
challenges as silly or over-ingenious. Descartes held that, pushed to the
limit, sceptical arguments showed the way to the certain knowledge
sought by dogmatists; he saw himself as the first philosopher to
overthrow the doubts of the sceptics.

Why does Descartes adopt this strategy? There is no simple answer,
and we shall come to a fuller understanding of this as the chapter
progresses. But there are several points that can be stressed now. The
traditional claim that Descartes seized upon this as a suitable weapon for
attacking Aristotelian science cannot be the whole story, not least
because this doctrine was already under attack from Gassendi and other
mitigated sceptics. An alternative view is that Descartes was disturbed
by the spread of fideism and of Pyrrhonist views of science and was thus
responding directly to the spread of scepticism. Popkin reports that in

1628–9, Descartes attended a meeting organized by Cardinal Berulle at which a defence of a sceptical, empiricist, probabilist approach to science received general approbation. Descartes attacked this consensus, arguing that probability and appearance could not provide a stable basis for science, and Berulle encouraged him to develop his own dogmatist anti-sceptical alternative (Popkin 1979 p.175). This suggests that Descartes' principal adversaries were various sceptics and Pyrrhonists: his aim was to provide foundations for science and religion by refuting scepticism.

This is plausible, bearing in mind that Montaigne, Gassendi and Mersenne were probably as influential as Descartes in the seventeenth century. Moreover Curley has illustrated many correspondences between Descartes' arguments and those employed by Montaigne (Curley 1978 ch.I). But it, too, is at best an incomplete account of Descartes' motivation. The full title of the *Meditations* may suggest a religious motivation, stressing as it does that the book contains proofs of the existence of God and the immortality of the soul. Although we should not question the sincerity of Descartes' desire to provide dogmatic foundations for religious belief, or his wish to integrate the foundations of science and religious belief, this is somewhat disingenuous. In a letter to Mersenne, dated 1641, he wrote that, besides these advertised themes:

> I think I have put in many other things; and I will tell you, between ourselves, that these six Meditations contain all the foundations of my Physics. But please don't say so; because those who favour Aristotle would perhaps make more difficulty about approving them; and I hope those who read them will accustom themselves insensibly to my principles, and recognize their truth, before noticing that they destroy those of Aristotle.
>
> (1970 p.94)

Descartes' physics was already developed during the 1620s, and although it was not Aristotelian, it seriously attempted to discern the real natures of things and to find the hidden, non-evident, causes of appearances. Since he proposed a dogmatic science which conflicted both with appearances and with conventional Aristotelian lore, he required a basis for both criticizing these mistaken views and certifying his own as correct. It is important to note that Descartes does not present sceptical challenges in order to shoot them down. In the light of the realist science that he defends, many appearances and common sense certainties do not survive: the senses prove a highly unreliable means for discovering the truth about nature. The strategy enables Descartes to use sceptical arguments to attack what cannot be sustained and exploit their limits as a device for providing a criterion to support his own dogmatic position. Although we should not discount the claim that sceptics were among his targets – since he could expect Gassendi and other mitigated sceptics to question his scientific views – his fundamental goal is to vindicate a realist dogmatic approach to science which conflicts with current scientific orthodoxies.

There is not room for a detailed examination of all the arguments of the *Meditations*, but it will be useful to offer a very brief sketch of its strategy and to indicate those topics that I shall discuss further. In the first *Meditation*, Descartes undertakes to extend sceptical doubt as far as it can be taken, in order to find some foundation for knowledge which is resistant to such doubt. In *Meditation II* he finds this in the *cogito*: he cannot doubt his own existence, or that he is a thinking thing. Reflecting upon this certain knowledge, he sees that it is restricted to those things that he clearly and distinctly perceives – a very Stoic view. Constructing proofs which enable him to perceive, clearly and distinctly, that God exists, he is assured that, in view of God's benevolence, he will not fall into error unless he misuses his reason and judgment. God would not allow him to be deceived in what he clearly and distinctly perceives. Hence – in some fashion – scientific knowledge is rescued from the sceptical onslaught.

We need not seriously consider whether Descartes has defeated scepticism. His proofs of God's existence do not carry conviction, and internal problems with Cartesian metaphysics led the tradition which Descartes founded to all but disappear by the end of the seventeenth century. For example, his dualist insistence that mind and body comprise two wholly distinct substances with distinct properties made it impossible to explain how modifications of the mind could resemble (and thus represent) states of body – he could not explain how minds could think about physical states of the world. But Descartes' philosophical significance outlasted the Cartesian tradition: his emphasis upon the *importance* of responding to scepticism survived if the details of his own response did not. Execution of his strategy called for a search for the most powerful sceptical arguments, for it is only by overcoming the most powerful sceptical arguments that scepticism can be put to rest. Hence, part of his legacy is a realization of how powerful the sceptical arguments can be. And it is tempting to draw from his failure the lesson that scepticism cannot be defeated. Moreover, the sceptical arguments he employed redirect sceptical discussion in an important way. Linked to his dualist theory of the relation of mind and body, Descartes insists that our knowledge of the contents of our own minds is indubitable while knowledge of external things is not. Hence, the central question becomes one about how we can advance from certain knowledge of our own mental states to knowledge of the physical world.

In this chapter and the next we discuss some issues arising out of Descartes' discussion of scepticism. The first of these concerns the importance of defeating scepticism. We have seen that scientists like Gassendi found a secure common sense basis for continuing with their scientific activities without responding to sceptical arguments. Descartes, in contrast, proposes that some of us should, at least once in our lives, devote time to studying the foundations of knowledge and inquiry, and he claims that we should do this by facing up to, and defeating, scepticism. This is, so to speak, a practical recommendation: one could dissent from Descartes' philosophical enterprise simply by denying that this was an interesting or important project; or one could accept the need for foundational epistemological study but deny that this need take the form of defeating scepticism. Hence we need to see how persuasive Descartes' arguments are for the rationality of undertaking this project.

Second, we must examine the sceptical arguments which Descartes employs in the first *Meditation*: how do they go beyond those available to earlier sceptics?; how do they work? And third, we must discuss some general strategic features of Descartes' response to scepticism. Reflection on the modes of Agrippa suggests that any attempt to propose a criterion which authorizes acceptance of some ideas or appearances is doomed to failure. Once the criterion is itself subjected to sceptical challenge, its defender is faced with an infinite regress of sceptical challenges unless he argues in a circle. Descartes fiercely resisted the accusation that his own response to scepticism involved such a circle, although reflection upon the brief description of his position offered above will reveal why his readers were unconvinced. Our belief in God is grounded in the fact that we clearly and distinctly perceive that he exists; and our understanding of why things which are so perceived are true is grounded in the benevolence of God. Even if the details of Descartes' arguments cannot be accepted, we may learn from the general character of his attempt to avoid the Agrippan problem.

This chapter examines the range of sceptical arguments employed by Descartes: they are introduced in section 2, and two receive more detailed discussion in sections 3 and 4. The issue of why Descartes thought that this ordeal through scepticism should be undergone is raised in section 2 and developed further in section 5. The final section considers the extent to which 'Cartesian' scepticism moves beyond Hellenistic scepticism through its focus on doubts about the existence of an external world. The following chapter is concerned with the logical character of the route Descartes uses to overthrow scepticism. The central issue there concerns not whether Descartes is correct (we have already admitted that many details of his position are unsound). Rather Descartes clearly believed that he was able to avoid the charge of circularity that would traditionally have been pressed using the modes of Agrippa. If he could avoid such charges of circularity, then this would be of great importance for our attempts to develop a non-Cartesian response to scepticism. It will also throw light on the relations between Cartesian science and Cartesian epistemology.

2. *Levels of doubt*

Descartes begins the first *Meditation* thus:

> Some years ago I was struck by the large number of falsehoods that I had accepted as true in my childhood, and by the largely doubtful nature of the whole edifice that I had subsequently based on them. I realized that it was necessary, once in the course of my life, to demolish everything completely and start right again from the foundations if I wanted to establish anything at all in the sciences that was stable and likely to last. But the task looked an enormous one, and I began to wait until I should reach a mature enough age to ensure that no subsequent time of life would be more suitable for tackling such inquiries.
>
> (1641 p.12)

This passage has several notable features. First, the sceptical worries that prompt Descartes to carry out his philosophical investigations are not crippling: he continues to live and do science for 'some years' before judging himself sufficiently mature to carry out the required exercise. Moreover from this pre-philosophical standpoint, he can reason about the value of these investigations. Second, he judges them to be necessary for a particular project, doing scientific work that was 'stable and likely to last'. Third, from the beginning, this project is described in terms of an architectural metaphor: he must 'start right again from the foundations'.

These features are even more evident in the lengthier discussion of philosophical procedure in the *Discourse on the Method*. Here too his concern is with providing foundations for putting science on a secure foundation. And he stresses that 'buildings undertaken and completed by a single architect are usually more attractive and better planned than those which several have tried to patch up by adapting old walls built for different purposes' (1637 p.116). The foundational architectural metaphor is here developed: the town or building prepared by a single architect is preferred to a town, for example, that has grown through the work of different hands, some of it building on the constructions of others. Before putting the method of doubt into operation, Descartes takes an *individualist* approach to epistemology and he takes the system of knowledge to need *foundations*. The most self-conscious use of the architectural metaphor ('Throughout my writings I have made it clear that my method imitates that of an architect') is in *Seventh Replies* (1641 p.366 ff.).

This has an important bearing upon the role of argument in responding to Descartes' views. Those who exploit powerful sceptical arguments can seem to be in possession of weapons which pre-empt any attempt to argue against them. Once it is put in question whether reason and the senses are reliable, why should we trust reason when it pleads its own case? But Descartes' discussion makes clear that reasoned argument has a role at an earlier stage: Descartes has to make good his claim that the pursuit of sceptical doubts and the search for secure foundations are justified. If somebody is convinced that science, although fallible, does make progress; and if that person believes that its progress rests upon the fact that it is a communal endeavour, each person learning from the fallible inquiries and testimonies of others: then they will not be persuaded that Descartes is right to urge each individual to seek secure foundations for his own system of belief. One might imagine constructive sceptics responding in exactly that fashion, and refusing to play Descartes' game. Once we abandon the secure basis of common sense certainties, we abandon any hope of dealing with sceptical arguments successfully; and these 'certainties' are a sufficient basis for science.

Several sorts of arguments could be used to justify Descartes' procedure. It could be argued, for example, that our ordinary conception of justification or knowledge naturally moves us to raise these sceptical concerns: we resist them only by a form of self-deception or through failing to exercise our reason in a full and responsible manner. If this were correct, then responsible rational agents could not fail to be disturbed by the sceptical arguments once they were aware of them; only ignorance or self-deception can enable us to avoid confronting these issues. Some thought of this sort is involved when philosophers take engagement with scepticism as, in some way, definitive of the task of epistemology (see for example, Stroud 1984, Cavell 1979, Clarke 1972). This strategy receives little support from Descartes' explicit claims in defence of his procedure, although he does remark that what pleased him most in his philosophical method was 'that by following it [he] was sure in every case to use [his] reason, if not perfectly, at least as well as was in [his] power' (1641 p.121).

Alternatively, Descartes could argue that his procedure was appropriate to particular cognitive projects. Participation in science, for example, may involve adopting goals with the property that we could have no confidence that progress can be made in pursuit of them unless we are confident that the Cartesian procedure can be carried through. A more plausible third possibility is that our experience of the obstacles in the way of cognitive progress in different areas suggests that only the Cartesian procedure can eliminate them. Several of Descartes' own arguments, including the first that he employs (one that is familiar from the Pyrrhonist canon) are of this character. His despair of progress in philosophy rests upon the familiar observation that 'it has been cultivated for many centuries by the most excellent minds, and yet there is still no point in it which is not disputed and hence doubtful' (1637 p.115). Finding a similar diversity in the views of non-philosophers, he 'learned not to believe too firmly anything of which [he] had been persuaded only by example and custom' (p.116).

We find here the first stage of sceptical argument used by Descartes. Reflecting upon the diversity of both philosophical views and 'common sense' opinions, he mistrusts anything which depends upon those philosophical views, and anything he might have acquired through education, example or custom. This application of a near relation of Sextus's tenth mode only motivates a partial scepticism: it challenges beliefs which depend upon the testimony of teachers or other people. It serves as a filter excluding beliefs which have this potentially corrupt origin. Its role in forming the structure of Descartes' thought is, importantly, twofold. First, since it is not always easy to determine

47

which beliefs do result from education, example or custom, it provides a reason for undertaking the methodological investigation proposed in the *Meditations*: unless these corrupt influences can be identified and eliminated, we can have no confidence in the truth of any of our opinions. And, second, it encourages the individualist character of Descartes' project: if the testimony of others is a source of cognitive corruption, we should be wary of trusting others to show us how to purify our corpus of beliefs. Once it is admitted that we may have acquired from parents and teachers many beliefs which appear certain but which threaten to distort all of our inquiries, an investigation characterized in Descartes' individualist and foundationalist terms can seem attractive. This first sceptical challenge is thus used to justify the project of the *Meditations*. Further and deeper challenges emerge as he tries to execute the project.

As is well known, the further development of sceptical arguments in the first *Meditation* goes through three stages; at each stage, more is put in question. The argument's structure reflects the assumption that all his most certain and secure beliefs 'I have acquired either from the senses or through the senses' (1641 p.12, see Descartes 1648 pp.3, 53–4). A merit of the method of doubt is that it provides 'the easiest route by which the mind may be led away from the senses' (1641 p.9) The first stage of this process involves the observation that the senses are not generally trustworthy since they often deceive, and meets the familiar response that this will not warrant any *general* scepticism about the senses since we are normally only deceived in highly abnormal or unfavourable circumstances. A square tower may appear round in the distance, but we make no mistakes about its shape when it is close by and well lit.

Hence Descartes presses his doubts further. Unwilling to base a sceptical challenge on the fact that the mad can be convinced of things which are plainly absurd, he observes that even the sane can be deceived when asleep and dreaming. Unless we can eliminate the suspicion that our experience is no more reliable than a dream, he urges, we cannot take sensory beliefs seriously. This is discussed in section 3. The dream argument introduces radical doubts about the deliverances of the senses, and it gives way to a deeper doubt still. Unless we can eliminate the possibility that we are the victims of an all powerful evil demon, we can have no confidence in either the senses or those rational principles which seem most evident. This challenge, further discussed in section 4, is supposed to present the deepest possible scepticism.

3. *The dream argument*

Sextus mentions dreaming:

> Sleeping and waking, too, give rise to different impressions, since
> we do not imagine when awake what we imagine in sleep, nor in
> sleep what we imagine when awake; so that the existence of our
> impressions is not absolute but relative, being in relation to our
> sleeping or waking condition.
>
> (PH1 104)

Rather than casting doubt upon our ability to tell whether we are awake
or sleeping, he draws a relativist conclusion from our lack of a criterion
for determining whether it is waking or sleeping impressions which
reveal the nature of reality: 'in dreams we see things which to our
waking state are unreal, although not wholly unreal; for they exist in our
dreams, just as waking realities exist, although nonexistent in our
dreams' (ibid.).

The argument about dreams in the *Meditations* is different. Descartes
notes that while asleep he can seem to be apprehending things in highly
favourable ways, although they are not really so: it can seem to him that
he is 'here in [his] dressing gown, sitting by the fire' when he is really
'lying undressed in bed' (1641 p.13). He may feel his waking experience
to have a vividness lacking in dreams:

> Indeed! As if I did not remember other occasions when I have been
> tricked by exactly similar thoughts while asleep! As I think about
> this more carefully, I see plainly that there are never any sure signs
> by means of which being awake can be distinguished from being
> asleep. The result is that I begin to feel dazed, and this very feeling
> only reinforces the notion that I may be asleep.
>
> (1641 p.13)

The suggestion is that, since there appear to be no features of our waking
experience which clearly distinguish it from a dream, we should
suspend judgment on all sensory judgments, even those concerned with
nearby objects in circumstances which are highly favourable for
observation.

We most naturally take Descartes to be claiming that we have no
right to rely upon our own perceptions unless we have a criterion that
will enable us to tell whether we are dreaming or awake: the sceptical

doubt will be met only when we have a rule for determining whether we are dreaming. Such a rule might enable us to do two things: when we are awake, it would enable us to establish that we were not asleep and dreaming; and, when asleep, it would enable us to recognize that we are dreaming and not awake. It is very implausible that a dreamer should, while asleep, be able to detect that he is dreaming, and fortunately Descartes does not require this. For his purposes, it is enough that someone who is awake can establish with certainty that this is the case (see Williams, 1978 app. 3); although it may also be desirable that someone who is awake can recognize which remembered experiences derive from dreams rather than from sensory experience. Hence, replying to Hobbes, Descartes takes it as evident that we can deceive ourselves when asleep – although, once awake, we can detect the error (1641 p.137).

In the sixth *Meditation*, when Descartes dismisses 'the exaggerated doubts of the last few days' as 'laughable' he returns to 'the principal reason for doubt, namely my inability to distinguish between being asleep and being awake'(1641 p.61). This confirms that his concern is with the argument just described. However passages in the *Discourse* suggest a different argument: 'For how do we know that the thoughts which come to us in dreams are any more false than the others, seeing that they are often no less lively and distinct?' (1637 p.130, see Wilson 1978, p.24). This is closer to Sextus' dream argument: the challenge it provides would remain in force even if we could establish with certainty that we were 'awake'. Suppose that waking experience does have a phenomenological feature distinguishing it from dreams; we might question whether that feature serves as a mark of *truth*. Although this argument is suggested by the passage quoted, it is not explicitly presented. For the passage in the *Discourse* also carries the implication that the features we rely upon in recognizing waking experience are also present in dreams and are thus not sufficient to warrant treating only the former as cognitively reliable sources of information about 'real existence'. Descartes' arguments thus focus primarily on the lack of a phenomenological mark to distinguish veridical experience from dream and delusion. The apparent lack of such a mark can be employed in sceptical challenges in two ways. First, as in the *Meditations*: what reason have we to suppose that we are not now dreaming? Second, in the passage from the *Discourse*: what reason is there to regard either dream or waking experience as a source of reliable information about 'real existence'?

According to Barry Stroud, the dream argument exploits the principle that unless we can eliminate all possibilities incompatible with the truth of what we claim to know, we lack genuine knowledge (1984 p.25). Suppose that I claim perceptual knowledge of a purple book in front of me. If I were dreaming and no purple book were around, my 'experience' might be just as it is and the belief be false. So unless I can rule out that possibility, my claim to knowledge of the book cannot be sustained. Since, for most ordinary perceptual judgments, it is implausible that they could issue from a dream only if they were true, our ordinary claims to perceptual knowledge are seemingly undermined if we cannot rule out the possibility that we are dreaming. Descartes' emphasis is on 'certainty' rather than 'knowledge', so this does not apply directly to his formulation of the dream argument, but it is easily adapted to fit his version. If we claim to be certain of a proposition, but we cannot rule out a possibility which is inconsistent with its truth, we have no response to the challenge that our certainty is unwarranted. Our certainty in our perceptual judgments reveals that we take it for granted that we are not dreaming (*Meditations* argument) and that waking experience is true to the nature of reality (*Discourse* argument): our certainty appears to rest on presuppositions which are groundless. It is important, of course, for the sceptical force of the dream argument that it threatens all of our perceptual beliefs if it threatens any: unless it can be defeated (in both of its forms) we are, apparently, not warranted in any of our perceptual beliefs; any or all could be the result of a dream or fail to provide truths about reality.

One way to present a sceptical challenge to a belief is to conjecture a (causal) explanation of our holding it which is compatible with its falsity. The *Meditations* version of the dream argument effectively does that. If we admit that dreams are caused subjectively (in some sense, we construct them ourselves), then we cannot rule out the possibility that what seems to be waking experience has a similar subjective cause. A response to such a challenge might have to rely upon a version of the Stoic doctrine that an experience contains traces of its causal history, so that we could tell from inspecting the experience that it was caused by the state of affairs which it represents. It is a strength of this version of the argument that it exploits a possibility which we find genuinely intelligible: we might at any time be deceived in a way in which we sometimes are deceived. As Descartes notes, the possibility that all this is a dream produces a sort of intellectual vertigo – we are almost convinced by it. It seems to be a real possibility.

The *Discourse* argument is more abstract. It does not offer a genuine possibility which, it alleges, we cannot eliminate. It, rather, uses the comparison of dream experience and waking experience to question whether any of our experiences bear what we might call the 'mark of truth'. In that case, it may not be possible to formulate the possibility which has to be eliminated in terms other than 'the possibility that this experience is deceptive'. If this makes the argument more powerful and more general, its weakness is that the alternative possibilities invoked are so abstract as to have no grip upon the imagination. It is easy to envisage how people who are persuaded that the dream possibility must be defeated would take less seriously the abstract suggestion that we do not know that there is not another possibility that we have not formulated. Yet the more abstract argument seems to rely upon such suggestions.

Since Descartes is concerned here with scepticism about knowledge derived through the *senses*, the sceptical use of these observations seems clear. The discussion, recall, grows out of the observation that what we take to be our most certain and useful information is acquired 'from the senses or through the senses'. If our sensory input cannot inform us of whether we are asleep or awake, then 'our most certain and useful information' is placed in doubt. Our right to our confidence in our beliefs about ordinary empirical states of affairs and about the reality of the external world is put into question. We have no warranted certainty that there are external things, that we have bodies, and that our surroundings have the character we take them to have.

In order to meet this challenge head on, it would be necessary to provide a criterion – to point towards a feature of our waking experience which cannot be replicated in dreams; and (presumably) to provide a defence of this criterion – a demonstration that this feature is indeed indicative of our experience having the proper kind of cause. As we discover by the end of the *Meditations*, the greater coherence of our waking experience does have a role in justifying our reliance upon it. But the certainty in question is not given directly by the senses; it is guaranteed by the power and goodness of God. Descartes' guiding assumption that our most useful and certain knowledge comes from the senses has, by then, been abandoned. He still accepts that our experience does not bear an infallible mark that it is not a dream; and he still accepts that sensory experience does not bear a mark of its cognitive reliability. The mind has been 'led away' from the senses, and our right to rely upon what we take to be waking experience is derived from reason.

Descartes insists that there are limits to the sceptical doubts instigated by the possibility that I am dreaming. When I dream of fantastic creatures, corresponding to nothing in everyday waking experience, all I do is to re-arrange simple elements which are common to dream and waking experience. I combine the head of a lion with the body of a man, and so on: there are limits to how far dream experience can differ from waking experience. He alleges that a range of simple conceptions and fundamental principles cannot be touched by the dream argument: for example, 'corporeal nature in general, and its extension, the shape of extended things; the quantity, quantity or size and number; the place in which they may exist, the time through which they endure, and so on' (1641 p.14). Descartes finds it natural to conclude from this that while sciences which deal with 'composite things', such as physics and medicine, are rendered doubtful by the dream argument, those, like geometry and arithmetic, which are solely concerned with simples are untouched:

> For whether I am awake or asleep, two and three added together are five, and a square has no more than four sides. It seems impossible that such transparent truths should incur any suspicion of being false.

> (p.14)

Some of this is implausible. Descartes merely asserts that the dream argument does not ground sceptical doubts about our knowledge of simples and mathematics. It is hard to deny that a geometric proof or calculation which was, in fact, invalid might compel assent in a dream. So perhaps the dream can extend sceptical doubts further than Descartes allows. It is likely that Descartes is partly guilty of allowing his positive metaphysical views to influence his description of how the methodological reflection of the first *Meditation* will develop. However this need not matter for he has a good reason not to investigate how far dream scepticism can extend.

This depends upon the fact that Descartes advances to a further, stronger sceptical challenge: the evil demon. Since this is supposed to provide the strongest possible scepticism, it will enable him to doubt anything which a more rigorously developed dream argument could challenge. Since there are bound to be contingent limits to how far dream experience can differ from everyday experience, there are bound to be limits to how far dream scepticism can extend. So, since the demon argument will be required anyway if the strongest scepticism is to be secured, there is little point delaying its adoption by staying with the dream argument. Moreover, Descartes uses the dream argument to warrant scepticism about the senses and then employs the demon argument to press his scepticism beyond the senses. Hence the role of the arguments reflects the different stages of sceptical doubt.

This helps to explain why there is no anticipation of another popular argument: even if I possessed a criterion which distinguished dream experience from waking experience, would I need a further criterion to establish whether, on some particular occasion, I merely dream that I have applied it successfully? Such a use of the dream possibility extends doubt beyond the senses. It may also explain why the *Discourse* dream argument has little role in the *Meditations*: the more abstract issues about truth which it appears to raise receive a clearer formulation in the suggestion that we might be deceived by an evil demon.

4. The demon

The dream hypothesis seems to be unable to induce doubts of those ideas and conceptions whose clarity and evidence seem to make it impossible to suspect them of any falsity or uncertainty. Our assurance that the origin of these ideas does not lie within us results from the apparent psychological impossibility of our doubting their 'truth'. However, the fact that I find these ideas or principles indubitable does not guarantee their truth: I take myself to have been created by an all-powerful God, and it would surely have been within His capacity that I be deceived in what seems most certain. We might suppose this to be incompatible with His goodness; but since He sometimes does allow people to fall into error, even permitting them to make mistakes in elementary arithmetic, it is not self-evident that Divine benevolence could not lead Him to ensure that we are always deceived. So Descartes proposes an explanation of our finding such ideas so clear and certain which is compatible with their falsehood. And, as he remarks, if there is no God, it is all the less surprising that we be imperfect and prone to error even about what is most certain. In general, my finding a proposition indubitable is no guarantee of its truth.

The doubt in simple ideas and mathematics thus induced is 'very slight, and so to speak metaphysical' (1641 p.25). According to Descartes, this distinguishes them from doubts arising from the possibility that we are dreaming. The force of the distinction is not altogether clear. However we can bring out two relevant considerations.

First, the ground of these doubts is wholly hypothetical. It is part of ordinary experience that dreams occur and can produce mistaken beliefs about reality: the dream argument challenges our right to determine how far such deception extends. Since we accept that it sometimes occurs, it is a real possibility that it occurs more often than we suppose. However, as Descartes stresses, at this stage of the inquiry, we have no positive reason to suppose that God would deceive us, or, even that he exists (1641 p.25). The present doubt lacks the dream argument's connection with ordinary experience: we are faced with a bare possibility which we have no inclination to take seriously. The second consideration is more important. If these ideas and principles are psychologically indubitable, then (obviously) they cannot be doubted: all I can entertain is the abstract possibility of doubt, a reflective recognition that indubitability-for-me is no guarantee of truth (Schouls, 1980 p.96). The 'slightness' of the doubt then might reside in a complex form of cognitive dissonance: there are propositions which (psychologically) I *cannot* doubt but which (reflectively) I judge that I *ought* to doubt if error is to be avoided. That something of this sort is involved is clear from Descartes' strategy for escaping from his sceptical doubts. He insists that these ideas or principles can be doubted only when we are not attending to them properly. While attending to them, our certainty cannot be shaken; when our attention turns elsewhere, suspicion of this certainty can intrude. But this suspicion is likely to be highly unstable: once we attend to the idea again, our certainty re-asserts itself. Our judgment that the idea *ought* to be doubted is, presumably, made when the idea is not itself a focus of full attention (see chapter IV, section 2).

Since such doubts are so unstable, we risk pressing these sceptical arguments incompletely or inexpertly by acquiescing in some natural belief which should be challenged by this final level of doubt. To reduce this risk Descartes reformulates his proposal making it easier to appreciate the force of these doubts. Rather than suspending judgment about whether the sum of two and three is five, for example, we are tough-mindedly to regard anything dubitable as false: however certain something may seem, we are to pretend that it is false if we possibly can. And as an aid to this – and to remind us that so far the existence of God is dubitable – we are to pretend that our experiences are engineered by the demon, a malign spirit whose single-minded concern is to ensure that all of our beliefs and ideas are mistaken. This additional twist does not affect the range of the sceptical doubt, but helps us to resist the temptation too readily to conclude that some judgment or other is absolutely indubitable: we now have to ask whether our certainty could have been induced by this malicious demon; and our beliefs must be defensible against an antagonist who holds not only that they are poorly supported but that all are false. An explanation of our assurances is proffered which entails their falsity: unless we can explain the right with which we reject this explanation of our beliefs, our certainty appears hollow and illegitimate.

Having described Descartes' sceptical arguments in detail, we should ask what he has added to the sceptical canon bequeathed by Sextus. Descartes sometimes suggests that the first *Meditation* contains nothing new (e.g. 1641 p.94 and comments by Hobbes and Gassendi ibid. pp.121, 180). However, in *The Conversation with Burman*, he explains that he wishes to go beyond the 'customary difficulties of the Sceptics' and raise and demolish 'every single doubt': 'And this is the purpose behind the introduction at this point of the demon, which some might criticize as a superfluous addition' (1648 p.4). As well as the heuristic considerations mentioned in the previous paragraph, this involves the non-piecemeal character of Descartes' doubts. Pyrrhonists employed an extensive compendium of modes; and they hoped that some of these could be used on any occasion to force someone to withdraw a dogmatic claim. Once the third stage of Descartes' argument has been reached, he seems to have one argument available which puts *everything* into question at once: the demon raises the possibility that *all* of our most cherished beliefs are mistaken. Hence he remarks in the first *Meditation*:

> So, for the purpose of rejecting all my opinions, it will be enough if I find in each of them at least some reason for doubt. And to do this I will not run through them all individually, which would be an endless task. Once the foundations of the building are undermined, anything built on them collapses of its own accord; so I will go straight for the basic principles on which all my previous beliefs rested.
>
> (1641 p.12)

Only general sceptical arguments of the sort Descartes proposes will contribute to an *exhaustive* search for sources of possible error in our beliefs (Williams 1986 p.124). If a dogmatic assertion fails to crumble before Pyrrhonist assault, this may be because the wrong modes were employed or because the Pyrrhonist manual is incomplete. There is no room for the parallel speculation that some belief may survive the demon hypothesis which could be undermined by further sceptical arguments. Its very abstractness can assure Descartes that he has pushed sceptical arguments to the limit: there are no contingent limitations to the causal powers of the demon. If a belief is not put into question by the demon hypothesis, there is no lingering possibility that it might be challenged in some other fashion: it is secure and provides Descartes with the Archimedean point he desires in order to reconstruct science.

If contemporary epistemologists are reluctant to ground their views in speculations about demons, modern versions of Descartes' grounds for metaphysical doubt are plentiful. Fanciful science fiction stories are introduced which, in one step, cast doubt upon all of our beliefs by raising the possibility that they have a cause outside ourselves which ensures that we are deceived. The best known of these is clearly expressed by Hilary Putnam (1981 pp.5–6; see also Pollock 1987 pp.1 ff., and Lehrer 1971).

> [imagine] that a human being (you can imagine this to be yourself) has been subjected to an operation by an evil scientist. The person's brain (your brain) has been removed from the body and placed in a vat of nutrients which keeps the brain alive. The nerve endings have been connected to a super-scientific computer which causes the person whose brain it is to have the illusion that everything is perfectly normal. There seem to be people, objects, the sky etc; but really all the person (you) is experiencing is the result of electronic impulses travelling from the computer to the nerve endings.

The machine can give the person the illusion that he is acting and experiencing the results of his actions; it can interfere with his memories; and, as Putnam conjectures, it can give him the experience of reading the paragraph quoted above and finding the supposition that he might be a brain in a vat utterly absurd (Putnam 1981, p.6).

This argument appears to rewrite Descartes' evil demon argument for a secular age, the two arguments having a similar structure. In so far as we can picture ourselves in the role of the scientist and reflect on the attitude we would then take towards the affirmations of the victim, the brain-in-a-vat possibility is less 'hypothetical' than the Cartesian one. However, for two reasons, this strength of the evil scientist hypothesis brings corresponding weaknesses. First, since a disembodied brain floating in a vat is wholly unlike a real human being, it invites the quick response that such a 'subject' could not really bear psychological states such as beliefs at all. In that case, it might be less useful than Descartes' original proposal for formulating deep epistemological problems. Second, the role of the demon hypothesis in producing the 'deepest scepticism' requires there to be no contingent limitations to the demon's power: if there were such limitations, we could admit the possibility of a stronger sceptical argument exploiting a deceiver who lacked these limitations. The brain-in-a-vat argument resembles the dream argument: there may be technological, physical and physiological limitations to the extent of the deception which the wicked scientist could induce; his power is more limited than that of Descartes' demon. Descartes needs a deceiver whose nature is described in the thinnest possible terms: he is all powerful, and he is malign; neither his power nor his propensity to deceive is subject to any contingent limitation.

The remainder of this chapter develops our understanding of the sceptical arguments of the first *Meditation*. We return to the question of why Descartes thought that trial through scepticism was philosophically important. And the final section examines how far scepticism about the existence of the external world, a characteristic focus of twentieth century discussions of scepticism, first enters the philosophical tradition with the work of Descartes. Themes arising out of Descartes' *response* to scepticism are the concern of chapter IV.

5. Cartesian doubt and the everyday criticism of belief

At the beginning of this chapter, we raised the question of what led Descartes to adopt the project of using scepticism to give birth to certainty. Is the project attractive to him because of particular characteristics of his other intellectual concerns? Or is it compulsory for any responsible inquirer, reflecting constraints implicit in our ordinary sense of reason or justification? There will be a fuller discussion of this in the following chapter. At this point, we shall draw attention to some relevant considerations which have emerged in recent sections.

In a famous passage, the pragmatist Charles Peirce described the distinctive features of Cartesianism. They included the doctrine that philosophy should begin with universal doubt; the claim that the ultimate test of certainty is to be found in the individual consciousness; and a stress that non-foundational beliefs were to be justified by 'a single thread of inference' tracing them to often 'inconspicuous premisses' (W2 p.211–12, 1868; for fuller discussion, see Hookway 1985 pp.20 ff.). Modern science, Peirce urged, requires us to abandon these individualist and foundationalist views. For example, he protested:

We cannot begin with complete doubt. We must begin with all the prejudices which we actually have when we enter upon the study of philosophy. These prejudices are not to be dispelled by a maxim, for they are things which it does not occur to us *can* be questioned. Hence this initial skepticism will be a mere self-deception, and not real doubt. ... A person may, it is true, in the course of his studies, find reason to doubt what he began by believing; but in that case he doubts because he has a positive reason for it, and not on account of the Cartesian maxim. Let us not pretend to doubt in philosophy what we do not doubt in our hearts.

(W2 p.212)

Peirce claims, first, that the Cartesian method is psychologically impossible; the insulation of these philosophical doubts from everyday life shows that they are insincere or pretence. Second, he denies that the legitimacy of these doubts flows from our pre-philosophical understanding of truth, justification, or inquiry. And, third, he holds that there is nothing in the character of modern science which requires us to adopt the Cartesian strategy.

There is much in this passage which would have appealed to constructive sceptics like Mersenne and Gassendi. In Peirce's work, this view is linked to a profoundly un-Cartesian view of science. He repudiates the individualistic and foundationalist viewpoint. We undertake scientific investigations as members of a community of like-minded inquirers, learning from the testimony of others, and subjecting their theories to critical scrutiny. Scientific theories are fallible: theories currently found plausible may subsequently be refuted, perceptual beliefs currently deemed certain may later be abandoned; but the practice of placing our confidence in theories currently certain, and subjecting them to severe critical tests enables the community of investigators to eliminate error and eventually progress towards the truth. Science does not fit the foundationalist pattern: 'Its reasoning should not resemble a chain which is no stronger than its weakest link, but a cable whose fibers may be ever so slender, provided they are sufficiently numerous and intimately connected' (W2 p.213).

This picture of scientific activity as making fallible progress by building on the successes of earlier inquirers conflicts with Descartes' view. The two pictures employ contrasting analogies to capture the structure of intellectual criticism. Descartes announces that 'if we have a basket or tub full of apples and want to make sure that there are no

59

rotten ones, we should first tip them all out, leaving none at all inside, and then pick up again (or get from elsewhere) only those apples in which no flaw can be detected' (1641 p.349). But of course modern philosophers are aware of other metaphors: our position is that of a sailor who rebuilds his ship at sea, placing rotten or damaged planks while the remaining timbers keep his ship afloat. This is contrasted with a nautical version of the apple analogy: the shipwright removes the leaky vessel to a dry dock and strips it down completely before rebuilding it from the keel up (Neurath 1932–3 p.201, Quine 1969 pp.126–7, 1981 p.72). We may all agree that if a body of knowledge can triumph through the Cartesian foundationalist programme, then its claims to our respect are unimpeachable. But the availability of the alternative fallibilist picture with its attendant metaphors, may suggest that the success of the Cartesian programme is not a necessary condition of our being able to take our scientific knowledge seriously.

A Cartesian could respond that the fallibilist picture is unstable: unless we have a demon-proof assurance that we are contributing to eventual progress towards the truth, then our participation in the community of scientific investigation is ungrounded. Towards the end of the following chapter, we shall address such an argument. For the present, we should note some features of Descartes' intellectual projects which might provide a special reason for his individualist foundationalist approach. He was attempting to construct a new dogmatic scientific theory which had few continuities with the work of Galileo or sceptical empiricists. This individualistic and revolutionary character of Descartes' own scientific activity may itself explain the appeal of the Cartesian strategy: if he seeks to replace an emerging tradition of scientific research which has not evidently run into the ground, he cannot rely upon the customary standards of any scientific tradition. Moreover, somebody impressed by Descartes' avowed theological targets may point out that fallible religious knowledge provides too tentative a basis for living faith; or that it conflicts with the view that man is made in the image of God, that our knowledge is so feeble and fallible in comparison with His. Hence it may not be merely anachronistic to criticize Descartes for failing to adopt a fallibilistic conception of science that was not clearly formulated in the seventeenth century. In his view, the failings of prevailing scientific beliefs and methods of inquiry were so extensive that there were no grounds for confidence that further inquiries of the same sort would eliminate these errors. If our fundamental standards for evaluating methods of inquiry are themselves among the rotten apples, we have no reason to expect scientific 'progress' to yield methods which will filter the rotten from the sound.

This provides the context for evaluating the complaint that Descartes' doubts are unreal or a pretence, and the related view that simply adopting the 'maxim' of taking as false anything which could be the result of the demon's deceptions cannot produce a 'live' doubt in anything. We have already noticed that Descartes acknowledges that these doubts are 'slight' or 'metaphysical', and we have suggested that they may involve little more than the sense that we ought to doubt what, psychologically, we find indubitable. They are 'insulated' from ordinary life, having no impact upon domestic concerns or planning our activities. Does this destroy their philosophical importance? Suppose that we are working within a community of philosophical investigators that is aware that its 'knowledge' is incomplete and flawed in unknown ways. However we are confident of the possibility of scientific progress and hopeful that we can contribute to it. From this perspective, it is natural to look upon the Cartesian challenges as empty and pointless, as blocking the road of inquiry by impeding the use of fallible methods to arrive at truth. Suppose, by contrast, that we are not confident of scientific progress and fear that science is running into the ground or weaving an illusory picture of reality sustained by self-deception about its methods and achievements. In such circumstances, it seems, the sense that we cannot embrace doubts whose legitimacy we cannot undermine can lead to a sense of estrangement from the practice of scientific inquiry. Descartes' first level of doubt was supposed to make the reliability of science a matter for investigation, and this may be sufficient to give the later 'slight' doubts psychological force. Moreover, the method of doubt may serve as a filter to separate the mind from the senses and hence help us to understand the sources of our knowledge without producing any really live doubt. In contrast, Peirce wrote from a nineteenth century perspective that was confident of both the achievement and promise of science; from that perspective it is less clear that such doubts are to be taken seriously.

The fact that these doubts are not real, that we are not really convinced, may still be significant in responding to those who believe that the need to respond to these doubts is implicit in the ordinary conceptions of knowledge and justification. Our response to the dream hypothesis is peculiarly indeterminate. We feel the force of it; it is easy to alert students to the need to respond to the challenge. But it makes absolutely no difference to our lives: we retain all our old certainties when making assertions or planning actions. (These issues are discussed in Hookway 1988 pp. 192–9.) The view that these sceptical worries are implicit in our ordinary practice requires us to see the retention of these certainties as somehow irrational or pretence. We might respond to this that their 'insulation' from practical concerns casts doubts upon the analyses of justification and knowledge which the 'sceptic' employs. Lacking a detailed explanation of what these errors consist in, however, this may serve only to signal a commendable suspicion of philosophical arguments which appear to challenge what most people find obvious. Its characteristic philosophical force derives from the arguments found in the common sense tradition (see chapter II, section 7 above and chapter VI).

6. Conclusion: the external world

As we have seen, Descartes develops sceptical arguments in a more systematic fashion than the Pyrrhonists, and he attempts to formulate the strongest possible sceptical challenge. Both of these features of his work reflect his ambition to attain certainty by overcoming the most powerful sceptical arguments. In this section, we consider an aspect of the scepticism of the first *Meditation* which seems less radical than earlier scepticisms. It connects to a point mentioned above: for much contemporary epistemology, what is characteristic of 'modern' post-Cartesian philosophy is the special importance it attaches to sceptical worries about the existence of the external world. Philosophical engagement with scepticism can seem indistinguishable from a concern with refuting solipsism, the doctrine that all that exists are myself and my own psychological states. If all is a dream, then my experience could be just as it is although no external thing corresponds to it. The status of anything which is not 'in' some mind becomes exceedingly problematic.

In one respect, the problem of the external world was not new. Suspension of belief about the existence of external things could presumably be achieved through the Pyrrhonian modes. There is no reason why they could not be used to compel a dogmatist to suspend judgment on the claim that there are physical objects and human beings other than himself, or the claim that he has a body or that he is not the only existing thing. The change we are considering is evident in the *importance* that such sceptical targets acquired in the modern era.

Perhaps because the Pyrrhonist's dogmatic opponents were primarily interested in defending general principles and laws, such existential judgments do not have a prominent role in *Outlines of Pyrrhonism*. Why, then, do they become more central for the modern discussion?

The development is linked to a change in the understanding of 'appearance'. In chapter I, we distinguished two ways of understanding the Pyrrhonist's insistence that he can assent to appearances. One employed a unitary notion of 'assent' and admitted that Pyrrhonist doubt was restricted by subject matter; the other saw 'acquiescing in appearance' as a distinctive kind of non-dogmatic propositional attitude which could be taken towards a proposition with any subject matter. It was argued that the latter best fits Sextus' use of this notion and pointed out that employing the former would have committed Pyrrhonists to a distinctive (dogmatic) theory of mind and perception, contrary to their sceptical position. Appearances are not distinctive *objects* of knowledge; accepting appearances is a distinctive sceptical manner of assent to propositions about ordinary things (see chapter I section 4). Descartes' position seems closer to the first of the two interpretations of Pyrrhonism. Appearances are a distinctive ontological category, they are modifications of the mind. By the second *Meditation*, Descartes argues that we do have certain knowledge of these subjective appearances. His developed position holds that our immediate certainty about the nature of our own ideas provides the evidential base for our perceptual beliefs about external objects. External things cause modifications of our minds which we immediately perceive. This makes the task of showing how awareness of our own subjective states licenses beliefs about external objects wholly central to epistemology. The solipsistic possibility that we cannot advance beyond these subjective certainties articulates this new version of the worry that we cannot legitimately judge how things are in their nature on the basis of appearances. The related doctrine ('subjective idealism') that all that exists are ideas and modifications of mind ('subjective idealism') can be formulated too (see Burnyeat 1982).

In view of this, it is natural to worry that Descartes' presentation of his sceptical arguments relies upon a distinctive theory of mind and perception; and Michael Williams has argued that the Cartesian metaphysical scheme is already, and illegitimately, taken for granted in the first *Meditation* (Williams 1986). If that were so, we might suppose that he had not developed the strongest possible sceptical argument. I shall illustrate this by reference to the dream argument. That appeared

63

to rest upon the claim that dream experience and waking experience could be qualitatively identical, that the immediate objects of dream 'experience' and sensory experience could be the same. We could imagine a sophisticated Pyrrhonist challenging Descartes' right to make such judgments of qualitative similarity: how can he justify his assurance that his judgments about the contents of his mind carry authority? It might be argued that this 'transparency of mind' (its self-intimating character) is taken for granted in the ways in which the doubts of the first *Meditation* are introduced, and that it is a potentially questionable feature of the Cartesian metaphysical scheme.

The dream argument could probably survive this criticism; it is easy to construct versions of it which do not rely upon our ability to acquire certain knowledge of the contents of our minds. When dreaming, I have often mistakenly taken myself to be perceiving things in a waking state; how do I know that I am not now similarly deceived? This rests upon the plain truth that we are often deceived about the causes of our opinions, and it remains neutral on the question whether both dreaming and waking involve immediate acquaintance with subjective appearances. Or, dream experience *appears* to be qualitatively similar to waking experience, and it does not appear to us that we have any defensible criterion which will enable us to discriminate the two. Descartes' claim that he sees 'plainly that there are never any sure signs by means of which being awake can be distinguished from being asleep' (1641 p.13) is less tentative in its claims about the contents of his mind, and it is this which grounds the suspicion that his scepticism is less deep than it might be.

We might suppose that these more tentative versions of the dream argument would serve Descartes' purposes as well as the argument that he does use. Moreover doubts about external reality would be as well grounded by the recognition that we do not know whether we have the right to discriminate dream experience from waking experience as by the assurance that we know that we do not. However, abandoning the assumption of the transparency of mind could prevent the sceptical arguments serving Descartes' further philosophical purposes. It appears to be required for the development of his argument after the first *Meditation*, and it may be implicated in the ways in which Descartes develops his doubts in *Meditation I*. The dream argument is supposed to demonstrate the unreliability of the senses as a source of information about our surroundings. This requires the premiss that the senses cannot determine whether we are awake; and this premiss is available only if we have the ability to determine what information the senses provide, and this calls for the transparency of mind. Without this assumption, Descartes could draw only the disjunctive conclusion: either the senses do not unaided provide reliable knowledge of reality or we lack the ability to discover what information the senses actually deliver.

As I have suggested, the sceptical force of the dream argument – and the demon argument – is not touched by this challenge. What is rendered questionable is Descartes' use of his sceptical arguments. Moreover we have not considered how far it may be possible to vindicate something like the transparency of mind without relying upon a distinctive dogmatic or metaphysical position. I shall, in fact, argue below that a proper understanding of the role of sceptical arguments in challenging our cognitive powers may provide room for a version of the transparency of mind doctrine which avoids the criticisms sketched here. This argument will be better presented after we have discussed some issues arising out of the strategies Descartes employs in responding to the sceptical challenges he has mounted.

CHAPTER IV

Descartes' Legacy: Science and Circularity

1. Introduction: foundations and the circle

Having secured the deepest possible sceptical doubt, Descartes finds 'foundations' for science which enable him to win through to certainty. By the second *Meditation* he has established: '*I am, I exist*, is necessarily true whenever it is put forward by me or conceived in my mind' (1641 p.17). He is equally certain that he is essentially a thinking thing with indubitable knowledge of his own mental states. Relying upon principles of reason which are equally undeniable, he obtains proofs which establish the existence of God. Once he is certain of God's existence, the demon hypothesis is defeated, and he is warranted in trusting his reason and senses so long as he does not wilfully misuse them. God would not allow him to be deceived so long as he makes proper use of the faculties with which God has endowed him.

As mentioned above, the Cartesian position cannot survive detailed critical analysis. The value of continuing our discussion of it lies in the strategy Descartes employs which is more sophisticated than some modern commentators have allowed. Our focus in this chapter will be the structure of Descartes' 'foundationalism' and his response to the common charge that his anti-sceptical strategy is circular. This accusation of circularity takes a form that will be familiar from chapter I. When an opponent of scepticism proposed a criterion which could be used to identify which appearances were veridical, a Pyrrhonist would question the credentials of that criterion. The modes of Agrippa suggested that the only real alternative to setting out along an infinite regress (by appealing to a further criterion to support the criterion that had been questioned) was to argue in a circle, defending the criterion by reference to beliefs which themselves required validation by that very criterion. This pattern of argument was so central to the sceptical tradition that a philosopher could not seriously claim to have an answer to scepticism unless he believed that he could avoid both regress and circle. Descartes clearly believed that he was able to do this, but few commentators have thought his strategy successful: indeed, there is little consensus about what his strategy against the charge of circularity is.

First, what form does the charge of circularity take? Having 'proved' God's existence, Descartes asks what the evidence of God's existence provided by the proof consists in. He notices that the proof furnishes a clear and distinct perception of God's existence: this grounds his psychological certainty that God exists and is the source of his assurance that this certainty is legitimate. This yields a proposition which Descartes appears to employ as a criterion of truth:

Anything which is clearly and distinctly perceived is true.

A sceptic would challenge this: surely the demon could deceive us into believing, falsely, that clarity and distinctness was a mark of truth. With what right do we treat clarity and distinctness as a criterion of truth? Descartes' answer to this question appears to be that God would not permit us to be deceived in what we clearly and distinctly perceive; for us to be so deceived would conflict with His goodness. The apparent circularity is plain: our assurance that God exists rests upon our clearly and distinctly perceiving that He does; yet our right to trust our clear and distinct perceptions depends upon our assurance that God exists and is benevolent. The problem is, of course, that once our criterion of truth is put in question, we cannot rely upon beliefs whose acceptance is conditional upon the adequacy of that criterion. This question about the appearance of circularity was introduced in the *Objections* to the *Meditations* by, for example, Arnauld (1641 p.150), and it was much discussed at the time.

Since the problem of circularity was so central to discussions within the sceptical tradition, it is very unlikely that Descartes succumbed to such an obvious form of it. It was predictable that Descartes' critics would have anticipated just such a circle in any response to scepticism; and it is also obvious that avoiding such circularities would have been central to Descartes' understanding of his task. His attempts to explain why the circle does not arise must thus be seen, not as desperate attempts to shore up a sinking position, but rather as an effort to elucidate a logical structure that was present in his position from the beginning.

Those who were sympathetic to sceptical positions would not expect Descartes to avoid the problem of circularity; but, if they are right in this, we should not expect the circle to be as plain and open to view as the diagnosis offered above suggests.

In the following section we shall introduce a reading of Descartes' response to the charge of circularity. Before doing so, some preliminary observations are required. Descartes is avowedly looking for 'certain foundations' for science, and we must offer some elucidation of both 'certainty' and 'foundations'. What, for Descartes, is involved in the claim that something is 'certain'? The term is sometimes used to describe a subjective attitude towards a proposition: we are certain of it if we are pretty sure that it is true. So understood, certainty can be misplaced and even unwarranted: it is not primarily a term of epistemic appraisal. Since Descartes does use 'certain' as a term of epistemic appraisal, he must use it to describe more than such a subjective attitude. It seems that something cannot be 'certain' unless it is true; and I am not certain of something unless I am legitimately sure of it. Indeed, Descartes' description of the 'slight' doubt which undermines the certainty of beliefs whose credentials are challenged by the demon argument illustrates these remarks about the relations between certainty, psychological indubitability and legitimacy. Certainty is a kind of rational warrant; but a proposition is not certain for someone unless he can recognize that it can pass the severest possible tests. Being certain of something acknowledges no possibility of error: the possibility of doubt must not arise.

If our aims in inquiry are to arrive at the truth and, perhaps, to hold beliefs only where there is warrant for doing so, it is hard to see why it is *necessary* for any of our beliefs to have this rather extreme degree of warrant. So long as our beliefs are justified, why do we need certainty? The answer to this question may rest on the need for foundations: perhaps only certainties can serve as foundations. This leads us to examine what is involved in Descartes' search for foundations for science. 'Foundationalism' can suggest two different pictures of the structure of knowledge. Contemporary 'foundationalist' theories of justification articulate the first of these. Typically, when we defend a belief and are asked to justify it, we introduce further beliefs which provide our reason for accepting it. Given Descartes' concern with obtaining sceptic-proof beliefs and with securing certainty, it is natural to attribute to him the view that propositions P1, P2, ... Pn, justify (serve as adequate reasons for) a belief Q only if Q is warranted conditional upon P1, P2, ... Pn all being true. Of course, I am thereby justified in accepting Q only if I am justified in all of P1, P2, ... Pn. I can justify these by offering further reasons which support them; but then the same problem arises about how I can be justified in accepting these further reasons. Unless, illegitimately, I argue in a circle, this process of justification must lead eventually to beliefs which serve as foundations: they are justified, but their warrant does not depend upon other beliefs which serve as reasons for accepting them. Rather they are self-evident, or self-justifying. If this is the picture Descartes has in mind, then the role he assigns to certainty may be explained by suggesting that it provides one way in which beliefs could be justified non-inferentially. Hence this reconstruction of the Cartesian picture of knowledge suggests that all justified beliefs rest upon a foundation of self-evident certainties. It is possible, but not necessary, to augment this with the view that such basic certainties justify other beliefs by making them in turn certain.

The second version of 'foundationalism' avoids the implausible claim that I am justified in a belief which I now hold only if I can provide it with a justification grounded in non-inferential certainties. Indeed, it can even endorse the fallibilist picture of a community of investigators progressing toward the truth by criticizing the theories and opinions which are found plausible at a given time (see chapter III, section 5). We can distinguish the body of logical principles, inductive methods, standards of plausibility and methodological principles employed by inquirers from the scientific opinions and current theories which have been arrived at by the use of these methods. If we treat the former as the 'foundations' of science, we can see how there might be a foundationalist picture which allowed for beliefs to be accepted on the basis of the overall coherence of the body of scientific lore of which they formed part. The picture would be foundationalist because we could do this only because the reliability of doing so is underwritten by the methodological and metaphysical framework which serves as the foundation of science as a whole.

A consequence of this second foundationalist picture is that we can occupy two distinct contexts of inquiry. The 'methodological context' is taken up when we ask:

> If we are careful in using our faculties, can we obtain knowledge of reality?

Since methodological foundations are required to be certain, epistemological investigations into how we should carry out inquiries if we are to discover the truth would proceed according to different rules from those followed when carrying out empirical investigations against the background of these methodological rules. The Peircean picture of inquiry might apply to the latter but not to the former: indeed, Peirce's mature writings employ just such a bipartite picture (see Hookway 1985 ch. 2).

There is evidence that Descartes' foundationalism fits this second pattern. He distinguished the metaphysical and methodological investigations of the *Meditations* from ordinary scientific inquiry: he plainly saw the former as a different kind of inquiry subject to different constraints. It is doubtful that he thought that ordinary science should forswear propositions which could not be grounded in absolutely certain foundations. In his scientific writings and even in the *Meditations* Descartes appeals to fallible hypothetico-deductive inferences to ground his views. In *Meditation VI* he offers a probabilistic argument for the existence of body – it provides the best explanation of the constitution of the imagination (1641 p.51). And his final resolution of 'that very common uncertainty respecting sleep, which I could not distinguish from the waking state' is that the hypothesis that he is now awake provides a better explanation of the coherence found in all of his experiences than the alternative that all is a dream (1641 pp.61–2).

So we shall address the question of how Descartes proposed to answer the charge of circularity on the assumption that his foundationalism was of this second kind. We shall take seriously the distinction between two contexts of inquiry; and we shall assume that the search for certainty is primarily appropriate to the methodological context.

2. *Is there a circle?*

The problem of the Cartesian circle involves the role in justifying our beliefs of inferences with the following form.

I   I clearly and distinctly perceive that *P*.
II Whatever I clearly and distinctly perceive is true. So, *P* is true.

The difficulty is that our acceptance of (II) depends upon the certainty of (III):

III An all powerful, benevolent God exists.

And, it is alleged, an argument of the form in question is involved in the justification of (III). It seems clear that Descartes can avoid the charge of circularity only if this allegation is unfounded. It is plain that he does assign such inferences a role in the justification of beliefs. This role must be limited: we must understand how they can have a role in justifying our beliefs while not being relevant to establishing the conclusions reached in the (early) *Meditations*.

There is much evidence that Descartes denies that we use such inferences in order to vindicate our certainty of simple ideas and fundamental principles. We find claims not wholly unrelated to Peirce's remarks on the insincerity of professions of sceptical doubt: a general sceptical doubt seems possible only for those who are inattentive, or for those who do not perceive things clearly. Descartes holds that when we perceive something clearly and distinctly we find it absolutely indubitable, finding no need for reasons to support our assurance. Hence, scepticism is possible only for those who have never attended to, or concentrated upon, these indubitable claims (1648 p.1). Sceptics have 'never, *qua* sceptics, perceived anything clearly. For the very fact that they had perceived something clearly would mean they had ceased to doubt it, and so ceased to be sceptics' (1641 p.321). The evidence and simplicity of claims such as that I, while I think, exist, ensure that 'we cannot ever think of them without believing them true':

> For we cannot doubt them unless we think of them; but we cannot
> think of them without at the same time believing they are true ....
> Hence we cannot doubt them without at the same time believing
> they are true; that is we can never doubt them.
>
> (1641 p.104)

Although, as we subsequently observe, the propositions we find absolutely indubitable are precisely those which we clearly and distinctly perceive, the judgment that we clearly and distinctly perceive them does not provide part of our reason for accepting them. We simply find them indubitable.

Descartes famously remarks that the key to the circle lies in the fact that God's benevolence has a role in satisfying us about beliefs which, in some fashion, involve memory. Consider a simple arithmetic proposition: $23 \times 47 = 1081$. The position of someone who is now completing this calculation, so that they see, clearly and distinctly we might suppose, that this is correct, can be contrasted with the position of

71

someone who recalls that, yesterday, they obtained such a clear and distinct perception. As Descartes uses the notion, I suggest, only the first is currently 'properly attentive' to the proposition: the other alludes to it in a more superficial manner. Their epistemic relations to the proposition are different. The first possesses an unshakeable certainty that requires no justification: the question of *why* the result of the calculation should be accepted does not arise. Since the second does not 'see' the truth of the proposition, he can ask why he should take the fact that he previously found the proposition irresistible in this manner should provide a reason for accepting it. The inference pattern described at the beginning of this section contributes to the warrant the belief has for the second of these people; it makes no contribution to the warrant it has for the first. Thus although I cannot doubt a proposition *while* I clearly and distinctly perceive it, it is possible for me to doubt a proposition which I *recall* clearly and distinctly perceiving. And this is not because I might doubt the reliability of memory, but rather because I might question whether being clearly and distinctly perceived is, in fact, a mark of truth. For when I recall the clear and distinct perception I clearly and distinctly perceive neither the fact in question nor the nature of clear and distinct perception.

In the following section, we shall examine how this is reflected in Descartes' attempt to provide foundations for science. Before doing so, we note some consequences of this picture for a view of what can be doubted. First, it might be objected to this diagnosis of Descartes' position that it prevents our making sense of a distinction which is fundamental to his argument. According to Descartes, we can achieve a 'slight' doubt in simple ideas or fundamental principles by employing the hypothesis of an all powerful but deceitful spirit. The *cogito*, by contrast, is absolutely indubitable: even the demon could not lead me to be deceived about my own existence. Yet all of these ideas can be clearly and distinctly perceived, so all should be absolutely indubitable: only inattention could lead us to doubt them. Why does Descartes insist that simple ideas are dubitable? And how can his doing so be consistent with his denial of the dubitability of the *cogito*?

The possibility of doubting simple ideas or fundamental principles requires that we can contemplate such ideas or propositions, or use them in reasoning without 'attending' to them properly. Two distinct phenomena can be involved. Often we may use a concept like 'isosceles' or 'gravity' without explicitly thinking of its content: a word may label the concept, collecting a variety of properties together, and although we *could* clarify the concept explicitly, we do not bring its analysis to consciousness every time we make use of it. Alternatively, we might have acquired the concept from our teachers or from books, and although our grasp is sufficient for our practical purposes, we have never achieved a clear understanding of it. Much philosophical analysis is grounded in the assumption that achieving such clarification requires hard work: the full clarification of the concept is not possessed by many ordinarily competent speakers. We may think we have a clear understanding of the concept when we do not do so; or we may be aware that our understanding is superficial. If philosophical work is required to achieve a clear and distinct perception of an idea or proposition, then one might judge it dubitable in advance of carrying out that work but find it indubitable once the philosophical work is complete. Since our understanding is superficial, our finding it dubitable does not rest upon a clear understanding of how we could be in error; it rests on no more than not being able to see it as indubitable. I suggest that the demon-induced doubt in simple ideas and the like has this character: our lack of attention to the ideas and our superficial understanding of them are two sides of the same coin. Once we acquire a perspicuous representation of the functioning of these ideas, the doubts simply disappear.

The special role of the *cogito*, then, depends upon its simplicity. Such is our acquaintance with our 'selves' that a superficial or confused apprehension of our own existence is impossible. We cannot contemplate the *cogito* without 'attending to it' and contemplating it clearly enough to perceive its truth; we cannot believe we grasp the proposition clearly when we do not. This is why the demon hypothesis cannot induce doubt of one's own existence. The demon possibility permits 'slight' doubts when inattentive, confused apprehension of an idea or proposition is a possibility. This accords with Descartes' careful formulation of the *cogito* in the second *Meditation*:

> I am, I exist, is necessarily true whenever it is put forward by me or conceived in my mind.
>
> (1641 p.17)

It is useful to note the range of such indubitable truths. We have seen that they include one's own existence, the contents of one's mental states, simple ideas and primary notions. Descartes holds quite generally that simple ideas can be clearly and distinctly grasped by *intuition*. Descartes comments that doubt of primary notions and simple ideas was

Scepticism

possible only because he was not attending to them properly: it is absolutely impossible to attend to such an idea and doubt its validity. Moreover, even when something is known by *deduction*, we can, if its proof is sufficiently short, grasp the whole of it in a single intuition and thus clearly and distinctly perceive the truth of the conclusion. In these cases, it seems clear, our certainty is complete and needs no further support. It is because we clearly and distinctly perceive these truths that we are certain of them; but we do not need to be reflectively aware that we clearly and distinctly perceive them, and *a fortiori* such reflective awareness does not enter into the *grounds* of our certainty.

Descartes appears to allow that, in principle, the whole of science could be established *a priori* in a system of derivations from axioms whose truth is intuitively evident. God's knowledge of physics may take just this form. Indeed, there might be a creature who clearly and distinctly apprehended any physical truth which he contemplated. Our science does not work in this fashion; and we are not creatures of this sort. Hence we rely upon God's benevolence in order to accept scientific results. Descartes informs us that, when he said we have no science in advance of knowing of God's goodness, 'I was speaking only of knowledge of those conclusions which can be recalled when we are no longer attending to the arguments by means of which we deduced them' (1641 p.100). But this is not to assign a minor role to God's benevolence: apprehending such conclusions is essential to human science. Some proofs are too long to be grasped in a single intuition: we can attend to a portion of them while remembering that we were convinced by earlier parts, but we cannot grasp the whole proof in one act of attention. So if we are to make investigations which involve long proofs, Descartes claims, we must then appeal to the benevolence of God. Normal scientific practice relies upon a stock of recorded results without questioning their credentials on each occasion of use; and we frequently rely upon the discoveries made by others without checking the proofs or evidences that ground their claims. Thus although we have certain knowledge which escapes the sceptical arguments, we are left well short of a systematic theoretical science relying on complex proofs and providing a corpus of established results. And unless we can clearly and distinctly perceive the existence of bodies (which Descartes doubts), the benevolence of God will be implicated in our belief in the external world. To understand the strategy underlying Descartes' appeal to the benevolence of God, we must examine the structure of his 'foundationalism' in more detail.

74

3. Are there foundations?

We suggested in section 2 that we should understand Descartes' 'foundationalism' by distinguishing two contexts of inquiry: the first of these is concerned with answering the methodological question: If we are careful in using our faculties, can we obtain knowledge of the world?, and the second, taking for granted an affirmative answer to this first question, attempting to describe the substantive character of reality. In so far as this way of drawing the distinction suggests a sharp distinction between 'methodological' and 'substantive' issues, it is misleading: Descartes investigates the distinction between mind and body, the essential character of these substances and the existence of God in the course of answering the questions posed in the first *Meditation*. However, this requires only a minor qualification of the distinction: the first context answers the fundamental methodological issues; the second investigates those substantive issues which are not resolved in the course of explaining the adequacy of our faculties.

We could classify investigations differently, distinguishing those which establish conclusions that can be clearly and distinctly perceived to be true from those essentially involving memory. Investigations of the first sort, grasping simple ideas in intuition, establishing conclusions by short proofs, would make no use of the inference described at the beginning of section 2. Conclusions would not be accepted on the grounds that God would not allow us to be deceived in what we clearly and distinctly perceive. Rather, our clear and distinct perception of the conclusions would render them indubitable to us. Our applications of results obtained in inquiries of this kind in further scientific inquiries would, of course, rely upon our memory that we clearly and distinctly perceived these things to be true; and then the benevolence of God would have a role in our reliance upon them. But while engaged in such inquiries – while 'attending' to proofs and ideas – no reason would be required for accepting them.

This again does not coincide with the distinction we wanted: the first class of inquiries would involve the grasp of elementary mathematical results of little methodological interest, for example. However if the circle is to be avoided, it seems that the methodological investigations of the *Meditations* must fall in this first class. The proof of God's existence, and the proof that He would not allow us to be deceived in what we clearly and distinctly perceive must be short. If they are short, they simply render God's existence indubitable: understanding them merely enables us to 'attend' to the proposition that God exists. If they are not short, then we should have to appeal to the memory of our clear and distinct perception of lemmas involved in the proofs in order to arrive at the ultimate conclusion. And God's benevolence is required for us to trust this memory.

So the key to defending Descartes against the charge of straightforward circularity is that so long as the proofs involved in the *Meditations* are short, they involve no inferences which are validated by God's benevolence. The role of the thought-experiments described in the first *Meditation*, and the arguments found in succeeding ones, is to provide a clear and distinct perception of God's existence and benevolence, and hence to ground certainty of the reliability of our faculties if they are properly used. If we follow the discussion properly, we simply find its conclusions indubitable so long as we attend to them and their (short) proofs.

As I understand Descartes' position, when we enter the first context, in the first *Meditation*, and attempt to conquer scepticism, we use no inferences whose complexity requires us to rely upon God's goodness in accepting their conclusions. We are absolutely certain of our first principles (because we clearly and distinctly perceive them); we are absolutely certain of God's existence, because the proof is sufficiently short to be grasped in intuition; and we are absolutely certain of our ability to obtain knowledge of the world because we grasp in intuition the implications of the goodness of God. All the time we are in this first context, none of our conclusions is an inference which depends upon the premiss that whatever is clearly and distinctly perceived is true. Within this context, the circle does not arise because our clear and distinct perceptions are simply self-evident. They require no further rational support.

Inquiries within the second context are often fallible, but we are usually confident that where we make mistakes, further investigation will eliminate our errors. Within this context, Descartes can rely upon fallible hypothetico-deductive inferences confident that, since he knows that reliable knowledge of reality is possible, his errors will not prove disastrous. However, his ability to live with his fallibility in this context depends upon his assurance that an affirmative answer to the question raised in the first context is correct. This means that fallibilism is inappropriate when we conduct an inquiry within the first of the contexts: if we erroneously decide that we are (not) capable of reliable knowledge of reality, we have no grounds for assurance that we shall eventually discover whether we have made a mistake. Such an argument suggests that even if we do not regard certainty as a prerequisite for something counting as scientific knowledge, we can only participate in science confident of the value of what we are doing if we are certain of an affirmative answer to the methodological questions raised in the first context.

Our sense that the problem of the circle has not been solved by these remarks might be sharpened when we consider our cognitive position when engaged in ordinary empirical inquiries – when we are in the second context. For at that stage we are rarely 'attending' to God's existence or His benevolence. In that case, our memory that these things have been clearly and distinctly perceived does appear to be involved in our acceptance of these truths. And, of course, our memory that we clearly and distinctly perceived that things clearly and distinctly perceived are true is involved in our acceptance of this last claim. So if no circularity is involved in the argument of the *Meditations* itself, it may intrude when Descartes attempts to rely upon those arguments in conducting ordinary empirical inquiries.

When we enter the second context, seeking substantive knowledge of reality, the position is more complex. Having completed our epistemological inquiries, we retain our assurance that knowledge is possible; we continue to believe that God underwrites our certainty in clearly and distinctly perceived propositions; and we continue to believe that epistemological inquiry led to an unshakeable certainty that all of this was true. However we no longer clearly and distinctly perceive these things to be true; at best we remember that we have previously so perceived them. Presumably we remain certain of these things, although we lack the unshakeable certainty that would be ours were we now clearly and distinctly perceiving them. How secure is our cognitive position? Are we better placed than before the process of trial by doubt began?

The crucial question is: how does someone's memory of having successfully completed the epistemological investigation described in the *Meditations* modify their attitude towards their ordinary scientific beliefs? In the previous chapter we noticed that the first level of sceptical argument in the first *Meditation* pointed to unnoticed prejudice found among Descartes' beliefs especially where they result from the testimony or training provided by his teachers. Without the live doubt produced by this reflection, he would have had no reason to employ the method of doubt at all. So if his memory of the *Meditations* stills these doubts, he can be confident that further trial through scepticism is unnecessary. If he is ordinarily certain that the effect of such prejudice has been filtered out, then he has no further reason to carry out such investigations; if he is ordinarily certain that were he to carry out such investigations, demon scepticism would be easily defeated, then he has no reason to undertake them. His confidence that scepticism can be defeated quells the doubts which persuaded him to devote time to epistemology in the first place. Dream-doubts and demon-doubts are forceful only *within* the methodological context: stronger doubts are required to persuade us to enter that context in the first place.

4. *Appearance and reality: Cartesian science*

Remarks about the problem of circularity take us back to the question of why the method of doubt should be adopted at all. The discovery that we have many confused or erroneous beliefs which may infect the results of other inquiries that depend upon them does not, unaided, require us to abandon our fallibilistic hope that further scientific inquiry will enable us to eliminate those errors. Even if it suggests a course of self-criticism, it is unclear why this should take the form of Cartesian trial through the deepest scepticism. The rest of the chapter returns to the issue of why we should take sceptical challenges seriously, and this section considers how far specific features of Cartesian science may be involved in Descartes' adoption of his method.

In the *Rules for the Direction of the Mind*, Descartes distinguishes four mental faculties: intellect, memory, imagination and sense-perception (c1628 pp.32, 39 ff.). While stressing that 'it is the intellect alone which is capable of knowledge', he claims that in this activity it can be both aided and obstructed by the other three (ibid.). The intellect grasps simple ideas and short familiar proofs by *intuition*; and it forms complex ideas by *deduction*. When we grasp a simple idea or short proof by intuition, then, as we saw above, we find it absolutely indubitable. Faced with an obscure complex idea, we use the intellect to analyse it into its simple elements and, through deduction, produce an intelligible reconstruction of the original. If we can grasp the resulting whole in intuition, then we have a clear and distinct idea of it: we see clearly and distinctly all of its elements and how it is constructed out of them (see *Rule* 12, pp.39 ff.). Imagination can provide suggestions as to how to analyse the complex idea and how to reconstruct it deductively out of simple elements. When science moves to analysing and reconstructing ideas too complex to be grasped in intuition, we rely upon memory as well. Of most concern here is the role of sense-perception.

Sensations are produced by motions or patterns in the brain resulting from the mechanical action of external things upon us. Descartes' dualist metaphysics prevents him from treating this as ordinary causal interaction, but he insists that it is a very *intimate* link – there is more than a correspondence effected on each occasion by a benevolent God. John Yolton has suggested, plausibly, that we understand this in semiotic terms: the motions in the brain function as natural signs which are interpreted in the sensation – the mind 'reads' the signs of external reality present in the motions of the brain (1984 pp.22–31). This interpretation helps us to understand Descartes' insistence that sensations have no resemblance either to the cranial motions that occasion them or the external objects that they refer to. In *The Optics*, he compares the ways we learn of objects through visual sensation with the way that a blind man learns about his environment by feeling his way with a stick (p.153). Our experiences of manipulating the stick, like our visual experiences, provide us with information about our surroundings. Our colour sensations give us information about external objects although – since there is nothing in the objects but patterns of motion – the object is not coloured as it appears to be in our sensations.

Assuming that sensory appearances reveal how things really are therefore leads to error: sensory experience yields highly confused ideas of its objects. But the empirical sciences, such as physics, depend upon sense for providing their materials, and in order to apply their abstract theories to external things. Although Descartes is often mistrustful of experience (mostly of experiment rather than ordinary observation), his censures concern uncritical use of sensory information:

> When we say 'the reliability of the intellect is much greater than
> that of the senses', this means merely that when we are grown up
> the judgments which we make as a result of various new
> observations are more reliable than those which we formed without
> any reflection in our early childhood; and this is undoubtedly true.
>
> (1641 p.295)

Experience is necessary for science, but will mislead us if not subjected to careful rational and theoretical scrutiny. Indeed, although in his earlier writings Descartes conceives scientific theory solely as the attempt to find clear ideas of things which are cast in terms of intuitable, and hence intelligible, simple ideas, his later writings allow a larger role for hypotheses tentatively accepted on the basis of their agreement with experience.

So science exploits both intellect and the senses to move beyond confused sensory experience and acquire an intelligible grasp of the nature of reality. This requires a clear understanding of the authority with which the intellect criticizes sensory ideas, and of how it employs sensory information in developing and applying its theories. Descartes proposes to replace our everyday understanding of reality and the prevailing conception of science with a view which finely distinguishes the roles of sense and intellect. The legitimacy of the new methods must be established, and the sceptical challenges provide a means to establish the distinctive roles, and cognitive authority, of these different faculties. If sceptical arguments are used to help us to understand the role of intellect or reason in correcting sensory ideas, we must understand why intellect is not itself threatened by analogous sceptical arguments. The authority of reason and experience to yield scientific knowledge in the way Descartes proposes must be established in the face of the rival methodological prescriptions provided by common sense and established scientific traditions.

I am not suggesting that Descartes illicitly took this conception of science for granted in the first *Meditation*: it is in the background in a more acceptable fashion. In the previous chapter, it was observed that there is a role for reasoned discussion concerning whether one needs to go through the exercise of the *Meditations*: Descartes needs grounds for judging it necessary. If someone reasonably expects (or hopes) to be able to construct a body of scientific knowledge *of this sort*, then they have a special reason for employing the method of doubt. For unless they can be confident that intellect can free itself from sensory obscurities and secure clear ideas of simple notions; and unless they can be confident that what seems clear and distinct to them contributes to knowledge of reality; then they cannot continue with such inquiries confident that they know what they are doing, and confident of the adequacy of their means to their cognitive ends. A kind of assured self-confidence is required to pursue such activities as free autonomous inquiring agents, and the Cartesian search for certainty through doubt is attuned to the task of obtaining such security in the pursuit of such an activity. Whereas this might provide a reason for adopting the method of doubt for someone disposed to adopt this Cartesian picture of science (which requires reason to free itself from the senses), it provides no such reason for those not so disposed. Descartes has a particular picture of dogmatic inquiry, and he holds that a suitable process of preparation enables us to carry out such inquiries with confidence in its success. Here lies the motivation for the method of doubt. This further clarifies our earlier observation that slight or metaphysical doubts may be genuine in the context of Descartes' project, even if it would be wrong for other philosophers to be impressed by them.

5. Inquiry and autonomous self-control

In chapter I, we saw how sceptical challenges were used by Pyrrhonists to question the possibility of a distinctive kind of activity, the attempt to discover how things are 'in their nature'. An erstwhile dogmatist is encouraged to conclude that he lacks the defensible criteria required for carrying out such activities: he cannot take responsibility for how such inquiries are carried out; he cannot arrive at a clear formulation of their goal; as an information gatherer, he is a passive recipient of appearances rather than an autonomous agent engaged in seeking scientific knowledge in a responsible and self-controlled manner.

The previous section suggested that Descartes' conception of scientific inquiry required such autonomous self-control: he required a clear specification of the aims of science and an explanation of how he should control scientific activities in order to achieve those aims. Otherwise he would possess only a vague hope that he could achieve goals that could be grasped in a confused manner. Since he proposed an alternative to contemporary scientific practice, he needed to provide a basis for confidence or optimism that his proposal is intelligible and feasible. The need for trial through scepticism then emerged from distinctive features of Cartesian science: his claim that the *Meditations* contained the foundations of his physics is unsurprising.

Our readings of the Pyrrhonists and of Descartes both emphasize, then, that inquiries are distinctive kinds of activities and that the sceptical arguments challenge the possibility of carrying out certain sorts of activity in a reflective self-controlled manner. They suggest that we can only continue with such projects while failing to exercise our rational autonomy, failing to seek clear specifications of our goals and defensible evaluations of the means we adopt to achieve those goals. In that case an examination of underlying assumptions about the structure of responsible self-control may help us understand the philosophical importance of sceptical challenges: perhaps our sense of their importance rests upon a mistaken view of what autonomous agency requires. We must also consider how far the relevance of sceptical challenges depends upon specific features of the kinds of inquiry (dogmatic inquiry, Cartesian science) so far considered. Are moderate empiricists warranted in ignoring sceptical challenges in conducting their inquiries? Do they present a challenge to everyday knowledge employed for domestic purposes? Under what circumstances is a defeat of the deepest scepticism (one that takes into account even slight metaphysical doubts) necessary if we are to be confident of our cognitive goals and our ability to pursue them?

Bernard Williams suggests that the 'absolute conception of inquiry' necessitates taking scepticism seriously (Williams 1978 pp.65–70). The beliefs we acquire about the world depend upon our perspective on it. Taking this literally: our location in the world determines what we see and hear, and how we see and hear these things. Less literally: our perceptual experience is determined not only by the objects we perceive but also by the character of our perceptual apparatus; how we think about things depends upon the structure of our system of thought and concepts. As Pyrrhonists have insisted, these relativities in thought and perception impede knowledge of things 'as they are in themselves'. We naturally suppose that things do have an 'intrinsic nature' our awareness of which is moulded by our perceptual and conceptual apparatus to yield our view of the world.

Hence we aspire to a kind of 'pure' inquiry which will provide knowledge which escapes these relativities: we overcome the limitations of our own nature to discover how things are 'in their nature'. If this aspiration makes sense, it requires us to filter out the influence of features of our cognitive apparatus which are potentially distorting or idiosyncratic. Since what seems most certain to us could be distorting, yielding information which is useful for our practical concerns without describing the true nature of things, the mere metaphysical possibility of error is just as much a matter of concern as possibilities of error that seem more plausible. For there is no ground for expecting reality to reveal its true nature to us: if we go wrong at the beginning of our search, then there is no reason why this should become clear to us later. If we leave the rotten apple in the basket, it will infect all the others before we notice it.

Whether this 'absolute' conception of the real nature of things makes sense is an important question: if it does, and if it is a proper aspiration for our knowledge, then scepticism may be difficult to defeat. It is an interesting question how far philosophers' concern with scepticism can survive abandoning the 'absolute' conception. Challenging judgments which are relative to the cognitive constitution of the knower, or the context of the object known, or the relation between knower and known, is certainly central to the sceptical arguments of the Pyrrhonists. It is less clear that Descartes is guided by an explicit recognition of such a conception, although the way in which God's undeceitful nature is supposed to underwrite our knowledge suggests that what is knowable to us will also be true from His (and hence the widest possible) perspective (see Craig 1987 pp.22–7). These questions will occupy us increasingly in later chapters.

In concluding this chapter, we shall return to the 'transparency of mind' in the light of these comments about rational self-control. It is often claimed that Descartes' certainty of the contents of his own mind is both questionable and presupposed by the argument of the first *Meditation* (pp.64–5 above). For example, the dream argument rests upon the surely debatable claim that dreams are qualitatively identical to waking experiences. In Descartes' defence, it may be observed that psychological concepts can be introduced in two distinct ways. They may be theoretical concepts within an explanatory theory of the mind. In that case, it seems to be a contingent matter whether people are authoritative on issues such as the qualitative relations between dreams and other experiences, and Descartes' argument is open to criticism. But they may also be introduced as the fundamental concepts employed in ordering and controlling our inquiries. What is then fundamental are the discriminations that we can make, rather than the theoretical identities and differences which explain those discriminations. According to this second conception, the claim that dreams and waking experiences are identical means no more than that we cannot discriminate them in qualitative terms: they are equivalent from the point of view of rational monitoring and self-control. Given the interest which guides this classification, which is to control inquiry in the light of appearances, a distinction between real qualitative similarity and apparent similarity has little role. We think of the qualitative content of sense in terms of the information which is made available to the monitoring cognitive agent.

If these comments can support a defence of the transparency of mind, they do so in a limited way which fails to justify all of Descartes' use of the notion. For he assumes that the classifications which are best suited to rational self-control provide the basis for an explanatory theory of the mind; this is involved in his argument for dualism in the second *Meditation*. It is far from obvious that this assumption is justified: if transparency of mind is justified in the fashion just described, it may enable Descartes to develop his first *Meditation* arguments without begging questions but it will have little role in clarifying the metaphysical status of the mental.

We learn from Descartes that confident self-controlled participation in inquiry requires a basis of evident certainty: our ability to make progress in scientific activity must be assured. In addition, our confidence or optimism about the possibility of cognitive progress must endure even when we are not engaged in epistemological investigations and attending to this certain foundation. That we actually make recognizable progress may have a role in this confidence, but more is required: when not attending to the basic certainties, we must be confident that we were not deceived in so relying upon them. Descartes' writings are not circular, but rather display a sophisticated awareness of what is required from a response to scepticism, and show that he sees that we should leave the epistemological context with an enduring assurance that there is no need to return to it. However it should be remembered that I do not defend his epistemology in its entirety. 'Clarity' and 'distinctness' are far from clear and distinct; we have yet to be persuaded that the method of trial by scepticism is obligatory once we move beyond the Cartesian scientific framework; and many of the details of his constructive arguments are unconvincing.

Moreover even if the position does not succumb to the traditional charge of circularity, there is a related problem which will occupy us further at a later stage. That we find a proposition indubitable is a psychological statement whose truth is compatible with the proposition being false. Even if we cannot doubt a proposition while attending to it, subsequent reflection may make us wonder whether this is due to an irrational psychological compulsion rather than due to rational insight: why should the fact that we *cannot* doubt something show that our reliance upon it is *legitimate*? Somebody might question the desirability of trial through scepticism because they believe that undertaking Descartes' thought experiment opens us to psychological compulsions which are an obstacle to discovery of the truth. If we observe that the experiment cannot be replicated, that other philosophers dispute Descartes' arguments and fail to see what ought to be evident, then special reason is needed to take his arguments seriously. What was supposed to provide foundations is then seen to need foundations in its turn. Unless in endorsing evident foundations we legitimately speak for all, the foundational exercise fails, and it is fair to conclude that

Descartes' epistemology fails at this point. When we examine common sense responses to scepticism in chapter VI, we shall consider this difficulty more fully.

CHAPTER V

Hume: Scepticism and the True Philosophy

1. Introduction: naturalism and scepticism

As with Descartes, we approach the writings of David Hume with two concerns. How far does he enlarge or transform the canon of sceptical arguments? Do his writings present sceptical arguments that would have been unfamiliar to earlier writers? And, second, what is there that is distinctive about his response to sceptical challenges? As before, we shall be highly selective; our treatment of these topics focusing on questions of general strategy rather than the details of Hume's philosophical position. Whole books have been written about the role of sceptical themes in Hume's writings (Fogelin 1985, Norton 1982); and space here is limited.

Hume's attitude towards scepticism is not a straightforward matter. From the publication of *A Treatise of Human Nature* in 1739–40, he was denounced as a sceptic. The tone of eighteenth and nineteenth century interpretation was set by Thomas Reid's claim that Hume had developed a *reductio ad absurdum* of the familiar doctrine that we have immediate knowledge only of our own subjective ideas only to embrace the absurd sceptical conclusion (Reid 1785 p. 210). Such interpretations survive in the writings of philosophers influenced by Reid. Richard Rorty, for example, talks of Hume's 'veil-of-ideas skepticism based on the view that "nothing can ever be present to the mind but an image or perception"' (Rorty 1980 p.140n).

A more recent tradition of interpretation, deriving from Kemp Smith (1905, 1941), and defended more recently by Stroud (1977) and Capaldi (1975), denies that Hume was a sceptic at all. In Stroud's words: 'the key to understanding Hume's philosophy is to see him as putting forward a general theory of human nature in just the way that, say, Freud

86

or Marx did' (1977 p.4); and he planned to obtain this through 'the experimental method of reasoning'. Hence Hume subtitled his *Treatise* 'an Attempt to introduce the experimental Method of Reasoning into Moral Subjects.' On this view, Hume is not joining the philosophical struggle with sceptical arguments at all. He is rather an early cognitive scientist trying to develop an empirical account of mind.

When expressed in this blunt manner, both of these interpretations are over-simplifications, but Hume's exposition of his views does not aid understanding. We have already criticized his dismissal of traditional Pyrrhonism, and we shall find below that his attitude towards this position was importantly ambivalent. Indeed, Popkin has described Hume as the only consistent Pyrrhonist, remarking that the naturalistic and Pyrrhonist elements in his thought cannot be distinguished (1966). We can begin to grasp these complexities by noting two respects in which Hume's epistemological writings are 'naturalistic'.

In *An Enquiry concerning Human Understanding* (1748), Hume distinguished what, following Fogelin, we can call *antecedent* and *consequent* scepticism (Fogelin 1985 pp.5–6). The former adopts the Cartesian method of extending doubt so far as is possible *before* attempting to extend our scientific or philosophical knowledge. It is a prerequisite of scientific responsibility, it is alleged, that we assure ourselves of the reliability of our faculties and methods 'by a chain of reasoning, deduced from some original principle, which cannot possibly be fallacious or deceitful' (1748 p.150). It is characteristic of a certain kind of 'naturalized epistemology' to resist the demand that we proceed in this fashion. Rather, we simply get on with developing a scientific theory of mind and nature, expecting this to provide the tools we can use to understand and evaluate our inquiries. Philosophy is thus not prior to (and hence distinct from) the science of nature.

In this spirit, Hume describes his strategy in the *Abstract* to *A Treatise of Human Nature*: 'to anatomize human nature in a regular manner, and ... to draw no conclusions but where he is authorized by experience' (1739–40 p.646). This discipline 'comprehends' logic, morals and criticism, and politics. In particular: '*The sole end of logic is to explain the principles and Operations of our reasoning faculty, and the nature of our ideas.*' (ibid.) However even if the defeat of scepticism does not thus become the prior focus of epistemology and logic, sceptical problems can arise in a different fashion. For the empirical logic thus developed may reveal to men 'either the absolute fallaciousness of their mental faculties, or their unfitness to reach any fixed determination in all those curious subjects of speculation, about which they are commonly employed' (1748. p.150). Such concern with scepticism arises as a consequence of the experimental science of nature rather than as a prerequisite of proper concern with it. In similar vein, Quine recommends that we abandon Cartesian methodology but admits that science *could* teach the sceptical lesson that it is a miracle that we know any science at all (1975 p. 68).

Part of the importance of stressing that Hume was a philosophical naturalist is to remind us that his writings are not organized around a confrontation with antecedent scepticism. This is compatible with their issuing in a deep consequent scepticism: indeed, we shall see that Hume held that philosophy could only present us with unanswerable arguments for the strongest Pyrrhonism. We can have no reason for our everyday beliefs or for our philosophical convictions. This introduces the second element of Hume's naturalism: 'Philosophy would render us entirely Pyrrhonian, were not nature too strong for it' (*Abstract*, 1739–40 p.657). Our nature compels belief where science and philosophy show that it has no support. The core of Hume's response to scepticism is that it is simply incredible:

> [The] sceptic still continues to reason and believe, even tho' he asserts that he cannot defend his reason by reason; and by the same rule he must assent to the principle concerning the existence of body, tho' he cannot pretend by any arguments of philosophy to maintain its veracity. Nature has not left this to his choice, and has doubtless esteem'd it an affair of too great importance to be trusted to our uncertain reasonings and speculations. We may well ask *What causes induce us to believe in the existence of body?* but 'tis is vain to ask, *Whether there be body or not?* That is a point which we must take for granted in all our reasonings.
>
> (1739–40 p.187)

Whether the resulting position counts as a form of scepticism or as an anti-sceptical stance is a question to be discussed below. It can immediately be seen that its stress upon what we naturally find ourselves believing and its rejection of the prospect of achieving an active rational control over our reasonings are very close to Pyrrhonism – and Hume's emphatic repudiation of Pyrrhonism reflects a misconception of Sextus' position. Indeed, our concern with the character of Hume's response to scepticism must focus on two separate topics. First, what attitude should the Humean take to his unshakeable confidence that (for example) there is an external world? Is there anything in this attitude which can be described as sceptical?; does he feel alienated from his disposition to assent to these things? Second, what attitude should he take towards his philosophical speculations? This involves two problems. In so far as a kind of conflict emerges between our everyday assurances and the teachings of theory, how does theory retain any claim upon our acceptance? If the epistemological theory entails that we can have no justified belief in (for example) the external world, one might take that to show that the theory is at fault. The second problem concerns the reflexive impact of consequent scepticism: if logic casts doubt upon the reliability of our faculties, it casts doubt upon itself – for it is a product of those very faculties. So even if we cannot suspend judgment upon whether there is an external world, should the Humean position lead to sceptical suspension of belief in science and philosophy?

These topics will be pursued in the later sections of this chapter. We close this introduction with two general observations about Hume's response to them. The first is that one respect in which Hume's position differs from ancient Pyrrhonism is that it holds that the search for philosophy is itself part of our nature: we naturally reflect upon our own cognitive activities, seeking to clarify the rational support of our opinions. In the *Dialogues concerning Natural Religion*, Hume has Philo pronounce that 'everyone, even in common life' develops some kind of philosophy:

> [From] our earliest infancy we make continual advances in forming more general principles of conduct and reasoning; and the larger experience we acquire, and the stronger reason we are endued with, we always render our principles the more general and comprehensive; and that what we call *philosophy* is nothing but a more regular and methodological operation of the same kind. To philosophize on such subjects is nothing essentially different from reasoning in common life, and we may only expect greater stability, if not greater truth, from our philosophy on account of its exacter and more scrupulous method of proceeding.
>
> (1779 p.9)

This continuity between the concerns of 'life' and the development of theory may make it difficult to rest with everyday certainties and sceptically abandon the search for science.

Second, Hume's conception of the nature and value of philosophy emerges through a kind of natural history of philosophical theories, presented in the fourth section of book 1 of the *Treatise*: 'Of the sceptical and other systems of philosophy'. Hume describes 'a gradation of three opinions, that rise above each other, according as the persons, who form them, acquire new degrees of reason and knowledge' (1739–40 p.222). The first of these is the conception of the world defended by the 'vulgar', the view of pre-philosophical common sense. Although philosophical criticism shows the vulgar view to be deeply flawed, those who developed these criticisms were led to a distinctive philosophical position – the 'veil-of-perception' empiricism which Reid finds in Hume. According to Hume, this 'false philosophy' is itself misconceived, and his own position – the 'true philosophy' – advances beyond both of these positions, retaining the merits of each while avoiding their errors. Although Hume does not exploit his natural history of philosophy when he restates his position in the *Enquiry*, it provides a valuable clue to his considered attitude towards scepticism.

Section 2 examines the kinds of sceptical arguments which emerge from Hume's philosophical writings, and section 3 provides a sketch of his natural history of philosophy. The final two sections attempt to understand and evaluate the response to scepticism which Hume wishes to adopt.

2. *Hume's sceptical arguments*

Our treatment of Hume's sceptical arguments will be highly selective: it attempts only to elucidate the *kinds* of arguments he employs. In the *Enquiry* he alludes to the Pyrrhonist modes, asserting that while those modes which point to the fallibility of the senses are weak and unconvincing, those which rely upon the absence of any criterion for settling conflicts of judgment are irrefutable (1748 pp.124 ff., Popkin 1966 pp.58 ff.). Since it provides the framework in which he discusses these matters, it will be best to introduce his naturalistic theory of mind before examining his own distinctive contribution.

According to the first section of the *Treatise*, 'all the perceptions of the human mind' fall into two classes, impressions and ideas. The first part of Book I is devoted to an analysis of different members of these classes and of the causal principles according to which they emerge and succeed one another in the mind. Hume takes the distinction between ideas and impressions to be sufficiently familiar for it to require little explanation. We can take it that both involve mental states with an intentional content: we have an idea of something when we think about it reflectively; impressions enter our minds 'with most force and violence' and include 'all our sensations, passions and emotions, as they make their first appearance in the soul' (1739–40 p.1). So a perceptual experience, a pang of hunger, and a violent emotion are all impressions; and thoughts about these things are mere ideas. Like the Stoics, Hume believes that the same intentional content can be present in the mind in different ways: 'an idea assented to *feels* different from a fictitious idea, that the fancy alone present to us: And this different feeling I endeavour to explain by calling it a superior *force*, or *vivacity*, or *firmness*, or *steadiness*' (1739–40 p.629); similarly, the evident difference between a perception and a judgment with the same intentional content (an impression and an idea) is a difference in the way that content is impressed upon us, in how it feels.

Hume is initially non-committal about the ontological status of impressions. His eagerness to distance himself from Locke's 'perverted' use of terms like 'idea' (1739–40 p.2n), should unsettle those who favour Reid's interpretation of his work. His first explanation of these notions is compatible both with the phenomenalist view that impressions are inner states, images or sense data which represent external objects, and with the realist claim that they are external states of affairs, that what we are directly aware of is not mental or mind-dependent in any way.

To clarify some questions of strategy, we shall look briefly at Hume's familiar claims about causation. The vulgar conception of causality involves the idea that the cause necessitates the effect: one event may be prior to another and contiguous to it, but still not be its cause – 'There is a NECESSARY CONNECTION to be taken into consideration' (1739–40 p.77). Hume's demonstration that this is a mistake employs two complementary argumentative strategies.

The first, negative, argument rests upon Hume's 'first principle', stated right at the beginning of the *Treatise*: all of the simple ideas that we employ in having any thoughts at all – simple or complex – make their first appearance in the mind in impressions. The conceptual materials of thought all issue from sensory experience, passions and emotions. Since he finds no impression of a necessary connection in his perceptions of causal interactions, Hume denies that a simple idea of necessary connection is involved in our idea of one event causing another. All we *see* is one event being followed by another contiguous one.

The second argument supplements this with an explanation of how the 'vulgar' confusion arose. Noting that we think of one event as cause of another only when we expect all events like the former to be followed by events analogous to the latter, Hume suggests that we form habits of expectation: on experiencing an event of the former kind, the imagination produces a vivid idea of an event of the second kind. Our vivid internal impression of this transition is reflected in the cluster of ideas that surround our thoughts about causation. This is the source of our error: we mis-identify an idea that results from our own cognitive functioning as a sensory impression – the mind projects its own functioning on to reality. Thus Hume's psychological theory helps to free us of the illusion that the 'experience' of causal necessity reflects a feature of the world of our experience: our primitive attempt to reflect upon our own cognitive functioning is undermined. The role of custom in unreflectively setting up habits of anticipation exposes casual reflection to error even about the most familiar aspects of our lives: we fail to notice that the idea of causation has a subjective source.

The most famous use of this strategy to an apparently sceptical end is Hume's discussion of belief in a world of external independent objects. Before discussing this in the following section, we shall note his sceptical doubts about some forms of reasoning. In each case, he criticizes the assurance that these practices are justified in a straightforward way; and then he explains our practice by tracing it to forms of mental functioning which are incompatible with viewing the practice as 'rational'. For example, he examines the causal reasoning underlying our inductive practice of forming beliefs about unperceived things on the basis of our experience. No rational justification for this practice can be provided, he claims, employing arguments of a familiar Agrippan form:

> all our experimental conclusions proceed upon the supposition that
> the future will be conformable to the past. To endeavour, therefore,
> the proof of this last supposition by probable arguments, or
> arguments regarding existence, must be evidently going in a circle,
> and taking that for granted, which is the very point in question.
>
> (1748 p.35–6)

His theory of mind allowing for no other rational basis for these causal reasonings, he offers an alternative explanation of our use of them:

> Our judgments concerning cause and effect are deriv'd from
> habit and experience; and when we have been accustom'd to

see one object united with another, our imagination
passes from the first to the second, by a natural transition,
which precedes reflection, and which cannot be prevented
by it.

(1739–40 p.147)

The source of our disposition to make inductive or causal reasonings does not lie in reason or wholly in experience: imagination and habit guide us. That our *imagination* guides us thus to make inductive inferences provides no reason at all for thinking that the practice of making such inferences takes us to the truth: the foundations of induction are arational. The role of imagination in induction also explains why our practice is untouched by philosophical criticism: imagination neither contributes to, nor accepts the authority of, reason. The practice is pre-reflective.

A parallel structure is found in Hume's discussion of deductive reasoning. Although he has earlier claimed that only demonstration (in arithmetic or geometry) can provide true certainty, Hume points out that we are fallible when we assess the validity of a proof, and he uses this to argue that even our acceptance of mathematical results depends upon the arational imagination. Before accepting a conclusion, he asserts, we must assess the probability that we have made an error in our assessment; and this assessment must rest upon an estimate of error in computing that first probability of error ... and so on. It is not to our purpose that Hume's discussion is confused: he sees the cumulative effect of these probabilities as eventually reducing the appropriate degree of confidence in the proposition to zero, and thus appeals to the imagination to explain our failing to be impressed by this apparent rational demand that we suspend belief in mathematical results. Even when we recognize that the probabilities of error are likely gradually to become arbitrarily small so that the probability does not reduce to zero in this way, we can perhaps acknowledge the force of an argument from infinite regress related to the modes of Agrippa. Whenever we accept a step of proof we need a reason for thinking that such a step is a correct one, and we need a reason for thinking that *this* reason is a good one, ... and so on. A Humean who managed to avoid the confusions about probability noted above could construct an argument analogous to Hume's by pointing to custom and imagination to explain our failure to be impressed by the demand that we follow this infinite regress of justification.

The similarities between this position and Pyrrhonism are clear. Hume's arguments often resemble the modes of Agrippa, and his insistence that judgment results from custom and imagination rather than from reason or understanding amounts to an admission that there is no defensible criterion of truth. Judgment is a passive matter: we accept what we find ourselves accepting, and rational evaluation does not influence acceptance. The same holds for Hume's psychological theories. Since they rest upon causal reasoning, he cannot claim to be justified in accepting them; their appeal to him depends upon imagination and habit rather than reason and understanding:

> Can I be sure, that in leaving all establish'd opinions I am
> following truth; and by what criterion shall I distinguish her, even
> if fortune shou'd at last guide me on her foot-steps? After the most
> accurate and exact of my reasonings, I can give no reason why I
> shou'd assent to it; and feel nothing but a *strong* propensity to
> consider objects *strongly* in that view, under which they appear to
> me.
>
> (1739–40 p.265)

Hume's own theories result from the influence of habit on the imagination, the very mental operations which have led common sense to error and illusion.

In the following section we are able to focus upon what most distinguishes Hume from Sextus. Even if ancient Pyrrhonists were not, as Hume alleged, left without any basis for action, they did claim that the life without belief was one of tranquillity. Intellectual conflict disappeared with the decision to acquiesce in appearance and abandon the search for rationally defensible dogma. Hume's understanding of the force and role of his sceptical arguments does not allow him to conclude that appreciating their power can lead to tranquillity. We must now explain why this is and how Hume's 'mitigated' scepticism offers a response to it.

3. The external world: the natural history of philosophy

The 'vulgar' view that the senses inform us of a world of independent external objects is examined in the chapter of the *Treatise* entitled 'Of scepticism with regard to the senses' (1739–40 pp.187–218). According to Hume, our conception of an external object or body has two problematic features. First, we think of them as continuants: when I

94

notice a book that I used yesterday, or meet an old friend, I think that I see the *very same object* that I saw before. What I see is not something similar to the other object, or something that stands in some complex relation to it, but is the very same object that still exists. And, second, this means that the existence of objects is independent of their being perceived by anyone. They continue to exist even when unperceived.

The vulgar philosophy explains this, Hume thinks, by denying the mind-dependence of impressions; their account of the ontological status of impressions is a form of direct realism. Impressions themselves have an independent existence, continuing to exist even when unperceived. Perception involves standing in a direct cognitive or perceptual relation to a public entity such as a state of affairs or fact (pp.206–7). Hume believes that this vulgar view of perception is easily refuted; the independence and continued existence of impressions cannot be defended. Hence he offers an explanation, cast in terms of his experimental psychology, of how we come to make this mistake.

Belief in an external world cannot derive from the senses or from reason. Crudely, we cannot have an impression of an unperceived impression, because any impression we perceive is (plainly) perceived. And the abstruse reasonings that philosophers employ in thinking of these issues cannot be involved in the acquisition of this view by children or the uneducated. Therefore, it must have some other source, and Hume finds this in the imagination. When we observe an unchanging object over a period of time, "'tis evident we suppose the change to lie only in the time, and never exert ourselves to produce any new image or idea of the object' (p.203). The mind moves into a relaxed state so that it hardly notices the transition from one moment to another, since they are not distinguished by any difference in our ideas. Indeed, when we encounter an interrupted series of impressions which are otherwise identical, the imagination places the mind in a similar relaxed disposition: 'we are not apt to regard these interrupted perceptions as different (which they really are) but on the contrary consider them as individually the same, upon account of their resemblance' (p.199). We are then involved in a 'kind of contradiction', for we are disposed to treat as continuous a sequence of impressions which, observation assures us, is interrupted. 'In order to free ourselves from this difficulty, we disguise, as much as possible, the interruption, or rather remove it entirely, by supposing that these interrupted perceptions are connected by a real existence, of which we are insensible' (p.199). This supposition inherits vivacity from memory of the interrupted perceptions and the natural disposition of the mind to treat them as continuous. As with the case of causal necessity, the mind succumbs to a natural error.

The story has to be complicated to explain the fact that we claim to recognize objects which have changed since we last encountered them. One cognitive activity of the mind is to find order in our experience through forming habits of expectation about the future run of experience. The laws we uncover in the course of this activity guide our understanding of how things can change while out of sight. Hume insists, however, that in formulating laws about external objects, our activity goes markedly beyond what is involved in simply finding order in our experience. By positing unobserved events, and allowing that much occurs while unperceived, we are able to find more order in the world than is actually experienced: apparent disorder in our experience falls into place as part of a larger pattern. The natural assumption that this might be the *source* of our belief in unobserved existence is denied by Hume. Only the error described in the previous paragraph can produce such a belief. Once it is available, the practice here described exploits the idea to enlarge our knowledge. Of course Hume believes that the practice is unjustified: since, he thinks, all that is present to the mind is its own perceptions, habits of expectation can have no other source and cannot 'exceed that degree of regularity' that is present in our perceptions. The imagination must be involved in leading us into this error, so there is no basis for supposing that it corresponds to anything in reality (p.197).

So, as with the case of our causal beliefs, Hume employs two strategies in challenging the vulgar conception of the external world. He denies that reason or sense could provide us with the idea of externality, employing the principle that all simple ideas enter the mind through impressions. And he provides a causal explanation of the vulgar view of external things which shows that it is *false*; resemblance among our experiences 'seduces' the imagination into the 'false opinion' of the 'fiction' of continued existence (p.209). It is important to notice that Hume has not thereby established a sceptical position: he has attempted to *refute* a particular 'philosophical' explanation of our responses to the world. Abandoning the vulgar philosophy may leave us without an explanation of how the belief in an external world is justified, but it is psychologically impossible for it to shake our confidence in the belief. At this stage, Hume's critical endeavours serve simply to sharpen our sense of a fundamental philosophical problem: if the 'vulgar philosophy' fails to solve it, a different philosophy may do better.

With the rejection of the vulgar view, we seem forced to accept that impressions are interrupted and mind-dependent. In a brief paragraph on pp.210–11 of the *Treatise*, Hume employs arguments familiar from Sextus to show that appearances are relative to the state and location of the perceiver: appearances are altered by 'our sicknesses and distempers'; objects appear to change in size as we move away from them (see also p.226). And he offers what he sees as a knockdown argument. When I press one eye, I see double, one of the impressions changing its location: are both of the images external objects with continued existence?; if not, which? But the issue we must now face is: once the vulgar view is abandoned, what more sophisticated position is there that we can take up?

If the immediate objects of perception cannot exist unperceived, two positions are open to us. We could give up the idea that there is a world of independent objects existing even when unperceived, but this position has been defended only by 'a few extravagant sceptics; who after all maintain'd that opinion in words only, and were never able to bring themselves sincerely to believe it' (p.214). The philosophical tradition preferred a second alternative: they 'distinguish (as we shall do for the future) betwixt perceptions and objects, of which the former are suppos'd to be interrupted, and perishing, and different at every return; the latter to be uninterrupted, and to preserve a continu'd existence and identity' (p.211). This philosophical doctrine of 'double existence' holds that we are immediately aware of mere appearances, of fleeting mind-dependent entities. But it also insists that behind this veil of impressions there is an external world of independent objects which are, in some way, represented by the impressions. Belief in the external world is thus reconciled with the rejection of the vulgar theory of perception. Our knowledge of external reality is mediated through immediate knowledge of appearances.

As we have seen, Hume sees this philosophical outlook as the natural result of reflection upon the failings of the vulgar theory of perception, and he examines a number of other doctrines characteristic of this 'false philosophy'. However, as this name suggests, it too is flawed, succumbing to criticisms similar to those which sank the vulgar view. Before examining Hume's critique of these philosophical doctrines, we should note some of his other examples of this development from the vulgar view to the false philosophy. In the section following 'Of scepticism with regard to the senses', 'Of the antient philosophy', he examines philosophical thought about *substance*. Our impression of a particular object – say, a book – involves a cluster of qualities; there is a distinctive shape, colour, size, and the printing on the cover and so on. Moreover, through time, there seems to be a continuous sequence of clusters of qualities that remain fairly constant. What is involved in our thought of these qualities being clustered or unified, of them belonging to just one object? The vulgar view is that they are tied together by some sort of necessary link. As we have already seen, philosophical analysis leads one to deny that there are ever necessary connections between ideas, so the vulgar view is flawed. The philosophers acknowledge this but continue to feel the need to explain the unification involved in a number of qualities belonging to the same object. Thus, they posit a substance, distinct from any of its qualities, in which the qualities inhere. Although there are no necessary connections between the simple impressions that make up the object, they are unified by standing in some real connection to the same underlying substance.

The fourth section of this discussion, 'Of the sceptical and other systems of philosophy', discusses another doctrine that grows out of criticism of the vulgar view of impressions. Accepting that the character of our impressions is mind dependent, philosophers discriminate between qualities and offer a positive view of reality which holds it to be rather different from how it appears to be. Sensory or secondary qualities like colour, warmth, tastes and smells are relative to the sensory apparatus of perceiver and lack continued existence. Primary qualities which do possess continued existence are those less directly linked to particular senses: figure, motion, gravity, cohesion (p.227). The external world is simply composed of matter in motion: colours and tastes reflect how these independent existences react with our minds.

There is a common pattern to these and other 'philosophical' moves. The vulgar mistakenly think they find externality or necessity in their impressions. The philosophers see the error of the vulgar view but continue to find a place for necessity and externality: they do so by finding it in a reality which is not experienced but, somehow, explains or grounds our experience. The vulgar are not wrong to believe in necessity and continued existence; their error lies in the claim that they find these things in their impressions. The philosophers relocate them as an unexperienced substrate of impressions.

Hume attacks all these philosophical views, his onslaught continuing through the sections dealing with the immateriality of the soul and personal identity. Just as he criticizes the vulgar view by offering an explanation of it which shows it to rest upon an error, so he undermines philosophy by diagnosing the errors involved in arriving at these doctrines. The standard form of his attack is that the philosophical position is, in a way, self-defeating: it derives from a critique of the vulgar position; but its own position could be plausible only if it continued to take seriously elements of the vulgar position which have been wounded in the attack.

Consider his critique of the representative theory of perception. Hume makes two points. The first negative thrust alleges that the idea of a reality which cannot be experienced but which our impressions inform us of cannot be obtained from experience or from causal reasoning. It seems plain that we could have no impressions of such things, and it also seems clear that we could not discern them among the lawlike patterns we find in our impressions. Thinking of them explicitly involves going beyond what experience can teach. This is accompanied by an explanation of how the philosophers came to make this mistake. His view is that 'the philosophical system acquires all its influence on the imagination from the vulgar one' (p.213). Roughly: the idea of continued independent existence was a fiction which resulted from mis-identifying an impression of the imagination as one of external sense. The philosophers realize we have no impression of continued independent existence and so locate this outside appearance. They only do this because they have retained the concept of external continued existence when their arguments ought to have persuaded them that it was an illusion. Rather than wholly repudiating the vulgar system, they revise it in a piecemeal fashion, failing to free themselves of its deepest errors.

If we were to accept Hume's position we would appear to possess both:

1. An unshakeable conviction that we experience independent objects which continue to exist unperceived.
2. An explanation of that conviction which shows that it is unjustified and empty.

Given Hume's theory of ideas, there cannot be an idea with the content of our unshakeable conviction. And since that conviction arises from the operation of the imagination, our possessing it gives no reason to suppose that it is true. (2) appears to be a wholly sceptical position; but (1) is strongly anti-sceptical.

Both (1) and (2) arise from the natural development of our mental faculties – unlike the false philosophy which rests upon 'unnatural' illusion, since the philosophers fail to appreciate the destructive force of their own arguments against the vulgar philosophy. Where Sextus asserted that withdrawing from the search for dogmata and resting with what we found ourselves naturally disposed to believe, would lead us to discover a tranquil life, free of disturbing conflict, Hume's discussion suggests that we naturally arrive at a conflicting set of views. In the final section of book 1 of the *Treatise*, he provides a very vivid description of this position.

> When we trace up the human understanding to its first principles, we find it to lead us into such sentiments, as seem to turn to ridicule all our past pains and industry, and to discourage us from further enquiries.
>
> (p.266)

Our fundamental aim in inquiry is to discover causes and to uncover 'the original and ultimate principle':

> And how must we be disappointed, when we learn, that this connexion, tie, or energy lies merely in ourselves, and is nothing but that determination of the mind, which is acquir'd by custom, and causes us to make a transition from an object to its usual attendant, and from the impression of one to the lively idea of the other? Such a discovery not only cuts off all hope of ever attaining satisfaction, but even prevents our very wishes; since it appears, that when we say we desire to know the ultimate and operating principle, as something, which resides in the external object, we either contradict ourselves, or talk without a meaning.
>
> (pp.266–7)

Returning to (1), Hume admits that 'this deficiency in our ideas' is not noticed in common life; 'nor are we sensible that in the most usual conjunctions of cause and effect we are as ignorant of the ultimate principle, which binds them together, as in the most unusual and extraordinary' (p.267). Since this 'proceeds merely from an illusion of the imagination' we confront a practical question: how far ought we to yield to these illusions?

4. *Mitigated scepticism*

Given the potentially self-destructive character of philosophy (position (2) above), and the contemptuous attitude we naturally take towards it once we leave the study (position (1)), two questions arise. First, why should we continue to do philosophy and science at all? And how can Hume maintain his evident preference for the philosophical view of mind and reality over the everyday view or the vulgar one? The second question links our discussion of Hume with earlier remarks on the phenomenology of scepticism: how can the Humean investigator look upon his own participation in inquiry? Even if, in some sense, he believes his results, does he experience the kind of alienation from them which is characteristic of scepticism?

In the *Treatise* Hume presents a stark dilemma. Having observed that it is an 'illusion of the imagination' which hides from us the degree of our ignorance in normal circumstances, he asks how far we should yield to such illusions. If we assent to 'every trivial suggestion of the fancy', we are led into 'such errors, absurdities, and obscurities, that we must at last become asham'd of our credulity' (1739–40 p.267). But if we decide to assent to none of the illusions of the imagination, we 'cut off entirely all science and philosophy' and we contradict ourselves: 'since this maxim must be built on the preceding reasoning, which will be allow'd to be sufficiently refin'd and metaphysical' (p.268). In other words, if philosophy tells us never to trust philosophy, why should we trust its advice?

Of course Hume admits that nature 'cures me of this philosophical melancholy'(p.269): after an evening of backgammon and good company, his speculations 'appear so cold, and strain'd, and ridiculous, that I cannot find it in my heart to enter into them any farther'(ibid.). He is ready to burn his books and papers and 'never more renounce the pleasures of life for the sake of reasoning and philosophy'(ibid.). But this is not his last word on the topic: why does philosophy continue to have value? Part of the answer is that it is a natural development out of the practices of life. The condition of a country gentleman whose interest in hunting and farming introduces no intellectual interests at all may be enviable but is not available to everyone. The slightest reflection upon aesthetic, moral or political matters introduces an inclination to examine underlying principles (pp.270–1). And in 'Of curiosity, or the love of truth' Hume compares intellectual activity with hunting. In each case our pleasure in the activity derives only in part from its results: we enjoy the exercise of our skills, gaining more pleasure from tracing a complex proof than accepting it on the authority of a mathematician. We enjoy inquiry because we have to 'fix our attention or exert our genius; which of all other exercises of the mind is the most pleasant and agreeable' (1739–40 p.449). So the pleasures of doing philosophy lead us to return to the hunt.

Since, as Hume sees, these pleasures will not be obtained if we see no value in what is pursued or no prospect of success in our pursuit (p.450), more must be said about the value of philosophical inquiries. In the first *Enquiry*, he points out that common sense, too easily impressed by the surface of things, fails to recognize many exceedingly useful regularities in experience which the abstruse philosopher can uncover: scientific discoveries are very useful. Second, not least because of the continuities between reflective inquiry and common sense, the abandonment of philosophy would leave a gap that could be filled by the unbridled operation of the imagination. An awareness of 'the strange infirmities of human understanding' prevents people 'throwing themselves precipitately' into opinions with no concern for opposing arguments. This would, 'naturally inspire them with more modesty and reserve, and diminish their fond opinion of themselves, and their prejudice against antagonists' (1748. p.129). Even if Hume's arguments do not convince people that there are no external things, they make them cautious and more diffident, equipped with a greater sense of their fallibility.

So Hume believes that to be 'convinced of the force of the Pyrrhonian doubt, and of the impossibility that anything, but the strong power of the natural instinct, could free us from it' (1748 p.130) has a salutary effect. Once we are aware of the tendency of the imagination to take delight in 'whatever is remote and extraordinary' and lead us into error, we shall restrict our inquiries 'to such subjects as are best adapted to the narrow capacity of human understanding' (ibid.). Hume famously concludes that unless we restrict our attention to 'abstract reasoning concerning quantity or number' or to 'experimental reasoning concerning matters of fact', the imagination is not properly under control and we head for 'sophistry and illusion' (p.132). In the section of the *Treatise* entitled 'Of the modern philosophy' he distinguishes those operations of the imagination which are 'permanent, irresistible and universal' from those which are 'changeable, weak and irregular' (1739–40 p.225). Since the former are 'the foundation of all our thoughts and actions', they are 'received by philosophy'. The latter are rejected by philosophy: they are 'observ'd only to take place in weak minds' and can easily be subverted. A course of Humean philosophy leaves us alert to the dangers the latter represent.

It follows from this that common sense does not simply re-assert itself once Hume has left his study. Philosophical and scientific reflection leave their mark. The unanswerable Pyrrhonian arguments cannot induce total suspension of belief: their impact is mitigated by our nature. But they are not without influence. For example, the vulgar philosophy cannot be sustained: if belief in external objects survives, it is no longer supposed that these are immediately perceived; and people are cautious about their wilder imaginings and hypotheses. People become cautious in their expressions, replacing dogmatic claims of absolute certainty with tentative avowals that something is probable. 'A true sceptic will be diffident of his philosophical doubts, as well as of his philosophical conviction; and will never refuse any innocent satisfaction, which offers itself, upon account of either of them' (1739–40 p.273).

Hume's mitigated scepticism insists that nature mitigates the force of the Pyrrhonian arguments. Rather than showing how to eliminate the various contradictions described in earlier sections, Hume tries to explain how we live with them. His explanation has three components. First, as we have just seen, we experience a growing detachment from our beliefs and opinions: they are what we find ourselves disposed to defend; but we admit that they are highly fallible and may not survive. Second, we employ a kind of temporal segregation: once we leave the study our theoretical beliefs lose the force they then had; and the habits of expectation that guide everyday life lose their everyday vividness once we enter the study. At no time are both present to us with full strength or vivacity.

Third, we acquire a sense of our cognitive limitations. As well as curbing excess, this has an impact upon our understanding of our participation in inquiry. We are aware we have no criterion of truth; we are aware that our methods of inquiry rest upon 'the illusions of the imagination'. But so long as we forswear 'hypotheses embrac'd merely for being specious and agreeable', 'we might hope to establish a system or set of opinions, which if not true (for that, perhaps, is too much to be hop'd for) might at least be satisfactory to the human mind, and might stand the test of the most critical examination' (1739–40 p.272). And, vividly capturing the limitations of the understanding, he writes:

> their ultimate cause is, in my opinion, perfectly inexplicable by
> human reason, and 'twill always be impossible to decide with
> certainty, whether they arise immediately from the object, or are
> produc'd by the creative power of the mind, or are deriv'd from the
> author of our being. Nor is such a question any way material to our

present purpose. We may draw inferences from the coherence of
our perceptions, whether they be true or false; whether they
represent nature justly, or be mere illusions of the senses.

(1739–40 p.84)

5. *Humean Pyrrhonism*

As we noted at the beginning, there is not space for a detailed
engagement with Hume's arguments. Many of the details of his
naturalistic theory of mind have not stood the test of time and little
would be gained here by listing its shortcomings. In this concluding
section, we shall bring out some of the distinctive characteristics of his
discussion of scepticism, for it is these that are most relevant to our
purposes.

The first point to note is that Hume adopts a naturalistic approach to
logical and epistemological matters. His overriding goal is not to
provide logical foundations for our knowledge or to defeat scepticism:
it is to make progress towards an experimental science of human nature.
Although Hume does finish with a form of scepticism, it is not obvious
that a naturalistic approach to epistemology will always do so. If we
were convinced that philosophy must begin as Descartes recommended,
then we might suppose that the attempt to understand inquiry in
naturalistic terms was itself an admission that antecedent scepticism
cannot be defeated. But we noticed in chapter IV that the Cartesian
strategy was not obviously compulsory. If a naturalistic study of inquiry
were to explain to us how it is that we know as much as we do, it could
have an important normative role in helping us to improve our methods
of inquiry. In that case it could help to answer sceptical doubts,
confirming our pre-philosophical confidence in our cognitive abilities.

Hume's study of human nature has sceptical implications because of
its detailed claims. In particular, fundamental features of our methods of
forming beliefs and concepts are traced to faculties which appear not to
be attuned to the discovery of truth. Our belief that there are external
objects, our reliance upon induction and reason, all depend upon
operations of the imagination rather than sense or understanding. Hume
is, moreover, convinced that the immediate objects of perception are
internal or subjective, albeit by arguments that do not now carry
conviction. We could conceive of a science of human nature which did
not have these properties and thus did not have these sceptical
implications.

The second point to note is that Hume stresses that belief in the external world and in the possibility of knowledge of it are *irresistible*. Even a sceptic must 'assent to the principle concerning body, tho' he cannot pretend by any arguments of philosophy to maintain its veracity' (1739–40 p.187). The existence of body 'is a point that we must take for granted in all our reasonings' (ibid.). This too need not be a sceptical position; we saw at the end of chapter II that some common sense philosophers take the fact that a belief has these properties as an indication that it has a kind of evidence which suits it for a foundational role. But Hume is unable to use it for anti-sceptical purposes because his naturalistic study of human nature explains this irresistibility as the work of the imagination: nature deems this 'an affair of too great importance to be trusted to our uncertain reasonings and speculations' (ibid.). When Hume explains why such beliefs are irresistible, he undermines their intellectual authority. The science of human nature denies that such irresistibility is a sure indication of truth.

Third, Hume's work contains hints of a kind of semantic approach to scepticism, close to arguments employed by Berkeley and analogous to arguments from recent empiricism. His science of man does not only challenge the suggestion that we can have knowledge of (for example) independent objects; it also suggests that we can have no idea of them, no thoughts of them at all. It offers an explanation of our ideas of bodies which shows them to involve the projective activities of the imagination. This could serve an anti-sceptical purpose: analysis of our concept of an external object reveals that it lacks the features which make sceptical challenges bite. In a related vein, we have noted recommendations that a more modest conception of the goals of inquiry be adopted: we aim at opinions which find coherent pattern in our experience with little concern for whether the resulting opinions are 'really true'. Both of these strategies offer redescriptions of our practice of inquiry which show that sceptical arguments rest upon conceptions of the aims of inquiry which are not compulsory.

The anti-sceptical force of such arguments may be limited. As Hume develops them, they are unlikely to be effective against sceptical worries about induction although they may form part of a response to scepticism about the existence of external objects. More important, although such arguments may have an unequivocal anti-sceptical role in the writings of other philosophers, Hume's attitude to them is more complex. The texts suggest that our nature makes Hume's analysis of our idea of an external object as resistible when we are not engaged in philosophy as his other sceptical arguments. We cannot believe that we do not genuinely possess the concept of external existence, even if Hume convinces us that our possession of this concept is unintelligible. And our contentment with a coherent body of ideas seems to be accompanied by an acknowledgement that this is less than we really think we want.

To anticipate a topic to be discussed more fully in the following chapter: descriptions of how our nature prevents sceptical arguments immobilizing us and of how certain beliefs and practices are irresistible can be employed in two contrasting ways. A variety of common sense and naturalistic approaches to philosophy find in them a demonstration of the groundlessness of sceptical arguments. They support the view that special reason needs to be given for taking sceptical arguments seriously. Alternatively, within a sceptical perspective, they provide an explanation of how we live with the unanswerability of scepticism. Rather than answering sceptical challenges or preventing their becoming a matter for concern, they indicate how scepticism can be coped with in practice. Hume's discussion may offer material for philosophers defending views of the first kind, but his own writings fall into this second class.

Consider the Humean conception of the position of someone engaged in theoretical inquiry.Their scepticism is manifested in a kind of cognitive dislocation: they find themselves believing certain things, and they find themselves carrying out certain sorts of investigations; but they are unable to make clear to themselves why these beliefs are not illusions or why those methods of inquiry have anything to recommend them. The sort of rational control over inquiry, which is partly constitutive of the rational autonomy we aspire to, is presented as impossible. Our cognitive position is of being passively buffeted by different forces which lead us to hold beliefs which they cannot legitimate.

The main difference between Hume and Sextus is that the latter escapes these conflicts by abandoning the theoretical inquiries that produce them while Hume continues with (at least some of) them. Sextus offers a tranquillity which Hume supposes cannot be attained. Nature prevents our being traditional Pyrrhonists. But greater similarities underlie these differences. Both abandon the search for rational self-control in our inquiries; both assent to beliefs and practices in a passive fashion – recall Hume's claim that all he can say is that he has a *strong* propensity *strongly* to believe his theories. Moreover both employ practical or moral arguments to vindicate their cognitive stance.

Pursuit of Humean science is justified by the practical benefits it offers in teaching us pragmatically useful regularities and (most important) by the benefits of becoming more tentative and detached in our view of our capacities. Speculative and dogmatic metaphysics is abandoned by both. The temporal insulation of periods of scientific investigation and the concerns of 'life', too, provides for a slightly more sophisticated form of 'tranquillity'. Hume's philosophical outlook depends crucially upon the contingent fact that the benefits of scientific activity can be obtained without disruption to the assurances that guide life. We remarked that Sextus' position could not survive the growth of modern science, and that a Pyrrhonist ought to be able to find room for a more complex life than he allows: Hume's writings present a Pyrrhonist position that incorporates these developments.

CHAPTER VI

Common Sense and Legitimation

1. Introduction

This chapter introduces some approaches to sceptical arguments arising from subsequent attempts to respond to the tradition of sceptical discussion described above. It is only a slight exaggeration to say that, by the time of Hume, a philosopher could not place himself in relation to an increasingly self-conscious tradition of philosophical discussion without stating an attitude towards philosophical discussions of scepticism. Someone who denied that epistemology should be grounded in the kind of engagement with antecedent scepticism recommended by Descartes would feel obliged to justify this denial. And the claim that we can rest our inquiries upon irresistible beliefs and experiences was understood to be at risk from destructive explanations of this irresistibility like Hume's. We begin by considering the development of the common sense tradition in the writings of a contemporary critic of Hume, Thomas Reid (1710–96). After a discussion of the relevance of Kant's philosophy to understanding scepticism (section 4) we turn to some more recent thinkers.

2. Reid: common sense foundations

Reid's philosophical focus was straightforwardly epistemological. Although he opposed scepticism and tried to discredit a philosophical tradition including both Descartes and Hume, his picture of the structure of knowledge and justification was shared with that tradition. He was a foundationalist, holding that 'all knowledge got by reasoning must be built upon first principles' and appealing to a familiar regress argument:

When we examine, by way of analysis, the evidence of any
proposition, either we find it self-evident, or it rests upon one or
more propositions that support it. The same thing may be said of
the propositions that support it, and of those that support them, as
far back as we can go. But we cannot go back in this track to
infinity. Where then must the analysis stop? It is evident that it
must stop only when we come to propositions which support all
that are built upon them, but are themselves supported by none –
that is, to self-evident propositions.

(1785 p.435)

As Paul Vernier points out, Reid's use of self-evident principles
'which are the foundation of all reasoning, and of all science' reflects his
commitment to the axiom-system model of knowledge which, he
thought, had contributed to Newton's scientific successes. 'By laying
down the common principles or axioms, on which the reasonings in
natural philosophy are built', Newton had laid 'a solid foundation in that
science'(1785 p.231, see Vernier 1976). Reid aspired to provide similar
axiomatic foundations for knowledge in general.

Before considering how successful he was in this, we should
introduce some examples of claims Reid takes to be self-evident. He
takes many ordinary perceptual claims and memory claims to serve as
first premises for inference: they are evident, justified, and do not
depend upon inference or deliberation. He lists twelve first principles of
contingent truth (1785 pp.441–52). They include:

That those things really did happen which I distinctly remember.

(p.444)

That those things do really exist which we distinctly perceive by
our senses, and are what we perceive them to be.

(p.445)

That, in the phenomena of nature, what is to be, will probably be
like to what has been in similar circumstances.

(p.451)

That certain features of the countenance, sounds of the voice, and
gestures of the body, indicate certain thoughts and dispositions of
the mind.

(p.449)

That there is a certain regard due to human testimony in matters of fact, and even to human authority in matters of opinion.

(p.450)

Although listed as just one principle among others, the seventh expresses the general principle underlying all the others:

That the natural faculties, by which we distinguish truth from error, are not fallacious.

(p.447)

It seems clear that we find such principles reasonable; and if we are warranted in relying upon them, scepticism would be out of place. What is less clear is that their 'self-evidence' explains the legitimacy of such reliance.

One task for philosophy is to identify these first principles. Reid mentions three 'marks' supporting such identification (1785 pp.439–41). One is:

A consent of ages and nations, of the learned and the vulgar, ought, at least, to have great authority, unless we can show some prejudice, as universal as that consent is, which might be the cause of it.

(p.439)

Second, beliefs that 'appear so early in the minds of men that they cannot be the effect of education or false reasoning' are likely to be first principles:

The belief we have, that the persons about us are living and intelligent beings, is a belief for which, perhaps, we can give some reason, when we are able to reason; but we had this belief before we could reason, and before we could learn it by instruction.

(p.441)

Both of these marks, presumably, indicate that the belief was probably not influenced by individual idiosyncrasy or training, that it is the common possession of mankind. The third mark is that the belief in question is necessary for action and conduct (p.441).

What is involved in finding something self-evident? Vernier points out that once understood, such truths cannot be doubted (Vernier 1976 pp.14–15, Reid 1785 p.434). Acceptance of such propositions is non-inferential, and (in something like Hume's sense) they are irresistible: our nature will not permit us to deny them. Reid's description of per-

ceptual experience indicates some relevant features: we cannot perceive
something without having some notion or conception of it; we have 'an
irresistible conviction and belief in its existence' (1785 p.258) which:

> is immediate, that is, it is not by any train of reasoning and
> argumentation that we come to be convinced of the existence of
> what we perceive; we ask no argument for the existence of the
> object, but that we perceive it; perception commands our belief
> upon its own authority, and disdains to rest its authority upon any
> reasoning whatsoever.
>
> (p.259)

Perceptual judgments share this brute self-evidence while lacking the
clear intelligibility of axioms:

> [When] I remember distinctly a past event, or see an object before
> my eyes, this commands my belief no less than an axiom. But
> when, as a philosopher, I reflect upon this belief, and want to trace
> it to its origin, I am not able to resolve it into necessary and
> self-evident axioms, or conclusions that are necessarily consequent
> upon them. I seem to want that evidence which I can best
> comprehend and which gives perfect satisfaction to an inquisitive
> mind; yet it is ridiculous to doubt; and I find it is not in my power.
>
> (1785 p.330)

As it stands, this does not refute scepticism. Hume could accept many
such claims about what is psychologically irresistible, and the normative
issue – how far relying upon such foundations is legitimate – has not
been touched. Indeed, resting upon common sense certainties in an
uncritical manner would be sheer dogmatism. Insisting that such
'foundational' claims are irresistible does not show that our certainty in
them is legitimate: we might experience it as a psychological
compulsion, accompanied by the meta-belief that opinions depending
upon such foundations are not justified. Hence the interest of Reid's
position rests upon his explanation of why we are warranted in relying
upon opinions depending on these foundations. How does the appeal to
common sense establish that philosophers' doubts are unreasonable?

3. *Common sense and legitimation*

Reid's position has two fundamental components. The first is a view
about where the burden of proof lies: we are warranted in relying upon

these common sense certainties unless given reason to abandon them. This involves the rejection of what we might call 'neutralism' – the doctrine that the question of the reliability of our faculties is initially open. The second component is criticism of the presuppositions of particular sceptical arguments. Thus, for Reid, failure to explain why the senses *are* reliable provides no support *for* scepticism, while a demonstration that there are no good arguments for scepticism effectively refutes it. As Vernier puts it, 'our self-evident beliefs are warranted because there are no reasonable grounds for doubting them' (1976 p.20). Peirce's 'critical common-sensism' captures a stronger but related view: common sense beliefs do not depend upon reasons since they are non-inferential; but rationality requires us to try to doubt them in order to avoid those which depend upon prejudice; philosophical error (and scepticism) can result from being too ready to believe that we can doubt what is really certain (CP5.438–52, Hookway 1990). We find here a mirror image of Sextus' Pyrrhonism: Reid cannot provide a conclusive refutation of scepticism; but he maintains the hope that individual sceptical challenges can be met as they arise.

The point about burden of proof appears straightforward: our actions and habits of acceptance show that we believe these axioms; and our spontaneous attitudes towards our practice show that we do not find this irrational. Although we might *say* that we doubt these things, our practice shows that such announcements are insincere or self-deceived. Special reason is required for doubting what seems obvious, so unless sceptical philosophers produce good sceptical arguments, or Descartes offers good reason for taking seriously the thought-experiment of the first *Meditation*, we can rest with our unquestioned certainties. To a degree, both Descartes and Hume could agree with this; so the core of Reid's response to scepticism lies in his response to their writings. Ignoring chronology, we shall begin with the response to Hume whose scepticism emerges from an attempt (like Reid) to apply the insights of Newton to philosophical topics: his natural science of mind supposedly suggests that we cannot sustain our common sense understanding of our cognitive achievements.

Reid combats Hume by attacking the theory of ideas. When the philosopher tells the common man that 'there is no smell in plants, nor anything but the mind; and that all this hath been demonstrated by modern philosophy', the latter will suppose him drunk or mad. The blame for thus setting philosophy and common sense 'at variance' is the philosopher's:

if he means by smell what the rest of mankind most commonly mean, he is certainly mad. But if he puts a different meaning upon the word, without observing it himself or giving warning to others, he abuses language and disgraces philosophy, without doing any service to the truth.

(1764 p.112)

In similar vein, philosophers equivocate on 'idea', running together the common concept of an idea as a mental event (a noticing or a conceiving) with a philosophical concept of an idea as an object of perception. From the beginning of the *Treatise*, Reid argues, Hume ignores the subtleties of our common psychological vocabulary and exploits these and similar equivocations to win adherence to a theory of mind with no independent plausibility.

Reid notes too the tendency of empiricist philosophers to attach the wrong significance to perceptual illusion (see, for example, 1785 pp.303–4, 1764 pp.142–4 and Tebaldi 1976). Noticing that an object appears large and small according to its distance and location they conclude that only an appearance of the external object is perceived. Once we acknowledge that 'apparent magnitude' is a perfectly objective property of external things, this move seems plausible only to those with a prior commitment to the theory of ideas. For Reid, if irresistible common sense belief conflicts with Hume's theory of mind and the latter has sceptical implications, the theory of mind should be abandoned.

Descartes too is a victim of the theory of ideas but Reid has other criticisms of his work (1764 p.100. He urges on quite general grounds that once Cartesian challenges are admitted they cannot be met: once we doubt the adequacy of our faculties to provide reliable information, no defence of their reliability which is obtained through the operation of those doubtful faculties can be trusted. But this need not yield scepticism because Reid sees no need to ground our methods of inquiry in the way that Descartes describes in the *Meditations*: he denies that the conceivability of our being deceived by an evil demon shows it to be a real possibility, and even if it were possible, he denies that it could shake our certainty that the senses are reliable. Propositions can be self-evident, and can serve as foundations for our knowledge even if they are not indubitable. The source of such errors, he sometimes seems to suggest, is an excessively intellectualistic or rationalistic model of reason: in spite of Reid's predilection for axiomatic reconstructions of knowledge, he is mistrustful of epistemologies which focus on reasoning and the giving of reasons.

This emerges in several ways. First he exploits one of the characteristic metaphors of the common sense tradition. His certainty that there is such a city as Rome is as great as that attaching to a geometric proposition: although his evidence is 'of that kind which philosophers call probable', it would be odd 'in common language' to say that there is probably such a city 'because it would imply some degree of doubt or uncertainty'. The metaphor is introduced after commenting that the ability of probable reasoning to provide certainty 'depends not upon any one argument, but upon many, which unite their force, and lead to the same conclusion':

> Such evidence may be compared to a rope made up of many
> slender filaments twisted together. The rope has strength more than
> sufficient to bear the stress laid upon it, though no one of the
> filaments of which it is composed would be sufficient for that
> purpose.

(1785 p.482)

Many arguments which would be individually unconvincing when 'taken together may have a force which is irresistible'. In such circumstances, an attempt to give one's reason for accepting a proposition will distort its warrant, making it seem much slighter than it is: the demand to give one's reason for belief can be rightfully resisted (see Ferreira 1986 chapter 4). Ferreira suggests that Reid does not always view acceptance of an axiom as conscious assent to a proposition: common sense beliefs are manifested in our practices, in unthinking inferential propensities and in the grammatical structure of our language. They comprise a largely instinctive body of cognitive habits forming the background to our methods of inquiry: hence, once again, our avowed justification for a belief may distort its real support.

Reid also makes the *ad hominem* objection that Descartes uses principles of reason which are no more or less secure than those which he exposes to ordeal through scepticism. To this end, he makes the standard charge of circularity (1785 pp.447); and he urges that trust in the reliability of our faculties is manifested in Descartes' acceptance of his sceptical arguments, and in his acceptance of the *cogito* and statements about his own mind. In other words, Descartes accepts that it is rational to rely upon some standards and practices without noticing that these are on a par with those which are doubted in the first *Meditation*.

Reid allows other kinds of argument in support of common sense principles. Since a first principle (like any other belief) does not stand 'alone and unconnected', 'it draws many others along with it in a chain that cannot be broken. He that takes it up must bear the burden of all its consequences'. This can support a 'proof ad absurdum' (1785 p.439): the challenger may be forced to abandon all those beliefs in whose justificatory history the questioned principle had a role. Through tracing these systematic connections, the challenger is forced to see the systematic structure of his beliefs and the depth of his commitment to those that he challenges. If, as seems plausible, there is a systematic structure involving all of the axioms, a challenge to one would bring the others down with it. Hence we vindicate the principles underlying all of our reasonings by bringing out the systematic relations between them.

To summarize this discussion, we can describe the complementary strategies of Reid's responses to Descartes and Hume. Descartes and Sextus press the problem of the criterion: when someone makes a claim to knowledge, one can ask how they know and if their view cannot be defended against challenges, it is unwarranted. Reid objects that such demands rest upon identifying reason with reasoning or deliberation: it should be met by pointing out that we find the challenges ineffective, and reminding the challenger of the nature of probabilistic certainty and of the role of common sense in grounding certainty. Hume provides an explanation of our cognitive habits which makes it hard to take them at face value. Reid quarrels with the details of Hume's theory and defends the view that its conflict with our everyday conception of justification and knowledge provides a strong *prima facie* reason for questioning it. His own theory of immediate perception of external things is more plausible than the theory of ideas.

Even if we accept these points, the demand for explanation appears to remain: we seek a theoretical framework which explains why relying upon our natural faculties will lead us to the truth. If no such framework is available, our reliance upon common sense standards of inquiry will appear illegitimate. The description of such principles and standards as 'natural' might gesture towards such an explanation but is too vague to be helpful. Vernier quotes from a manuscript:

> The truth itself ... does not depend on my constitution, for it was a truth before I had an existence ... but my perception of it evidently depends upon my constitution.

Hume's writings appear to make vivid the possibility that the conception of reality which my constitution renders irresistible may be an illusion. Simply pointing out that a variety of standards are natural or 'self-evident' does not establish that we are not victims of such a systematic illusion. Why does Reid think that holding this common sense view of the world is legitimate?

I suspect that Reid's own response to this challenge invokes the goodness of a God whose existence is established through a version of the argument from design. Since God is known to be the benevolent creator of a world which displays intelligence and design, He would ensure that our instinctive standards of rationality were adequate for our developing intellectual aspirations.

These remarks have wrongly led some scholars to claim that Reid succumbs to circularity, grounding belief in the axioms in a belief in God depending upon those very principles. We can clarify these strategic issues by distinguishing three uses of the claim that God exists in epistemology. The first, straightforwardly circular, holds that our acceptance of first principles rests upon the *premiss* that a benevolent God exists. Both Descartes and Reid have been charged with committing this error. Second, according to Descartes, belief in God is required to ground our acceptance of long or complex arguments and truths the evidence for which we are not currently contemplating. So long as there is a proof of God's existence which is neither long nor complicated, I have argued, this is not obviously circular. In both of these cases, God's existence has a role in providing justification for (at least some of) our scientific beliefs. The third use (Reid's, I am suggesting), is not primarily one of justification. The reliability of our faculties is self-evident, and stands in no need of justification. However it is natural to seek a systematic understanding of ourselves and our capacities; the benevolence of God *explains* our possession of reliable faculties although it has no role in justifying our belief that they are reliable. This may *add* to the justification which these beliefs already possess but it has no role in warranting our initial acceptance of them.

This must be interpreted in connection with another theme: the unintelligibility of our cognitive achievements. For Reid justification and explanation are distinct. Holding that memory provides immediate and reliable information of the past, he announces that 'how it provides this information ... is inexplicable': such knowledge is 'as un-accountable as an immediate knowledge would be of things to come; and I can give no reason why I should have the one and not the other'

(Reid 1785 p. 340). Self-evidence can be a kind of brute, unintelligible evidence or plausibility. Appeal to God's benevolence is an affirmation of confidence in our cognitive faculties which provides no detailed explanations of them – they remain unintelligible. However this admission that no explanations of our cognitive success need be available, may seem a dangerous concession to scepticism.

The problem is that our ability to control our reasonings, directing them in accordance with our cognitive aims, seems to depend upon a kind of ungrounded trust: we hope that our natural faculties are attuned to discovering the truth without an explanation of why this should be. A believer can appeal to God's benevolence to underwrite this hope but a secular epistemologist appears to have nowhere to turn: finding that we rely upon an inexplicable certainty involves recognizing what may be arbitrary limits to our ability to take responsibility for the conduct of our inquiries or to control our attempts to uncover the nature of reality. Reid's view of justification is more satisfactory to the believer who subordinates his practices to the will of God than to someone who attempts to exercise autonomous self-control over his inquiries.

Reid may be correct in using the standards of rationality which are uncritically accepted and the distinctions which we find second nature as tools for undermining the grip which sceptical arguments can hold upon our imagination. However his own development of this theme is unsatisfactory. In order to see this, we should distinguish two contexts of inquiry. Everyday practical decisions rest upon methods of collecting information which are habitual and unreflective. Their success in enabling us to solve our practical difficulties vindicates their use; the suggestion that we are irresponsible in carrying them out unless we can reflect upon the means we use to obtain information and assure ourselves that they are reliable is absurd. We can contrast with this our concern with science. It is natural to see this as a disinterested search for the mechanisms and principles which underlie the appearances guiding everyday life. Such 'scientific' investigation is guided by systematic ambitions; it seeks ever more inclusive systems of laws and principles and attempts to explain the correctness of the laws and principles which it employs. Moreover, it is often critical of common sense truisms and can appear to open up to us a vision of reality which is radically at odds with all that is familiar to us. In chapters III and IV, we saw that this conception of science was required to motivate Descartes' employment of the method of doubt; in chapter V, we saw that such systematic ambitions drove Hume's attempt to construct a science of human nature;

and in the previous section, we noticed that Reid similarly sought to emulate Newton in searching for 'axioms'. Unless we are assured of God's benevolence, we may not feel confident that common sense principles will guide us towards the truth in scientific investigations.

4. Legitimation

In the *Critique of Pure Reason* (1781, 1787), Kant complained that it remained 'a scandal to philosophy and to human reason in general that the existence of things outside us (from which we receive the whole material of knowledge ...) must be accepted merely on *faith*' (B p.xxxix). Sceptical arguments, he thought, alert us to the danger of treating 'as a well earned possession what we perhaps only obtain illegitimately' (A p.379). Although his complaint that Reid's appeal to common sense 'was but an appeal to the opinion of the multitude, of whose applause the philosopher is ashamed' (1783 p.7) misunderstood Reid's position, his writings identify the deep problems facing common sense responses to scepticism.

Part of Kant's contribution is a more systematic attack on the theory of ideas and Cartesian theories of mind. Such views, as we have seen, hold that beliefs about the contents of our own minds (our ideas) are epistemically prior to beliefs about the external world: we could have knowledge of our own inner states while doubting all claims about external objects; and these claims about the inner provide evidence for judgments about external things. Kant argues that we can only conceive of our experiences as forming the temporally ordered experience of a single individual because we take ourselves to be embodied and standing in spatio-temporal relations to other external objects. If this is correct, our cognitive position could not be as the theory of ideas supposes. If we can think of our own minds at all, we think of ourselves as possessing knowledge of a world of external things.

Since my concern is not primarily with scepticism that depends upon the theory of ideas, I shall not examine this controversial argument in detail. It differs from Reid's discussion largely in being more systematic: they agree that our natural theory of perception holds that we directly perceive external things; and they agree in drawing on the systematic connections of our fundamental commitments to reveal a kind of inconsistency in someone who denies this realist stance. But the move to a more systematic approach reflects a better appreciation of the problem of legitimation.

Where Reid offers *ad hoc* refutations of particular attempts to draw sceptical conclusions from theories of mind which conflict with common sense, Kant elucidates systematic logical relations of dependence between different sets of concepts: his explanation of how it is possible for us to think of the temporal ordering of our thoughts and experiences shows that this depends upon our holding that we directly perceive causally ordered substances existing in space and time. For recent discussions of the use of 'transcendental arguments' to respond to scepticism see Strawson 1985 ch.1, and Grayling 1985 *passim*, especially ch.4. However this argument is not straightforwardly anti-sceptical. It offers a more sophisticated description of how we are constrained to think of reality, but the possibility remains that although, inevitably, it appears to us that we directly perceive causally ordered substances in space and time, this is all an illusion. Kant's second contribution to the defeat of scepticism responds to this possibility.

Unease about Reid's view can take two forms. In order for the propositions that serve as foundations for my knowledge to be acceptable, I must be confident that there is nothing idiosyncratic in my adherence to them. Ideally they should be accepted by all rational inquirers; or I should be confident that anyone who does not endorse them is prejudiced or self-deceived. We might object that the instructions Reid offers for identifying these principles carry no guarantee of success. Indeed, it is only despair at responding to scepticism otherwise and a pious nod towards Newton that assures Reid that such principles are to be found. Second, even if we accept that we are constrained to think of the world in accordance with these standards and assumptions 'by our nature' or 'by our subjective constitution' the possibility remains that they conceal reality from us rather than revealing its true character. Unless we have something more than stubborn resistance or 'mere faith' to back up our refusal to take these worries seriously, Reid's response to scepticism seems incomplete. As we saw in the previous section, we need an explanation of how our practice provides us with knowledge. Otherwise, the appeal to common sense leaves us convinced *that* we have knowledge of reality but unable to understand our right to this conviction.

Metaphysical realism is the doctrine that reality has a character which is independent of our cognitive constitution. It allows for the possibility, just alluded to, that *our* conception of reality is a distortion: an evil demon may have endowed us with an irresistible commitment to a collection of epistemic principles or Reidian 'axioms' which disguise from us the true nature of the world. Kant's project of legitimation must enable us to discount this possibility without resting upon 'mere faith'. So long as we can intelligibly raise the question whether our foundational commitments are actually true to the character of reality, and we acknowledge that an answer which itself depends upon those commitments would be question-begging, a gap opens which can be closed only by ungrounded faith.

Kant's greatest contribution to the discussion of scepticism lies in the suggestion that these fundamental claims are not *answerable* to an independent reality. They ground our epistemic criteria but no criterion is needed to judge their own correctness simply because the question of their correctness cannot intelligibly be raised. There is no logical gap to be crossed between elucidating how our cognitive constitution constrains us to experience and reason about the world and characterizing in the most general terms what it is to be a constituent of reality.

Kant's development of this idea exploits a distinction between the *form* and content of our knowledge and experience. For example, we see particular spatial objects at particular locations; space and time are not themselves perceived but rather provide the formal framework within which perceived objects are located. It is a consequence of this that our knowledge of the properties of space and time depends upon our capacity for perceptual experience but is not grounded in experiential evidence. The properties of space and time are presupposed in our perceptual judgments and not tested by reference to them. Similarly, the role of the concepts of substance and causation in our thought is manifested, Kant claims, not only in the particular predicates we use to describe the world but, most fundamentally, in the logical forms of our beliefs. Use of subject–predicate propositions and of conditional propositions already commits us to conceptualizing our experience as composed of causally related substances. If it can be demonstrated that these fundamental principles do have a *formal* status, an important step forward has been made. They have a distinctive character which can provide a focus for an explanation of the legitimacy of relying upon them. Reid failed clearly to indicate how their distinctiveness amounted to any more than the fact that they were irresistible and uninferred.

The second stage of Kant's position is a form of idealism, described as formal or transcendental idealism. The resulting position is very hard to formulate clearly; one naturally succumbs to potentially misleading metaphors or vague technical use of terms like 'constitution'. The metaphors emerge when one asserts that the world of 'appearance', which is the object of all our claims to empirical knowledge, is partly our own construction; the formal properties reflect the rules in accord with which we construct it. Whereas this makes vivid the respect in which no possibility of error faces these formal claims, it is barely intelligible. The empirical world is not 'constructed by us' in any *literal* everyday sense. So unless such talk of construction is, at best, a slightly helpful but potentially confusing metaphor, it invites us to understand processes of construction which are not straightforwardly empirical. Preferable is the claim that these principles are constitutive of empirical reality: they provide a framework of assumptions *within* which we can raise questions of truth and evidence. By giving sense to our terms of epistemic appraisal they determine our goals in seeking empirical knowledge. Our cognitive aims are to understand the causal regularities underlying the observable behaviour of spatio-temporal objects. In that case, the possibility that 'reality' does not have this character provides no challenge to our ability to participate in such inquiries.

The underlying contention that our fundamental commitments have a distinctive logical and epistemological status, that they are not answerable to reality but rather provide the framework within which investigations into the nature of reality make sense, is more important than Kant's own development of this view. If correct, it removes the element of 'risk' from our reliance upon these commitments; they do not provide a potentially arbitrary restriction upon our capacity for rational self-control. However such views face a dilemma. Our response to the evil demon hypothesis, or to the suggestion that all might be a dream, *suggests* that we understand the possibility that all may be an illusion. The Kantian strategy requires that we be able to employ arguments to show other philosophers that their response to the first *Meditation* is mistaken. But mounting such arguments is problematic: offering general claims about the metaphysical status of the world of appearance or about the logical status of our fundamental commitments appears to require us to step back from the commitments which, it is alleged, are presuppositions of all meaningful thought and speech. If somebody observes that we can have no conception of how things are in themselves but only of things as they appear to us, how are we to understand the distinction he draws? By his own principles, it should be unintelligible.

Rather than considering Kant's response to this challenge, we shall turn to some recent attempts to retain the benefits of Kant's approach. In spite of considerable philosophical differences, Carnap, Quine and

Wittgenstein all attempt to undermine the appeal of sceptical challenges by interpreting fundamental cognitive commitments as providing a framework of standards and assumptions which are presupposed by the goals of our inquiries and hence do not threaten the achievement of those goals.

5. Carnap and Quine

Kant's 'formal' or 'transcendental' idealism is a kind of 'internal realism': questions about what is real or true arise relative to, or internally to, a set of principles which fix the general character of reality and are used to validate methods of inquiry. Sceptical arguments, it is suggested, raise the question whether these principles (our 'framework' or 'conceptual scheme') might not serve as distorting spectacles constraining us to approach the world in terms which may not reflect its character. 'Internal realism' insists that once raised, only the sceptical response to this question is available; it accepts 'the conditional correctness of scepticism' (Stroud 1984 p.195). But it denies that framework principles should be evaluated in these terms. Since they are presupposed when we formulate our cognitive goals, the fact that our inquiries are conditioned by these principles does not threaten our ability to achieve these goals. Their irresistible character does not mean that our investigations may be distorted, so relying upon them does not challenge our ability to act responsibly or autonomously in our inquiries.

This section considers 'internalist' themes in two twentieth century philosophers, Carnap and Quine. The former makes two important contributions. First, he adopts a verificationist account of meaning, arguing that the question whether there are 'really' external objects is meaningless:

> *Neither the thesis of realism that the external world is real, nor that of idealism that the external world is not real can be considered scientifically meaningful.* This does not mean that the two theses are false; rather they have no meaning at all so that the question of their truth or falsity cannot be posed.
>
> (1967 p.334)

A statement is not 'scientifically meaningful' unless it is empirically testable, so the very fact that gives rise to traditional sceptical doubts supports Carnap's rejection of the question which they address.

Alongside the appeal to a theory of meaning to dismiss the problem of scepticism as a 'pseudo-problem', Carnap employs ideas much closer to those of Kant. We approach our investigations equipped with a 'linguistic framework' which contains a logic, including an inductive logic, and the fundamental classifications to be employed in describing our surroundings. 'Internal' questions arise relative to this framework which provides criteria to be employed in answering them. When we ask whether there are 'really' physical objects, or whether our logic is 'really' correct we raise an 'external' question which is better expressed in the meta-linguistic 'formal mode': should we employ a linguistic framework employing '... is a physical object' as a fundamental predicate and treating a particular set of sentences as fundamental logical truths? Such questions are not substantive: it is up to us to choose a framework guided by 'pragmatic' considerations; and we should allow many contrasting frameworks to flourish. Sceptical challenges misidentify questions calling for conventional choice of linguistic framework as questions about the nature of reality (Carnap 1937 *passim*, 1956 app. A; and see Hookway 1988 chapters II and III).

This position faces many difficulties (Stroud 1984 chapter V, Hookway 1988 pp.35–9). Carnap insists that scientific progress involves both internal and external changes; and the obstacles to disentangling them suggest that any view exploiting such a distinction between analytic propositions of the framework and substantive internal questions will be hard to sustain. Moreover Stroud emphasizes that using a verificationist theory of meaning against scepticism is question-begging. That we cannot empirically test the apparently intelligible possibility that we are the victims of an evil demon could be regarded as a *prima facie* counter-example to verificationism rather than as showing that scepticism is groundless: so we cannot assess the plausibility of verificationism independently of assessing the sceptical arguments which it was meant to assess (Stroud 1984 p.204).

Although Quine's position grows out of Carnap's, it avoids some of these problems and has interesting similarities to Reid's. I shall just introduce this approach here; it will be discussed more fully in chapter XI. First, Quine relies upon Neurath's anti-foundationalist ship metaphor: our cognitive position is that of a sailor who rebuilds a ship at sea, replacing individual planks while the rest of the fabric keeps the ship afloat (see chapter III section 5). No sharp distinction between framework and framework relative knowledge is drawn: the only (vague) distinction is between what is certain at a particular time and what is seen as open to question. But the position is close to internal realism because our concept of reality, our goals in undertaking inquiries, and our understanding of the methods available to us in pursuing these inquiries are a product of the amorphous system of beliefs holding firm at a particular time. No sense (or point) attaches to standing back and asking whether the whole system of scientific knowledge might not be an illusion.

This makes sense against the background of three Reidian views. The burden of proof lies with the sceptic who challenges our shared certainties: indeed Stroud's argument against Carnap may rest upon a 'neutralism' which Carnap would not share; the latter could argue that it supports his verificationism that it confirms our antecedent certainties. And Quine clearly believes that philosophical engagement with scepticism involves defeating particular sceptical challenges on an *ad hominem* basis while seeing no need to vindicate our right to what nobody seriously challenges (see Quine 1975 *passim*, Hookway 1988 pp.191–202). Finally, Quine's holistic account of meaning and confirmation accords with Reid's insistence that the certainty of many beliefs is the product of many confirmations and their contribution to the overall success of our cognitive activities, this being ignored when we accept the challenge to say *how* we know the things we do (Quine 1953 pp.42–3, and cf. Harman 1986 chapter IV on 'Coherence theories of belief revision').

If this supports Quine's repudiation of Cartesian epistemological strategies, a different element of his position distances him from Hume, and also from Reid's insistence that our ability to acquire knowledge need not be naturalistically intelligible. Quine proposes that a naturalized epistemology – a scientific account of the psychology and physiology of cognition – can answer to our philosophical needs (Quine 1969 pp.69–90). Hume's theory of ideas was confused, but a better science of cognition will explain why our investigations are successful. If we adopt a 'neutralist' position, this strategy will be circular; it depends upon agreeing with Reid about the burden of proof. If framework principles have a distinctive epistemological status then an empirical investigation of their credentials may again be circular. Quine's naturalism thus depends upon these other features of his position.

For the present, we can note two difficulties facing this position. First a naturalistic approach to epistemology describes how we *do* conduct our inquiries; epistemology is interested in legitimation, in understanding how we *ought* to conduct them or explaining why we are right to proceed as we do. It is sometimes argued that Quine simply ignores these normative issues and thus changes the subject (see Stroud 1984 ch. VI, Hookway 1988 ch. XI, Gibson 1988 ch. III, and chapter XII below). Second anyone who is convinced that Cartesian sceptical challenges *do* make sense, that they arise out of our ordinary practice of evaluating assertions and challenging people's claims to knowledge, will be dissatisfied with what appears to be a wilful turning away from fundamental issues. Asserting that the burden of proof lies with the author of sceptical challenges, or ignoring the naturalness of challenges which are alleged to put the anti-sceptic on the defensive, can look like ignoring the problem of scepticism rather than responding to it.

6. *Wittgenstein on certainty*

In the late writings published as *On Certainty* (1977), Wittgenstein provided an unfinished but challenging meditation on philosophical scepticism focusing upon Moore's attempt to quell sceptical doubts about the external world by listing common sense certainties which, he insists, he knows (see Moore 1959 pp.127 ff.). Although Wittgenstein is sympathetic to the thrust of Moore's rejection of scepticism he questions Moore's claim to know these things and claims, indeed, that Moore's discussion fatally accepts one of the presuppositions of the sceptical arguments that it challenges. Moore's claim to *know* these things is an error – and since it opens him to the challenge to explain *how* he knows them, he lacks the resources to meet sceptical counter-attacks. Wittgenstein writes: 'I should like to say: Moore does not *know* what he asserts he knows, but it stands fast for him, as also for me; regarding it as absolutely solid is part of our *method* of doubt and inquiry' (1977 para. 151). Moore is correct to point to the special role which claims such as 'I have a hand', 'I am a human being', 'I am in pain' have in our ways of justifying assertions and ordering our inquiries; but he is wrong to try to describe this role by saying that we *know* these things (see Wright 1985, McGinn 1989).

Wittgenstein relies upon some views about 'knowledge'. Claiming 'knowledge' makes sense only where doubt makes sense; it invites the challenge to explain how we know, a challenge which is most appropriate when the claim concerns something describable as an hypothesis; and I can intelligibly claim to know something only where the possibility of being mistaken makes sense. When I identify an object in my hand as a book, for example, none of these conditions is satisfied: I don't seriously admit the possibility that I have made a mistake; that it is a book is not an hypothesis that I proceed to test; and there is no intelligible response to a request that I explain how I know this. Of course we can imagine circumstances where identifying something as a book would satisfy these conditions – the book may lie in a shadow, or it may superficially resemble something other than a book, or we may have been told that there are containers which resemble books. But that should not deceive us that claims to knowledge are appropriate in the more central cases where the conditions are not satisfied.

We might suppose that we can give our grounds for identifying the object as a book: we can *see* that it is. But it is questionable whether this offers any *support* for our knowledge claim. Using a different example, Wittgenstein writes: 'My having two hands is, in normal circumstances, as certain as anything I could produce as evidence for it.' So 'I am not in a position to take the sight of my two hands as evidence for it' (250). If someone questioned my claim to have two hands we should treat that as evidence that their eyesight was defective before entertaining doubts about our hands. Were we even to entertain a doubt of such a proposition in normal circumstances, 'the foundation of all judging would be taken away' (614). So when Wittgenstein insists that such propositions 'stand firm', he gestures towards a kind of certainty which is the foundation of our ability to make judgments and entertain doubts, and he suggests that to look on this certainty as a special kind of 'knowing' fails to take account of how distinctive its role in cognition is: 'Not everything that has the form of an empirical proposition *is* one' (308); perhaps 'rule and empirical proposition merge into one another' (309).

Crispin Wright (1985 pp.449–50) refers to these claims as 'hinge propositions', because:

> the *questions* that we raise and our *doubts* depend on the fact that some propositions are exempt from doubt, are as it were like hinges on which those turn.

> That is to say, it belongs to the logic of our scientific investigations that certain things are *in deed* not doubted.

> But it isn't that the situation is like this: we just can't investigate everything, and for that reason we are forced to rest content with assumption. If I want the door to turn, the hinges must stay put.

> (341–3)

The 'hinge' metaphor would be appropriate for the views of Kant and Carnap as well as Wittgenstein. What is distinctive is Wittgenstein's characterization of what is involved in having this status. How does Wittgenstein allow for a kind of certainty which is not a kind of knowing, which is, as it were, prior to knowing?

Traditional sceptical arguments suggest that I can understand propositions like 'I have two hands' but be unsure of their truth value. For Wittgenstein, 'the *truth* of my statements is the test of my *understanding* of those statements' (80): the suggestion that I may understand 'hand' but be largely wrong in my identification of hands is incoherent. Treating certain propositions as standing firm, as certain and not in need of justification, is required for us to be able to talk and judge intelligibly at all. For a child to master a language game does not require that it possess knowledge, rather 'it must be *able to do* certain things' (534): it 'learns to react' in certain ways, and 'in so reacting it doesn't so far know anything. Knowing only begins at a later level' (538). This stress upon 'reaction' which is not 'knowledge' is important. The foundation of our system of giving reasons is 'not an ungrounded presupposition: it is an ungrounded way of acting' (110). Indeed Wittgenstein's version of the regress argument includes:

> Giving grounds, however, justifying the evidence, comes to an
> end;– but the end is not certain propositions striking us
> immediately as true, i.e. it is not a kind of *seeing* on our part; it is
> our *acting*, which lies at the bottom of the language game.
>
> (204)

Hence the use of '*in deed*' in the quotation from (342) above. So if someone were to wonder whether the earth existed a hundred years ago 'I would not know what such a person would still allow to be counted as evidence and what not' (231).

These, and many other related passages, point out features of our practice suggesting that we hold fast to propositions which serve as the 'scaffolding' (211) for our inquiries: 'The existence of the earth is ... part of the whole *picture* which forms the starting point of belief for me' (209); a claim which is 'removed from the traffic' and 'shunted onto an unused siding' 'gives our way of looking at things, and our researches, their form' (210-11). Wittgenstein holds that 'hinge propositions' are of many kinds: the existence of the earth, like 'Every human being has parents', has belonged to the scaffolding 'for unthinkable ages' (211); others, like 'the earth is round' (299) 'were once disputed' (211). We

127

inhabit an evolving body of variably stable certainties which give sense to our doubts and inquiries.

Rather than draw out all the similarities between the views of Reid, Wittgenstein, Quine and others, I shall conclude with three observations. Unsurprisingly, the anti-sceptical force of these arguments is problematic. First, many would take the fact that we feel the force of standard sceptical worries as indicating that something has gone wrong with Wittgenstein's argument. Somebody who admits that all may be a dream will be unconvinced that we talk of error or mistake only in the context of assessing the fit between a controversial opinion and an accepted view of the world (74). This is a general problem noted earlier about the dialectical complexities of a debate between one who uses sceptical arguments and those who refuse to acknowledge their force.

The second observation concerns self-control. Marie McGinn points out that 'the practice of employing descriptive techniques is something that we inherit through the training that constitutes our method of induction or acculturation' (1989 p.145). She points out that this practice is encountered 'as a natural phenomenon in the world: it exists independently of any particular individual, but it is something in which we all participate' (ibid). For Wittgenstein self-control rests upon something which is experienced as brute or even contingent: entering the practice is not something over which we have control; the rules of the practice cannot be evaluated:

> [It is] something that lies beyond being justified or unjustified; as it were, something animal.
>
> (359)

> [It] is not based on grounds. It is not reasonable (or unreasonable). It is there – like our life.
>
> (559)

We 'find ourselves' exercising self-control in particular ways. But where Sextus would conclude from this that an intelligible intellectual aspiration is unobtainable, Wittgenstein refuses to see it as limiting our rationality or our ability to control our inquiries.

This leads to the third observation, which involves Wittgenstein's admission that these fundamental certainties change, sometimes quite quickly, over time. This must mean that part of our current sense of our cognitive position should be a recognition that what now holds firm may subsequently be rejected. Indeed, our paradigms of cognitive 'progress' take just this form – 'The earth is round'. Our consciousness of many of our cognitive activities has an historical dimension: we recognize that our physical views, for example, have benefited from critical engagement with earlier theories whose inadequacies they have explained and overcome; and we are actively engaged in seeking further such progress which will undermine many of the hinges on which our present inquiries turn. While pointing out that many of these propositions serve as 'hinges' may illuminate our current attitude towards scientific certainties (see 599), it has little to say about our confidence that progress will continue: it can seem that Wittgenstein ignores the historical dimension of our consciousness of our historical position and the need for coming to terms with this dimension if we are to contribute to continuing traditions of inquiry in a self-controlled manner. (Peirce's 'critical common-sensism', which grounds all inquiry in 'acritical certainties' represents an attempt to combine a related view of the 'instinctive' character of our fundamental commitments with an awareness of this historical dimension – see Hookway 1990.)

This concludes the historical part of this book. Although we have discussed the views of only a few of the philosophers who have contributed to our understanding of scepticism, we have examined the most influential sceptical arguments, and we have attempted to relate them to the wider philosophical concerns of their authors. The present chapter has introduced the most important themes involved in recent attempts to defuse the challenge of scepticism. We now turn to the constructive part of the undertaking: an attempt to explain how sceptical challenges should be understood and to discover how their impact can be resisted.

CHAPTER VII

Scepticism and Inquiry

1. Why is scepticism a problem?

How important is it to defeat scepticism? How central is it to the tasks of epistemology? There is an attitude towards epistemological issues that can be expressed thus:

> Although we cannot answer the sceptical arguments, we are unconvinced by them. No one genuinely doubts his beliefs about his surroundings on the grounds that he cannot show that he is not a brain suspended in a vat of nutrients, sustained and manipulated by a brilliant scientist. Indeed, the more convinced we are that the arguments cannot be met head on, the more they look like pointless philosophical games. Consequently, let us leave them behind, and, making the best use we can of our knowledge of the history of science and the psychology of cognition, construct a plausible, scientifically informed, account of how we know as much as (we all agree) we do know.

This view exploits the fact that our puzzlement by sceptical arguments is apparently 'insulated' from our first order practice of conducting inquiries and forming beliefs. Since they have no impact upon this practice, we can ignore these arguments when we search for a philosophical understanding of our success in obtaining knowledge of reality.

The outlook just described insists that there is no need to see sceptical arguments as providing any kind of threat. Their lack of psychological impact confirms their innocuous character. Hence we can look upon them as interesting puzzles; we can try to see what is wrong with them. Or we can treat them as tools for philosophical understanding: since, plainly, we do know all sorts of things, they provide a criterion of adequacy for analyses of knowledge or justification. In other words, our task is to provide an analysis of knowledge which shows that the sceptical arguments are ineffective: if we cannot show where they go wrong, that means that our analysis of knowledge requires revision. The general assumption is that we know, before embarking upon philosophical analysis, that scepticism can be overcome. The interesting philosophical question concerns how this is to be done. And if we cannot answer this question, we are not inhibited from tackling central epistemological questions in a naturalistic spirit.

A dilemma for modern epistemology is presented by the fact that when we do examine sceptical arguments from the traditional canon, at least some of them exercise a powerful influence upon our imagination. Like our students, we readily succumb to the thought that all may be a dream or to the possibility that we are victims of an evil demon. Because of our ordinary practice of assent and investigation may lead us to wonder about the significance of this response, suggesting that it is a complex pretence grounded in our disposition to take pleasure from embracing fantastic possibilities, many philosophers find it hard to purge themselves of the thought that these arguments issue challenges that cannot be ignored.

Behind this response to sceptical arguments is the reasonable assumption that scepticism raises matters of central philosophical importance only if it would somehow make a difference if it could not be defeated. We have seen that for Sextus, Descartes, and Hume, it would make a difference. Both Sextus and (to a lesser degree) Hume admit that a Pyrrhonist or mitigated sceptic is transformed by his philosophical outlook. Descartes seems to have held that defeating the strongest scepticism was a precondition of being able to carry out certain sorts of scientific investigation. All these doctrines recognize 'being a sceptic' as committing one to living in a certain way, or having certain attitudes towards one's inquiries. If concern with scepticism is truly 'insulated' from the concerns of science and ordinary life, it may be correct to view it as a topic of secondary concern for epistemology.

I take it that scepticism is a position of central philosophical importance only if it either threatens our cognitive achievements or holds up possibilities of a readjustment in our attitudes towards our beliefs and investigations. Either way, acknowledging that sceptical arguments cannot be defeated should make a difference, phenomenologically. In that case, it is important to be clear about just what is threatened: what would it be like to be a sceptic? This chapter defends a view of the target of sceptical arguments: how should we describe the aspect of our ordinary sense of our selves and our activities which is threatened by sceptical arguments? Familiar sceptical arguments will be examined in the light of this suggestion in chapters VIII and IX.

An analogy with the free will problem may help to clarify these remarks (although it will subsequently turn out to be more than just an analogy). Arguments designed to show that, for example, physical determinism undermines our claim to be free responsible agents can be met by the insistence that our ordinary practices of assigning blame and holding people responsible for their actions are untouched by these arguments. If the notions of freedom and responsibility which govern our relations with other people and our evaluations of our own conduct are indeed not challenged by the arguments, it is urged, then they attack nothing of importance. Freedom and responsibility are compatible with physical determinism. If this compatibilist position ('soft determinism') is to be resisted, we need to show that physical determinism deprives us of something that matters. In the same way, an understanding of philosophical scepticism must begin by examining whether anything that matters is challenged by sceptical arguments. If not, we might see 'soft scepticism' – the retention of all of our familiar practices of inquiry and the criticism of belief in the face of the unanswerable sceptical arguments – as an attractive option.

2. Certainty, knowledge, justified belief

In this section, we shall examine some candidates for the target of sceptical arguments. The underlying question is: what should we see sceptical challenges as denying the possibility of ? What target best reveals the threat that sceptical arguments pose?

The suggestion that sceptical arguments show that we cannot be *certain* of anything, or that we cannot be *absolutely* certain of anything, gains support from a casual reading of Descartes. Descartes demands a degree of certainty in (at least some of) his beliefs which can overwhelm even the suggestion that he is the victim of an evil demon determined to lead him into error. We do indeed take ourselves to be certain of many things, but to see certainty as the prime target of sceptical challenges is a mistake. It is relevant here, as is often stressed, that philosophers' use of 'certain' is often both vague and ambiguous. In particular, our familiar subjective assurance, naturally expressed as 'certainty', is distinct from the absolute certainty often discussed by epistemologists. We are generally happy to admit to certainty while allowing the remote possibility (and certainly the logical possibility) that our confident claim may be defeated by subsequent evidence. In that case, we need an argument to show that a demonstration that absolute certainty is never warranted would shake our ready subjective confidence in all of our common sense 'certainties'.

Even if it could be shown that we could not be certain of anything in our familiar everyday sense, this may be no cause for alarm. It is often objected that sceptical arguments for the impossibility of certainty rest upon misconceptions about knowledge. This can take several forms. Peter Unger's defence of scepticism rests upon an analysis of knowledge which insists that the claim that someone knows something entails that they are absolutely certain of it (Unger 1971). Many philosophers argue that this is simply a mistake; and to support this they describe cases where we happily ascribe knowledge to someone who expresses a belief somewhat hesitantly or admits that it is defeasible. Alternatively, they may insist that although certainty may be necessary for someone to know that they know some fact, it is a mistake to hold that we cannot know something unless we also know that we know it. Hence certainty is not required for plain knowledge. It is not to my purpose to evaluate these arguments here. Rather, I wish to notice the underlying assumption that certainty is not important for its own sake. Rather, these philosophers hold that the fundamental issue concerns whether we *know* anything. Certainty is a suitable target for sceptical attack only because of some (real or imagined) connection between knowledge and certainty.

This suggests that certainty is not an intrinsic epistemic value. If it were possible to possess widespread knowledge while being certain, or absolutely certain, of nothing, then sceptical arguments suggesting that we are never warranted in being certain of anything would be of little interest. It is very common for epistemologists to treat knowledge as the fundamental epistemic value: sceptical arguments are of interest only in so far as they suggest that we do not *know* anything. This too, it seems to me, is a mistake. Scepticism might be held at bay even if we have no knowledge; and extensive scepticism is compatible with the possession of knowledge. I shall argue for these claims in turn.

Suppose we discovered that certainty *was* required for knowledge: if we were in the slightest degree doubtful of some claim, then although the claim to know it may have a rhetorical role, it is literally false. A philosopher may then argue from the impossibility of such certainty to the impossibility of knowledge, strictly so-called (cf. Unger 1971). He might point out that although knowledge is impossible, we are not prevented from holding large numbers of justified, albeit defeasible, beliefs. If we were to accept his analysis of knowledge, then we might stop claiming to 'know' things while continuing to endorse beliefs with the favourable epistemic evaluative property of being justified. If this is scepticism, it does not cut very deep and does not present much of a threat to our sense of being in cognitive contact with reality. We might conclude that whether our beliefs count as 'knowledge' is less important than we had supposed. The point I am making does not depend upon our accepting the view that knowledge requires certainty. The hypothesis that such an analysis was correct merely helped us to see that a proof of the impossibility of 'knowledge' has a sceptical impact only if we have a demonstration of the importance of 'knowledge' for our cognitive lives. If we can show that, unless we know some things none of our beliefs is ever justified, then attacks on the possibility of knowledge are disturbing. If if we cannot show this, and we cannot describe other respects in which knowledge is deeply embedded in our system of cognitive evaluation, then we may conclude that scepticism can indeed be held at bay even if we do not know anything.

The second argument, that proving that we have knowledge need not be sufficient to defeat scepticism, employs a similar thought experiment. Suppose we adopted a fairly crude account of knowledge which claimed, simply, that a true belief counts as knowledge if it is caused by the state of affairs which it describes. Suppose, too, that we have a philosophical argument which establishes that we know (say) at least one hundred things: a reasonable number of our beliefs are caused by the states of affairs that they describe. Although this argument establishes that we possess knowledge, it does not establish that we have any rational basis for identifying which of our beliefs it is that we know. We cannot make use of the fact that we possess knowledge of some facts in planning our actions or ordering our inquiries. Our possession of knowledge would thus have very little impact upon our ability to establish which of our beliefs are justified, or to decide which beliefs can be relied upon in testing further hypotheses. Unless we can make use of our knowledge in our deliberations, unless we have some idea of which things it is that we know, our possession of knowledge is powerless to disturb the threat of scepticism.

I should stress that this is not intended as a refutation of causal theories of knowledge: I have discussed a very unsophisticated and implausible version of the doctrine. My aim was solely to argue that if demonstrating that we know things is required for the defeat of scepticism, this is because of the importance of the possession of knowledge for a wide range of cognitive activities. If it turns out that our cognitive economy can survive the elimination of evaluations using the concept of knowledge, or if it turns out that it is impaired unless we know which things we know, then a simple demonstration that we possess knowledge is of minor importance for philosophical engagement with scepticism. If knowledge is the primary focus of sceptical arguments, we need an explanation of why knowledge is important.

We might suppose that the fundamental target for sceptical arguments is *justified belief*: they show that we are never actually justified in holding one belief rather than another. However this, too, does not go deep enough. First, it is an exceedingly vague and slippery notion. What suffices to justify a belief varies enormously according to the context of inquiry: the amount of evidence required for me to be justified in believing that it will rain tomorrow is much less than would be required for a medical researcher to be justified in believing that a drug is safe: the risk of error that is acceptable differs greatly. This suggests that, if talk of justification is helpful at all, it must be embedded within a range of cognitive concepts and evaluations which explain how we can decide how much evidence is required to justify us in asserting different propositions in different contexts. We do not have a unitary notion of justified belief which can be made the prime focus of sceptical attack.

A more controversial argument suggests that we can hold scepticism at bay even if deprived of justified belief. Both Popper (Popper 1972 ch.III) and Peirce (CP5.589, 7.606) insist that a responsible scientist need not *believe* his or her current theories at all. Science involves participating in a continuing process of co-operative inquiry. Currently accepted hypotheses and systems of concepts are not viewed as truths; they will almost certainly be replaced as inquiry proceeds. Rather, they are looked upon as assertable at the current stage of investigation, and the value of asserting them consists in the contribution that doing so can make to further progress. Although we might follow Peirce and describe such 'acceptance' as 'scientific belief', this is a misleading expression which conceals the detached uncommitted attitude that inquirers should take towards their assertions. Whether or not we are impressed by this picture of science, it points towards a wider perspective on cognitive life. We participate in *inquiries*, both scientific and everyday. The deepest scepticism may show that we are unable to do *that*. Sceptical challenges to certainty, knowledge and justified belief threaten our cognitive self-assurance in so far as those concepts are employed by us in ordering and evaluating our inquiries.

Other targets for sceptical arguments could have been considered here. Examination of certainty, knowledge and justified belief has, I hope, helped us to see that if scepticism is to be perceived as a threat, these specific targets must be understood in a broader context which enables us to see why they are important. The remainder of this chapter attempts to understand what this wider context is.

3. Some lessons of history

The epistemological focus upon what it is to *know* something, and upon what can be *known*, is largely a twentieth century phenomenon. It is not to be found in the work of Sextus, Descartes or Hume. The views examined in earlier chapters may provide guidance in our search for a better understanding of the impact of scepticism.

The Pyrrhonists challenged the possibility of an activity, the search for truths about the non-evident properties of things. Many people attempted to take part in this search and obtain dogmata. But Sextus revealed that we do not seem to understand how the attempt can be successful. We lack a clear understanding of the aims of the activity and we have no defensible conception of the criteria to be employed in evaluating dogmatic hypotheses and methods of inquiry. It appears that we can continue to participate in the activity only if we are ignorant of the nature of the activity and our participation in it. If somebody participates in dogmatic inquiry confident that he is in control and is ordering his actions in pursuit of a clear cognitive aim, he is the victim of illusion or self-deception. So the target of Pyrrhonist scepticism is the possibility of participating without self-deception in a cognitive activity that we take to require a measure of rational self-control. Two features of this position will be important for subsequent discussion: the focus on inquiry, understood as a particular kind of cognitive activity; and the idea that sceptical arguments suggest that we can only participate in the activity by compromising our rational autonomy, our sense that we are in control of our inquiries.

Our discussion of Descartes made a similar point. He held that defeat of the strongest sceptical arguments was required if we are to be confident of our ability to investigate the real nature of things. Unless the programme of the *Meditations* can be completed, scientists are not justified in their assurance that the methods they employ are adequate for their purposes.

The suggestion to be derived from our study of Hume complements this. We naturally seek to understand the goals of our attempts to investigate the causal laws that govern the behaviour of the external things that we perceive. We investigate the methods we employ in this investigation and try to account for our success. As we saw, Hume concluded that our success is unintelligible. Our explanation of our understanding of these aims and of our reliance upon familiar methods of inquiry threatens to undermine our confidence and trust in our ability to carry out those activities. We continue to carry out inquiries at the cost of a sort of dislocation of the self. We cannot integrate the views of our cognitive powers that compel our belief at different times. Continued investigation of our surroundings cannot be accompanied by the sense of rational self-control that we would normally take to be desirable. It is in this loss of integration between our first order inquiries and our beliefs about our inquiries that Hume's scepticism is manifested.

The lesson of these historical investigations is to direct our attention towards the fact that inquiry is an activity. Philosophers' tendency to distinguish theoretical and practical reasoning hides from us the fact that scepticism challenges the possibility of our participating in an *activity*. Moreover we are reminded of how scepticism can have an impact upon our consciousness even if it does not shake our confidence in our beliefs about reality. Its 'phenomenological' impact could be revealed in the fact that, for example, participation in inquiry must be accompanied either by ignorance of our cognitive position or by self-deception. Or it can surface in a dislocation or disturbance of the integrity of the inquiring self: we cease to be able to look upon ourselves as autonomous inquiring agents in control of our investigations.

4. *Scepticism and agency*

The idea that concepts drawn from the theory of action have a bearing upon epistemology is often dismissed for several bad reasons. It is pointed out that forming a belief is not an action. If it were, so that choice of belief reflected desires as well as other beliefs, we should construct a charter for wishful thinking. But we cannot believe whatever we wish to; indeed, it would undermine a belief if we thought that it originated in an act of will (B. Williams 1973 'Deciding to believe'). We don't want to choose our beliefs; we want them to be caused by what is the case. In a similar vein, we may be reminded that reasoning and inference are not actions. It is central to our experience of reasoning that we are drawn along by the force of rational considerations and forced to one conclusion rather than another. In similar vein, notions like autonomy and freedom are often taken to have a role in the moral assessment of agents but have no bearing upon epistemological assessments of their scientific or non-scientific inquiries.

The claim that we want our beliefs to be answerable to reality and thus not to be a matter of choice is correct. However there are ways of bringing out the importance of concepts from the theory of action for the understanding of epistemological problems which do not involve thinking that inference and belief formation are themselves actions. In this section, I shall describe two of these. Although the points I am making are familiar, I believe that they can be used to cast important light on the question of scepticism.

First, our actions depend upon our beliefs: we perform actions which we judge likely to lead to consequences which we believe to be desirable. This can have a bearing upon our practice of epistemic assessment in two ways. Our ability to act with integrity or to subject our activities to rational self-control depends upon our ability to look upon our beliefs as formed in the right way. If I suspect that my beliefs are produced in a distorted fashion, so that my possessing a belief is not an indication that it is probably true, then I may feel that I cannot act rationally when I rely upon them. Recognizing that I am forced to act on beliefs which reflect such distortions may challenge my assurance that I am a free, autonomous agent. For example, a roulette player who became aware that he could not not rid himself of a disposition to form beliefs in ways that were probabilistically unsound would sense that his gambling activity was deeply irrational. On each occasion when he responded to a run of red by placing a large bet on black, he would suspect that his conviction that this was sensible was improper. So the first relation between our agency and our practice of epistemic assessment is that if sceptical arguments cannot be defeated, so that we cannot dismiss the possibility that our methods of belief formation are distorted, then this may be reflected in the phenomenology of agency. If scepticism is correct, then we may feel that we cannot act freely; we are constrained by causal processes which may distort our beliefs about the world.

The fact that beliefs are among the antecedents of action may have a second bearing upon our practice of epistemic assessment; it may help to explain our standards of cognitive evaluation. For example, our understanding of the amount of evidence we require in support of an hypothesis before we can describe it as justified may reflect the degree of support that is required before we can feel that we are acting responsibly when we act upon it. This promises to explain some of the relativities involved in our concept of justified belief: the greater the disaster if our actions fail to achieve their purpose, the more evidence we require before we regard the belief as properly justified; the greater the risks attaching to inaction, the readier we are to act on limited evidence. Much epistemological writing which attempts to integrate the theory of knowledge with decision theory and subjective probability theory accords with this epistemological strategy.

We now turn to the second link between epistemology and the theory of action. Even if beliefs and judgments are not actions, the process of inquiry or investigation is, as we have seen, an activity. We travel from one location to another in order to make observations or consult works of reference; we carry out experiments; we ask advice from others and discuss our opinions with them, criticizing their views and defending our own. We inquire into the truth of a proposition by carrying out a sequence of actions which are structured or unified by higher order plans and intentions. The sequence of actions is seen as a means to securing purposes which contribute to achieving the goals which direct our inquiries. They are backed by a thought of the form:

If I perform actions A1, A2, ... An, then whatever I find myself believing concerning whether p will be true.

I decide which questions to investigate, and I decide when and how to carry out my investigation. I decide, too, when I have carried the investigation far enough, and abandon the search for further evidence.

The same holds for deliberation *in foro interno*. I can decide to work out the route I should take when I drive to Oxford. I then decide to spend time thinking through the criteria I should use for making this decision; and I settle in which order I should consider the different routes. If I cannot choose the answers to the questions I consider, I can choose which questions to ask and I can choose how to go about answering them. Once again, in approaching questions of truth, I am an agent, planning an activity of inquiry or deliberation.

139

We find here a focus for understanding the impact of sceptical arguments. If they show that we cannot carry out these activities as integrated, rational autonomous agents – if they challenge ideals we aspire to in exercising our agency – then we may understand how sceptical arguments can have a phenomenology without leading us to suspend belief or feel doubt concerning everyday beliefs. In section 6 we shall make a suggestion about how we should understand the threat posed by sceptical arguments. In preparation for this, the following section considers how we can use the concept of responsibility in making epistemic appraisals.

5. Inquiry and responsibility

I shall first consider some examples which indicate how we can hold people responsible for the ways in which they organize their inquiries or form their beliefs. Second, I shall describe some psychological phenomena which may be used to cast doubt on how far we can be held responsible for our cognitive failings.

The appropriateness of talk of responsibility to the products of investigation is evident when authors are criticized for failing to take into account documents which count against the conclusions for which they argue, or for failing to pursue lines of inquiry which might have shown their evidence to have been unrepresentative. Drug manufacturers are held responsible when patients are harmed because of flaws in their testing. Candidates for degrees have to affirm that their theses are all their own work, that they are responsible for the discoveries reported therein.

Lorraine Code (1983), in the course of an interesting discussion of Edmund Gosse's account of his father's scientific activities in *Father and Son*, concludes that it is 'difficult to deem [the father] wholly responsible from an epistemic point of view' (p.269). After a successful career as a zoologist, the fundamentalist Christian Philip Gosse was forced to confront the challenge to his views provided by the new evolutionary biology. Famously, Gosse's response was to repudiate the discoveries obtained by the new biology and to affirm the literal truth of the book of Genesis. Although he initially welcomed the biological advances, he was *unable* to absorb them into his religious view of the world and forced to deny them. Understanding why this occurred leads Code to judge him 'less than perfectly virtuous' and not 'wholly responsible' in his inquiries. This is because his response to his crisis betrayed a lack of self-knowledge and a complete absence of self criticism. His commitment to Genesis meant that to attempt to assess it from the outside would be blasphemy (Code p.271): no scrutiny from the outside was admitted. He was unable to recognize the conflict for what it was and ask the question: what criterion should be employed in choosing between these conflicting views? He was unable to take responsibility for understanding the character of the conflict he faced; and he was unable to acknowledge that it was for him to try to understand and justify to himself his grounds for resolving the conflict as he did.

A similar, but more mundane, example might emerge from a study of people who form expectations on the basis of their newspaper horoscope. In so far as they do not have a sense that they are acting irresponsibly or frivolously in doing this, we may suspect that this is only because they are unreflective, or negligent about what they are trying to achieve or about the adequacy of their method to obtain what they want. Alternatively, they deceive themselves about how their methods measure up to the standards which they employ in other areas of their lives, or they make no attempt to understand the relations between their different practices. Similarly, when people defend creationist science by insisting that 'evolution is only an hypothesis', one suspects that their view is only sustained by a wilful failure to explore the structure of hypotheses and the differences between creationism and Darwin.

We would be disturbed by the suggestion that our own position when confronting conflicts between our opinions did not differ in kind from Gosse's. This would suggest that we were not capable of taking responsibility for our beliefs and inquiries; we are always the victim of drives or compulsions which cannot be brought to consciousness or subjected to rational criticism. Work in cognitive science has led to a number of discoveries which yield this disturbing suggestion. Consider the following example, from Harman (1986 p.33). A student takes an aptitude test and is informed, in consequence, that she has an aptitude for science and music, but not for history and philosophy. Experience of college grades conflicts with this: she has done well in physics and history, badly in both philosophy and music. However, she decides to accept the results of the aptitude test and drops her history courses, taking more music courses instead. Pyschological evidence suggests that if she were subsequently told that she had been given the wrong set of results, and that her own results accorded with her earlier experience, the belief that she was better at music than at history could well survive. Once beliefs are in place, they can prove tenacious, even when the arguments that originally convinced us of them are discredited: 'it is clear that beliefs can survive ... the total destruction of their original evidential bases' (Ross and Anderson 1982 p.149, cited by Harman p.37). Awareness of this and related phenomena can shake our confidence that we act responsibly in basing our actions or inquiries on beliefs whose origin we now forget.

There is extensive evidence that we naturally handle probabilities very poorly (see Goldman 1986 pp.307 ff): 65 per cent of a sample of 'statistically naive' students judged that the percentage of a sample to have had one or more heart attacks was smaller than the percentage that were both over 55 and had suffered one or more heart attacks (p.319). There is more evidence that we naturally make errors when we rely upon memory, and we are all familiar with circumstances in which perceptual error is common. Of course, our confidence that we have a large body of correct beliefs about reality is not shaken by these observations. We are confident that their impact is limited and that when they do lead to error on matters of importance, our system of epistemic checks and balances soon alerts us to our mistake. In spite of this, we can use them to illuminate some features of the role of talk of responsibility in connection with belief.

The example of Philip Gosse illustrated how we can use this notion to criticize ways of forming or revising beliefs: Gosse failed fully to take responsibility for the ways in which he responded to the conflicts that emerged between his theological and scientific beliefs. The recognition that psychological processes of which we are unaware can disrupt our attempts to arrive at true beliefs might be used in two ways. First, somebody might use it as an excuse, arguing that they cannot be held responsible for the consequences of beliefs that were distorted in this way. Imagine someone who is the subject of a psychologcal experiment which involves providing them with a lot of misleading feedback about their success in performing a variety of tasks. Although they are subsequently debriefed, their misconceptions about their capacities survive the destruction of their evidential base. They have never learned that this doxastic tenacity is a feature of human psychology. Subsequently they act upon their misconception with disastrous results. Might they not disclaim responsibility for these results, either holding the experimenter responsible for what occurred or (more interestingly) complaining that their tendency to retain beliefs in these circumstances is simply a fact of psychology or physiology which they could not be expected to take into account?

The second response might be one of estrangement from their methods of belief formation: how can they be expected to take responsibility for their beliefs, and for the actions which rely upon these beliefs, when they are prey to a variety of psychological infirmities most of which are unknown to them? Even more than the first, this response seems an overreaction, although many people may respond in this fashion when exposed to the evidence of our inexpert handling of probabilities. It is enough, for my purposes, that we can appreciate the possibility of a response of this kind; and it will be important, subsequently, to investigate why it is an overreaction.

6. *The challenge of scepticism: a suggestion*

We aspire to a kind of autonomous rational control over our activities. If it is shown that there are limits to our self-control, that we are compelled to adopt certain goals or to pursue them in one way rather than another, this can challenge our assurance that we can act freely and lead us to deny that we are truly responsible for the consequences of our actions. 'Freedom', 'responsibility', 'autonomy', 'rational self-control': these are concepts that are central to philosophical debates over the freedom of the will and the impact of determinism upon our ability to see ourselves as responsible agents. As a single term to express this related set of ideas, I shall use 'autonomy': ideals of what is involved in acting autonomously govern our sense of rational self-control and our attempts to claim or avoid responsibility for the consequences of our actions.

There is a parallel between philosophical discussions of freedom of the will and scepticism. The differences between challenges to beliefs which all find acceptable and those that threaten to undermine our right to claim any knowledge of reality at all do not seem to be of the right kind to legitimate our ignoring the latter challenges. And the differences between 'excuses' which successfully enable us to disclaim responsibility and 'excuses' which suggest we can never be truly responsible for any of our actions are similarly not sufficient, it appears, to warrant our unreflective disregard of the latter. In each case, the philosophical challenges leave us uncertain that we are warranted in continuing with practices which we cannot seriously abandon. Once we recognize that inquiry is itself an activity, and that our attitude towards it can also reflect its role in providing information which we can use in planning our activities, we may begin to wonder whether this is just a parallel. An alternative perspective would hold that sceptical arguments challenge our ability to preserve our rational autonomy while participating in inquiry – or our ability to preserve our rational autonomy while planning actions that rely upon the products of our inquiries. The problem of scepticism emerges as a special case of the free will problem.

My suggestion is that we should examine sceptical arguments from the perspective that they challenge our ability to see ourselves as autonomous, responsible agents. Once we acknowledge that inquiry is a form of activity, this seems an obvious perspective to adopt. Our historical discussions support it too. We saw that Sextus and Descartes were concerned with demonstrating, respectively, the impossibility and possibility of participating responsibly in distinctive kinds of inquiry. And Hume's mitigated scepticism seemed to remove the possibility of a kind of psychological integrity which we normally judge to be essential to such autonomous agency. Our understanding of our own participating in inquiry cannot be used to control and underwrite our practice; it serves only to make us cautious in our assertions because we are aware that we are not fully in control.

This approach has several advantages. We have noted that philosophers' engagement with scepticism is generally insulated from their first order evaluations of their beliefs. It is rare for someone to feel even a slight tendency to suspend judgment in everyday or scientific opinions when challenged with the problem of the criterion, or by the possibility that all is a dream. Nobody seriously considers that our ordinary epistemic evaluations are threatened by these arguments. The perspective adopted here enables us to question the significance of this claim. It explains how acceptance of scepticism could have a phenomenology even if it does not lead us to revise our practice of epistemic evaluation. Scepticism threatens our sense of rational autonomy and integrity, and challenges our ability to manage our activities in ways that are required by our aspiration to self-control and our understanding of responsibility.

A second advantage is that it provides a perspective within which we can understand the importance of concepts such as 'certainty', 'knowledge', and 'justified belief' and which can help with explaining what certainty, knowledge and justified belief are. Finally, we can hope that concepts and distinctions from philosophical debates about agency

144

and freedom will prove useful tools in framing a response to scepticism. For example, a position which despairs of answering sceptical challenges but describes the ways in which we evaluate beliefs and assertions, suggesting that we can recognize their value without being able to defend them against sceptical onslaught, may be placed in a different perspective when it is seen as the epistemic counterpart of soft determinism: soft scepticism, as we may call it. The remaining chapters of this volume develop this perspective. Chapter VIII gives more content to talk of autonomous self-control and offers a diagnosis of how sceptical arguments work, and chapter IX explains this more fully by examining some contrasting diagnoses of the source of sceptical challenges. An explanation of our concept of knowledge in chapter X is followed by an attempt to show how scepticism can be avoided within the context of a naturalistic approach to epistemology.

CHAPTER VIII

Autonomy and Scepticism

1. Autonomy

After a general discussion of the notion of rational *autonomy*, this chapter examines some familiar sceptical arguments. Our aim is to formulate them in ways that reflect the suggestion made in the previous chapter and to obtain an overview of the strategies available for a response to them. There are many competing analyses of autonomy, and it would inhibit our discussion to commit ourselves to just one of them at this stage. We shall begin by noting some of the factors which are normally taken to be crucial to the valuations made using this notion (cf. Dworkin 1988 ch.1).

As etymology suggests, the underlying idea is one of self-rule or self-control. Scanlon asserts that an autonomous person 'must see himself as sovereign in deciding what to believe and in weighing competing reasons for action' (1972 p.215); and Lucas writes: 'I, and I alone, am ultimately responsible for the decisions I make, and am in that sense autonomous'(1966 p.101). R. S. Peters has remarked that children reach the stage of autonomy when they appreciate 'that rules are alterable, that they can be criticized' (1973 p.130). Although some of these claims relate specifically to moral or political rules and decisions, they are helpful for our more general purposes. Dworkin helpfully lists a number of features commonly related to (or identified with) autonomy:

> It is used sometimes as an equivalent of liberty ..., sometimes as
> equivalent to self-rule or sovereignty, sometimes as equivalent with
> freedom of the will. It is equated with dignity, integrity,
> individuality, independence, responsibility, and self-knowledge. It
> is identified with qualities of self-assertion, with critical reflection,

with freedom from obligation, with absence from external
causation, with knowledge of one's own interests.

(Dworkin 1988 p.6)

The connections between some of these elements emerge in his
characterization of what he takes to be central to autonomy: a capacity
to reflect critically upon our desires, etc., and to 'accept or attempt to
change these in the light of higher-order preferences' (p.20). By so
doing, 'persons define their nature, give meaning and coherence to their
lives, and take responsibility for the kind of person they are'. Critical
reflection and taking of responsibility are here closely linked; and few
people would deny the value of either.

How might we establish that someone lacks this capacity for
reflective self-control? I shall contrast three sorts of arguments, of
decreasing scope. The first relies upon general philosophical or
metaphysical doctrines to argue that autonomy, so understood, is an
impossible ideal. The second points to contingent features of human
nature or human experience which preclude (or limit) its possession.
The third argues that distinctive projects cannot be pursued
autonomously, either by anyone or by particular people.

We shall take for granted the following rough picture of our
participation in activities. We act in pursuit of goals, consequences
which we find desirable. This requires us to formulate ordered sets of
subordinate goals, the satisfaction of which we believe to be means to
the achievement of our overarching goals. We form intentions to act in
various ways in order to achieve these subordinate goals, and, at an
appropriate time, we attempt to execute our intentions. This provides
much scope for critical reflection. We can reflect upon:

1. Whether our overarching goal is a good one.
2. Whether the beliefs we use in selecting our goal and deciding
   which subordinate goals and means should be employed were
   responsibly formed.
3. Whether our course of action has other undesirable side effects.
4. Whether better means to achieving our goals are available, or
   whether it would have been better to have pursued a different
   one of our basic goals.
5. Whether our intention should have been revised between its
   formation and the time at which it was executed as more
   information becomes available.

147

6. Whether our beliefs about when, and how, the intention should be executed are correct.

In certain circumstances, people can be held to account for the failure of their actions if they have failed to reflect upon these (and other) factors. Of course, it should not be part of an acceptable model of agency that deep reflection upon all of these matters must precede every action. What is required is that such reflection is possible, and that responsible agents are sensitive to when it is required.

The first set of arguments is familiar from literature about whether we can really act freely. One such argument depends upon the truth of physical determinism. If physical determinism is true, then, had someone known the totality of physical laws and the disposition of every particle in the universe at some point during the sixteenth century, then only computational complexity would have prevented them from predicting every bodily movement involved in carrying out human activities. How can we claim active control over actions, or be ascribed ultimate responsiblity for them, when our doing them was determined before we were born, and (*a fortiori*) before we began our practical reflection? We are not sovereign to any degree. In similar vein, Ted Honderich argues that if we are convinced that our desires, beliefs, intentions and actions are bound by deterministic laws to neurophysiological events of which we are not aware, and which are beyond our control, our view of ourselves as pursuing our 'life hopes' by *initiating* courses of action cannot be sustained. It is natural to relate this talk of active initiation to the process of taking responsibility for one's activities, and to take from Honderich the thought that the pursuit of 'sovereignty' over our thoughts and deeds can yield only failure and 'dismay' (1988 pp.382 ff.).

A related argument, not depending upon determinism, is employed by Galen Strawson (1986). We act rationally and responsibly when our actions issue from our beliefs and desires. However, if we are simply determined to have a particular set of desires (say) it is implausible that we are truly responsible for actions which are caused by them. If they are not *determined* since they result from random or indeterminate processes, our responsibility is similarly undermined. Should these beliefs and desires issue from others by inference, we can step back and ask the same question about the desires, beliefs and inferential habits which produced them. It is only if these states are 'self-determined', or determined by an agent without his choice being either determined by his nature or wholly capricious, that he can really be held responsible for how he acts. This is an unintelligible (or at least unhelpful) suggestion.

Such an argument is potentially more powerful than those depending upon determinism, for it suggests a logical incoherence in the whole idea of free responsible agency, and hence undermines concepts which we thought were central to the understanding of rational autonomy. Moreover, it displays a fruitful analogy with some epistemological arguments discussed above:

> Responsibility for an action depends upon its possessing a feature (*A*). Possession of this feature depends upon its antecedents possessing the same feature. If these antecedents in turn have antecedents, so that possession of *A* always depends upon the possession of it by antecedents, then we face an infinite regress. If a state can possess *A* while having no antecedents at all, we can provide no rationale for the evaluative role of talk of responsibility. Hence, if *A* is to be applicable at all, some states and events must just be intrinsically *A*. No explanation has been offered of how this is other than unintelligible.

If we substitute 'justified' for *A* and 'beliefs' for 'actions', 'states' and 'events', and begin 'Acceptability of a belief depends upon its possessing 'justification', we arrive at scepticism based upon familiar regress argument concerning justification together with the unintelligibility of self-evidence.

The second set of arguments exploits contingent features of human nature. Pointing to the role of training and education in shaping people's beliefs and values, or the ability of television and the press to shape attitudes in ways of which the viewer or reader is ignorant, or the capacity of such institutions to lead people to deep misconceptions of where their real interests lie, or the role of unconscious drives in shaping our beliefs and desires, we may conclude that both our capacity for self-knowledge and our ability to criticize our activities in the light of our interests are profoundly limited. It can even be argued that a primary consequence of emphasizing autonomy as a moral and political value is to obscure the limited extent to which such informed self-control is possible for us.

A third sort of argument is less common but relevant to subsequent discussion. It can be argued that particular kinds of activities cannot be pursued autonomously. An example is Robert Paul Wolff's insistence that participation in some forms of political systems is incompatible with preserving individual autonomy because it requires the individual to see the law as 'binding' upon him: the 'rightness' of accepting political obligations is not a matter for reflection; accepting them is not something for which the agent can take responsibility (1970 p.14). Participation in some religious cults is similarly possible only if one is not open to reflection about the sources of one's commitment and the authority of those who direct the cult. And Philip Gosse's rejection of evolutionary biology in the name of fundamentalist creationist science apparently involved admitting a limit beyond which critical reflection could not proceed.

Epistemological issues have been surfacing throughout this section. Before turning to them in a more systematic way, we shall note some strategies that might be adopted in the face of these arguments. One possibility, of course, is to criticize their coherence or factual basis. Short of that, it is possible to argue that they rest upon misconceptions of what autonomous self-control requires. Indeed, reflection upon such arguments can help us to clarify the value we really attach to autonomy. We can describe the use we actually make of the notion and produce an analysis that vindicates this use. Alternatively, we can admit that they raise difficulties for our concept of autonomy (or for the most attractive one) and admit the necessity of retreating to a more limited, less attractive cousin of that conception. Real autonomy might be denied us, but we can pursue virtues which share many of its features. Compatibly with the two last mentioned strategies, we could discover that the value of autonomy lies in 'local' applications: we can raise questions about an agent's ability to take control of his life, and take responsibility for his actions, against a background of a set of shared standards or evaluations which are not put in question. A still further possibility is to abandon autonomy as a value, finding virtue in loyalty and a sense of community and tradition which suffices to give meaning to our actions and projects.

When arguments seem to challenge the possibility of pursuing distinctive kinds of projects autonomously, there are also several possibilities. We can simply abandon the activity, its alienating or self-destructive character having been revealed. Or we can try to reformulate our understanding of it, limiting the scope of our goals and accepting that there are limits to what we can achieve. There may also be the possibility of freely deciding to submit to the hope that all will prove for the best if we continue with the activity; it is characteristic of much religious practice that surrendering one's autonomy, accepting without question the guidance of another in the hope that a meaningful life will result, can be a reasonable choice. Indeed, in some circumstances, surrender of the desire for autonomy can yield the assurance that we have just that capacity to take responsibility for our lives which has been at issue.

2. Inquiries

It would be a mistake to assume that all of the activities describable as 'inquiries' or 'investigations' have the same structure. There is no reason to believe that they have similar goals, employ the same methods, or allow an analogous role for critical reflection. In this section, we describe a range of inquiries in order to illustrate some of these differences.

We can usually identify an inquiry by specifying the question that it attempts to answer. Consider my attempt to discover:

Ia. What time is the next train to London?

where this has a role in my planning a sequence of activity directed towards a further practical goal which can only be achieved if I can travel to London today. We are familiar with the range of methods (telephoning the railway station, consulting a timetable) which can be employed to answer the question. Compare two further inquiries:

Ib. Is that ball going out?

where I am a tennis player deciding whether to try to intercept an attempted passing shot. Here talk of employing 'methods' may seem out of place; but there is a resemblance between 1a and Ib. In each case, the quest for information is subordinated to a practical goal: catching the train, and winning at tennis or playing well. The third example is similarly internal to a wider activity, in this case, that of pursuing scientific investigations. We might consider:

Ic. Does theory T predict observation O ?

In each case, the 'inquiry' is directed towards answering a specific question; and in each case, we can specify a range of possible answers among which a selection must be made. In case Ia, this is given by a list of times. For Ib and Ic there are just the two answers 'yes' and 'no'. In each case, we approach the inquiry against a background of a set of assured methods for responding to them; we are not uncertain how to proceed (at least in the normal case). For Ib, we are likely to trust to the judgment we arrive at as we observe the ball in relation to the line: no conscious application of a method is involved. Thought may enter into the selection of a method for Ia, and into its execution, but we do not generally experience any doubt about the reliability of the method we select. Ic is more complex. But at least some inquiries of this form can be experienced as merely routine investigations, employing familiar methods which yield unambiguous results. If reflection is involved in pursuing these inquiries it has a limited role against a background of assurance that such reflections are adequate for their intended purpose.

The focus of the second group of inquiries is more indeterminate. Suppose somebody attempts to discover:

IIa. Why does water expand on freezing?

Here there is no determinate range of possible answers among which he must choose. In many cases, attempts to answer 'why' and 'how' questions pose the challenge to the imagination of discovering that certain sorts of answers are possible which were not previously considered. And this can involve reflection upon the circumstances under which an answer can be considered as a possible one. If we ask:

IIb. Is the suffering of animals morally relevant?

we find that there is a definite set of possible answers to our question – 'yes' and 'no'. However, there is no settled assurance about the methods which can be used to find a satisfactory answer. Hence there can be a role for reflection which goes beyond choosing which of a set of known methods is most sensibly employed on this occasion, and beyond its role in executing the method that we have adopted. It arises because the project of answering this question provokes a preliminary inquiry into which methods can be employed to answer this question.

My final three examples set goals for investigations which are not specified by stating questions. I could set myself to:

IIc. Contribute to the scientific understanding of the genetic code.

IId. Discover the nature of justice.

IIe. Explore the underlying structure of matter.

While I can adopt these general epistemic goals, and try to plan my activities in accordance with them, I can be unclear about which specific inquiries I am committing myself to undertaking. Other than in very general terms, I may be unsure which questions I must answer in order to achieve my goal; and even when I am aware that a question is relevant to my purpose, I may be unsure what this relevance is.

The division into two groups is not a hard and fast matter. First, inquiries directed at answering the same question can have a very different character in different circumstances. We can imagine telling a story that makes Ic appear to belong in the second group; and against a background of established scientific theory which limits the range of possible explanations, IIa may fit better with the first group. And second, once this limited range of examples is extended, we shall find cases forming a spectrum rather than falling straightforwardly into two classes. However my general point is unaffected by this. Inquiries of the second class may not be specified in terms of a definite question at all: our focus is, somehow, upon getting ourselves into a position where definite questions can be raised and settled (IIc, IId, IIe). Or we may be able to formulate a definite question while unable to agree upon a set of possible answers which can be taken for granted in our investigation (IIa). Or we may be able to agree upon a set of possible answers but be unable to agree upon how to evaluate methods for selecting among those answers, or unable to agree upon a range of possible methods to be taken for granted in making such evaluations.

Group II inquiries appear to demand critical reflection of a potentially open ended sort: the expectation of critical challenge and the sense that our ways of proceeding might be open to question appear to be internal to the investigations. We might distinguish the groups by describing group II inquiries as 'theoretical' while group I inquiries are rooted in our common sense practices. The term 'common sense' might be taken to exclude case Ic, so it is better to put the point as follows: when an inquiry of the first kind is carried out, we are guided by confidence about which answers are possible or how to find out which answers are possible; we possess an assurance about which methods can be employed, or about how to establish which methods can be employed; and we are confident that we can determine which answer a particular method warrants. In most cases this assurance will be, in Peirce's useful term, 'acritical': it is irresistible; it is not grounded in argument; and it does not naturally occur to us to question it. However, it is defeasible. We should lose confidence in our judgment if we made too many mistakes on the tennis court; we might be shaken by hearing that a new edition of the timetable has been published or that a bug in the computer system has led the railway employees to give unreliable information. And we are familiar with how scientific advance can challenge our standards of evidence and demonstration.

3. Scepticism and determinism: the 'Epicurean argument'

It will aid our understanding of the familiar sceptical arguments if we begin by examining some that have not been discussed in earlier chapters. There is a variety of arguments intended to show that acceptance of determinism is somehow pragmatically self-defeating because determinism has sceptical consequences: a number of such arguments are discussed by Honderich (1988 ch.6). He traces those that concern me here to an Epicurean fragment – although the interest of the arguments does not depend upon the accuracy of this attribution:

> The man who says that all things come to pass by necessity cannot criticize one who denies that all things come to pass by necessity; for he admits that this too happens of necessity.

The suggestion is that evaluation and criticism of beliefs and methods of inquiry cannot properly be sustained if we accept the truth of determinism. Since such an argument would parallel arguments to the effect that determinism undermines the possibility of free agency, an examination of some arguments of this sort will help to place the discussion of scepticism in the context I have suggested.

Honderich uses a thought-experiment to develop his 'Epicurean argument'. We are to consider four cases where lack of information prevents our deciding a question: a returning officer cannot declare the winner of an election because he lacks the returns from one polling station; somebody attempting a calculation lacks the value of one variable; a moral dilemma is irresoluble because the agent is ignorant of the consequences of his action upon a lover; and uncertainty about the coherence of one step of an argument prevents a philosopher deciding upon the acceptability of a philosophical theory (Honderich 1988 p.414). If our situation were *always* similar to one of these, then scepticism would be warranted. Honderich's view is that if I were to obtain the missing piece of evidence and, at the same time, to be convinced of the truth of determinism, then I should reasonably feel that the closing of one evidential gap has simply opened another. Considering the fourth of the cases described above, 'I may now feel that my final situation, including a view of the coherence of a part of it, and also including my contemplation of determinism, is in a way like my situation *before* I became clear about the coherence position' (p.414). I respond in this way because:

> I can suppose that there may exist facts such that different acts and actions, logically possible acts and actions never performed, would have issued indirectly or directly in their discovery, and that these facts would have provided further reasons for or against my conclusion about the theory. In particular I can suppose that these facts would provide reasons such that the reasons I actually have for my conclusions are not good ones, or are not sufficient.

(pp.414–15)

We are drawn towards scepticism, 'at least for a time, and indeed recurrently', because we come to view ourselves and those whose testimony has guided our inquiries 'as having been fixed to follow only certain of the logically possible paths of inquiry': 'They and we have not *explored* reality, but have been guided, however voluntarily, on one tour' (p.415). If we are to 'explore' reality, the activities that make up our inquiries must have resulted from our originating one course of action rather than another from among a wider selection of alternatives that are *actually* (not just logically) possible.

While I agree with Honderich that understanding in this area should exploit the observation that inquiry is a form of activity, and I agree, too, that determinism might engender scepticism by challenging our sense that we can participate in inquiry in a free and responsible fashion, I believe that a different thought-experiment is more revealing. Honderich's argument invites the response that the sceptical impact of his thought-experiment relies only on the fact that I cannot carry out *every* logically possible observation. This would be the case even if I could freely choose which observations to make: since observations and experiments take time, I can only carry out so many in the time available; since observations must be carried out at particular locations, I may not be able to travel from one to another in the time available; and even if I am not physically determined to carry out O1 and not to carry out O2, it may be physically determined that I can carry out only one of them. In order to appreciate how scepticism can result from acceptance of determinism we need to understand how my cognitive situation is better if I originate the selection of observations rather than having it forced upon me.

In line with the argument of the previous chapter, it is best to relate the notion of 'originating' actions to the idea that we can subject our activities to full rational self-control. 'Origination' is arguably necessary but not sufficient for such self-control, so it is preferable to find a version of the 'Epicurean argument' which focuses on the possibility of planning activities of inquiry in a responsible fashion rather than specifically upon the properties of particular acts and actions. So consider the position of someone who believes that determinism is true, but is largely agnostic about the neurophysiological antecedents of his thoughts and decisions. He is also agnostic about the laws that govern their determination. To sharpen the thought-experiment, consider a modern Cartesian who suspends judgment in all that can be doubted and exploits the possibility of determinism as a device for extending his doubt.

The experiment functions in a way analogous to the evil demon hypothesis. Both exploit the fact that the causal histories of our thoughts and attitudes are not manifest to us when they are employed in thought or deliberation. The evil demon was intended to suggest that our experience could have exactly its present character even if it totally failed to reflect the character of reality. If we are to rely upon our experientially produced beliefs in planning our actions and inquiries, we need some grounds for assurance that they track the truth – that our having these beliefs is a sign of their truth. The demon argument challenges our right to feel sure that there are such grounds. The determinist thought-experiment exploits the fact that our experiences and attitudes are fixed by complex neurophysiological processes whose character is not available to us. In deciding how to conduct our inquiries, we cannot rely upon knowledge of *how* these beliefs and attitudes are caused; the thought experiment supposes only *that* they are so-caused, and it exploits the fact that this is compatible with their failing to correspond with reality.

An argument along these lines may not induce scepticism about the external world since the hypothesis of determinism itself takes for granted much of our familiar world view. However, it is is clear that it could induce doubt about our ability to resolve complex philosophical and theoretical questions. If I have difficulty deciding upon the coherence of a step in a philosophical argument, then the possibility that any verdict I arrive at is the product of such complex neurophysiological causal processes, whose epistemic reliability is at best a contingent matter, may undermine my confidence in my responses. From the Cartesian perspective, I may well judge that I should suspend judgment in all such abstract and theoretical issues; and I shall leave it open just how far such a doubt should extend.

In the light of this discussion, we can consider the position of someone who actually *is* convinced by a proof of determinism. What should he then make of the line of sceptical argument which I have just sketched? If his assurance of the truth of determinism is unshaken, then, it can seem, this can only be because he acknowledges that he cannot attain the sort of autonomous self-control of his inquiries that I have described. He finds himself certain of a conclusion, with a clear sense of what makes him sure of this conclusion. But he has no assurance that being guided to such conclusions in this way contributes to his over-arching goal of tracking the truth. There is a sense in which he is alienated from the methods upon which he relies: he finds himself relying upon them; but he cannot make clear to himself the right with which he does so. The aspiration to rational self-control and the firm disposition to accept determinism are in tension. It is easy to see how this can produce the uneasy shifting between intransigence and dismay that Honderich describes: when attending to the evident truth of (say) determinism, the aspiration to autonomous rational self-control can appear an unnecessary ambition; when attending to the degree to which our cognition runs out of our control, the unshakeable disposition to believe is experienced as an external imposition upon our cognitive activities. In a phrase I have used above, it is something we 'find ourselves believing' rather than something we believe. Potentially, there is an imbalance between our aspiration to control our attempts to track the truth and the firm dispositions to believe formed by our nature.

Following this line of argument, someone convinced of the truth of determinism might thereby become alienated from their own cognitive activities and hence unable to view their conviction as the upshot of a responsible and controlled pursuit of the truth. So far, this does not undermine the proof: if it produces conviction, then (as we have noted) sceptical reflection is unlikely to shake it. However, since the issue of determinism is an abstract philosophical question, it is unlikely that anyone will experience a firm unshakeable conviction that the doctrine is true. Perhaps in these cases (where we can be genuinely uncertain of whether steps of argument are coherent), our sense that we are losing control of the inquiry can genuinely shake our confidence in the conclusion reached. Sceptical agnosticism is a possible response to metaphysical issues even if it is not available when we consider the reality of the external world.

My argument can be related to Honderich's as follows. An under-standing of the value attached to 'originating' agency must assert that it is a precondition of our properly taking responsibility for our actions and exercising rational self-control: Honderich may think that an action is not 'originated' unless it is controlled in this fashion. This requires that the standards of plausibility and evidence that guide us in deciding which observations to make and which hypotheses to accept should be ones that we can trust. By challenging the assurance with which we rely upon such standards, the hypothesis of determinism questions our ability properly to take control of our inquiries and thus allows that there may be a capricious element in the ways in which we arrive at our beliefs. The hypothesis threatens our participation in inquiry in a way that is parallel to its challenge to free agency generally (see Hookway 1989 for further discussion).

4. Challenges

The first group of inquiries described in section 2 were partly unreflective: we do not generally deliberate about the reliability of our methods and the nature of our cognitive goals in the course of carrying out such investigations. In the case of the tennis player, such reflection would be absurdly self-defeating; and it is related to this that describing the tennis player as conducting 'inquiries' or 'investigations' sounds strained. This is partly because of the practical role of the inquiries being considered: they are successfully carried out if the results contribute to the success of the practical projects they serve. Our confidence in our ability to settle these questions in a satisfactory way fits Reid's pattern: it is grounded in a history of success although all that can be said in its favour is that everything counts for it and nothing against it. Reflection cannot provide a doubt concerning whether I am good at detecting whether the ball is going out; although it may produce puzzlement concerning how I manage this. So long as the practice of arriving at opinions actually coheres with the other features of the practice, my confidence in it is wholly warranted and the puzzlement just mentioned remains an object of intellectual curiosity rather than a cause for concern that I am not in control of my actions. The Epicurean argument has no effect; and it is rational to wish for unreasoned spontaneous successful ways of gathering useful information; autonomous self-control requires no more.

Sceptical arguments are more effective as challenges to our confidence that we can carry out those investigations (more properly so-called) which involve deliberation. Both Sextus and Descartes were concerned with such inquiries, which fall into our second group. They focused upon particular kinds of inquiries: the search for truths about the non-evident natures of things; and the development of a science of nature which conflicted both with everyday experience and such established scientific practice as existed in the seventeenth century. Reflection is unavoidable in carrying out such inquiries. If somebody proposes that new methods of inquiry be adopted, it is incumbent upon him to defend them. If someone's claims about reality differ from those familiar to common sense or established science, they must be able to explain why their views deserve our assent. And if they propose to make progress in areas where apparently irresoluble dispute is pervasive, they must be able to explain why they are not just adding to the number of discordant voices.

One way in which participation in such activities can misfire is through failing to see how far this commitment to rational self-control and monitoring extends. If we were painstakingly to consider each method, principle or premiss we make use of in our inquiries, then we should make no progress at all. We generally hope for the best, confident that any further challenges that arise can be met, but feeling that to confirm this by anticipating each of these challenges in turn is obsessive. Trusting that challenges to our beliefs can be met, we hope that the need for reflective monitoring can be contained: we are satisfied that we have secured the legitimacy of those principles and methods which are problematic, and we rest upon our comfortable confidence in the others. The Epicurean argument may be sufficient to cast doubt upon this 'comfortable confidence'. What reason is there to suppose that those abstract standards of reasoning which are agreeable to our minds should put us into harmony with the underlying structure of reality? We saw that Descartes' attempt to legitimate his methods of inquiry derived from noticing how far his practice of inquiry was the product of his education and possibly unreliable testimony.

While it is probably a mistake to force all sceptical arguments into the same pattern, many share a characteristic form. As we have seen, they involve presenting challenges to our practice of forming beliefs: how can we defend our reliance upon induction?; how can we be sure that our everyday beliefs are not planted in our brains by deceitful scientists? These are challenges which we typically ignore; indeed most people find it hard to take them seriously. Moreover, many would agree that if we were to take them seriously – if we were to regard them as challenges requiring an answer like more familiar ones – then no satisfactory answer would be forthcoming. The sceptical introduction of these challenges must somehow suggest to us that we are in bad faith in ignoring them: our failure to take them seriously is not a sign that they are not serious. And a common, and attractive, way of supporting this suggestion begins by describing challenges to beliefs that we all do take seriously – unless we can answer them, we abandon the belief in question or are embarrassed by our retention of it. It is then argued that the resemblance between the sceptical challenges and the respectable ones is such that our responding to them differently is arbitrary: if the 'genuine' challenges are indeed genuine, then so are the unconvincing sceptical ones.

If the sceptical arguments do work in this way, then they suggest that we are mistaken in supposing that the scope for reflection in attempting to order our inquiries can be contained. In those inquiries where reflective monitoring of our performance does have an essential role, our unthinking reliance upon a distinction between those features of our practice whose legitimacy should be a matter for reflection and those which can comfortably be taken on trust is put into question. This distinction has no natural or intelligible foundation. And reflective criticism may even place in question our confidence that we know what we are doing in those inquiries which do not involve much reflection. Our habitual unthinking trust in these aspects of our cognitive practice is challenged.

We can illustrate this by working through an example. Consider a technician who employs a thermometer to judge the temperature of a fluid – as part of a scientific experiment or in order to monitor an industrial process. In general it will not occur to him to reflect upon the reliability of his 'method' of discovering temperatures. He was trained to use thermometers for this purpose, and he has obtained no surprising results which could suggest that something was amiss. However, his trust in his method relies upon an assurance that its reliability could be ascertained: he assumes that there is a body of theory which explains the workings of such instruments and which could assure someone that, unless his thermometer is malfunctioning, it provides the information he requires; and he assumes that, if he wished, the instrument could be tested for reliability. Although he has no doubt of the reliability of his method, he is also certain that its reliability could be demonstrated if necessary. The possibility of such demonstration is required here because there is a merely contingent link between the methods he employs and the aims of his inquiries. His goal is, let us assume, to measure temperatures rather than to record thermometer readings, and he must take himself to be justified in holding the second of these activities to serve as a means to his goal.

It is easy to imagine many circumstances which would challenge his assurance of the reliability of his method. Similar instruments have proved inaccurate due to a manufacturing defect; he discovers that the instrument has been placed in a powerful magnetic field and is unsure of the effect this might have upon its performance; examination of his results leads him to wonder whether he might be using the instrument to make much finer discriminations than it is capable of. In such cases a challenge is presented: others may become wary of relying upon his testimony; he may become wary of using his data in calculations. Critical reflection is required to establish the reliability of the method. In general, these challenges introduce the possibility that the instrument's reading is not determined by the temperature of the fluid being measured. Distortions in the causal processes involved mean that the thermometer reading is not a reliable sign of the temperature. Can we use this case as a model for understanding sceptical challenges?

A first step towards doing so involves noticing that we can be led to view our own habits of response to data and hypotheses as analogous to instruments. Suppose that it is made clear to me that my spontaneous judgments of probability are often unreliable. One effect is that I begin to distance myself from these spontaneous responses: I view it simply as a fact about myself that a run of heads makes me believe that tails is probable. The question can then arise under which circumstances I can trust these responses. It is as if I treat myself as a measuring instrument and my spontaneous responses to problems as the readings of the instrument. Indeed, my learning to trust my sense of whether the ball will remain within the court while playing tennis is easily thought of in the same terms: I rely upon my spontaneous responses just as I might rely upon an instrument. Should I regard these instruments as reliable? We have seen how there are circumstances in which I can decide that they are unreliable; and others where their reliability can become a matter for investigation. So, quite generally, reflection upon my capacities seems to involve treating myself as an instrument to be used in inquiry. And challenges to our cognitive reliability can exactly parallel those that can be pressed against the reliability of the thermometer.

But the challenges just alluded to are likely to differ from normal sceptical challenges. I demand a demonstration of the reliability of an instrument when it is introduced as a new way of establishing the value of some magnitude. I also ask for such a demonstration when given positive reason to suppose that the readings obtained are unreliable: background knowledge suggests that distorting forces are present or the results obtained clash with common sense or well supported theory. While it is easy to find cases where methods of inquiry are challenged for these sorts of reasons, they may not include standard sceptical challenges. It is a familiar point that sceptical arguments seem to rely upon the mere logical possibility that our methods are not reliable. Since there is no positive reason to suppose that we are deceived by an evil demon, it is commonly objected that philosophers' sceptical challenges do not parallel those that we make regular use of.

This objection should be resisted; I shall explain why before developing the parallel more fully in the next section. Suppose that I rely upon a measuring instrument, trusting in its reliability, and having no positive reason to suspect it of inaccuracy. What does this trust involve? Plausibly it depends upon our assuming:

1. If it were inaccurate, then this would probably be reflected in our experience.
2. If the question arose, it would be possible to check its reliability.
3. Although we may not be interested in discovering it, an account of the instrument's mechanism could be obtained which explained why it was reliable.

If somebody persuaded us that these statements were not true, then the question of the legitimacy of our relying upon the instrument would arise. Denial of (1) could weaken our trust in the instrument. If (3) is available, then inspection of the mechanism would provide a way of checking reliability. We would be puzzled by an instrument that unaccountably made accurate predictions but we would be warranted in relying upon it. But consider the possessor of a machine which, he believes, measures people's biorhythms. He provides predictions of his own moods and those of his friends, and he tries to anticipate the times at which he should avoid risk or decision. Facing little difficulty in persuading his friends of the powers of his machine, he finds his predictions accurate and his warnings valuable. He takes the reliability of the machine on trust. Suppose one day he reads a newspaper article which reports that the scientific community is somewhat scornful of the very idea of biorhythms. Even if he is not interested in persuading the scientific community of the reliability of his machine and remains highly impressed by the success of his predictions, he may be led to wonder how the 'success' of his device is to be explained. The realization that there may be difficulty providing the required explanation can lead him to re-assess his successes: has he been selective in ignoring failures and dwelling on successes?; has awareness of the prediction been a factor in its fulfilment? The suspicion that the success of the method may be inexplicable can be enough to raise the question of whether it is to be trusted, especially where there is no effective way of assessing its output.

If sceptical arguments suggested that our position was like that of the person just described, then they could occasion doubts about our right to proceed as we do. How far can they be understood as so doing?

5. Sceptical challenges

This discussion suggests a distinctive view of sceptical challenges. They begin from reflection on how we conduct our inquiries, bringing to the surface practices which are normally habitual or unreflective. We find ourselves accepting observational reports, we find ourselves drawing certain inferences and not others, we find ourselves relying upon induction and so on. We come to appreciate that these are judgments and inferences that we make 'naturally'. Once they become 'objects of reflection' for us, we recognize the intelligibility of questions about how reliable these 'instruments' are: how reliable is the information produced by the senses?; how reliable are the predictions we make through induction?; how good is our uncritical sense of plausibility? Are we right to employ these as means to our cognitive ends? Of course, it does not normally occur to us that we should question the right with which we 'rely' upon these things. But that need only mean that we simply trust that the questions can be answered, that the reliability of the methods can be demonstrated. If we can then suggest that the justifications or explanations whose existence we take for granted *cannot* be provided, then the case begins to look like that of the user of the machine for measuring biorhythms. Our trust is put into question, and our use of the method is challenged in a wholly familiar way.

If we then find that we are psychologically constrained to use these methods, then we conclude that we cannot take responsibility for the ways in which we conduct our inquiries: we are forced to place our trust where it may not be properly placed. The key to the argument appears to be the fact that any feature of our practice can be made an object for our reflection: if we can think about it, then we can think about the reflective attitude we should take towards it. In that case, we can consider it as a means to achieving cognitive ends and wonder whether it is a good one.

An interesting sceptical challenge must have three features. First, it alludes to part of our practice of obtaining information about our surroundings which we find natural, which it does not normally occur to us to question. Second, it must have a certain generality: challenges to the reliability of particular thermometers may lead us to lose confidence in that particular instrument; they do not lead us to lose confidence in ourselves as inquirers. And third, it must intimate that the feature of our practice which it draws attention to *could not* be defended. This is required not only to draw the negative moral about our abilities as inquirers which is the sceptical intent, but also (as we have just seen) to provide a complacent inquirer with reason to take the challenge seriously at all.

The point about generality is important: it must be difficult to confine their impact to the particular aspect of our practice which is attacked. A challenge to my intuitive probabilistic reasoning does not go very deep. Nor does the suggestion that I have a tendency to find theories plausible which are subsequently shown to be incoherent. This is because much of my practice is not touched by such challenges – I should be forced to be careful but not to conclude that my ability to conduct inquiries in a responsible manner is put at risk. Even if the challenge is directed at a specific aspect of my practice, its sceptical impact must involve the suggestion that it is contagious. For example, it must not exploit any of the *specific* features of the method or practice which is attacked, so that we conclude that if the challenge is effective against *this* method or application, then analogous challenges can be mounted against a large number of other methods or applications. Alternatively, we may judge that the specific method under attack is so deeply implicated in our methods for acquiring beliefs that its abandonment would leave very little.

For example, if we were to challenge the observational report that a passing car is a Ford by pointing out that another model resembles a Ford and requiring the observer to eliminate this alternative explanation of his experience, the challenge would be contained. It would not generalize to ground a sceptical worry, for the challenge is based upon a possibility which exploits the specific character of the report in question. If we challenge someone's claim to see a car or a rock by, for example, suggesting he may be a brain-in-a-vat, it is easy to see that if the challenge is effective against this specific observational report, then it puts all of our perceptual judgments into question.

A second example of this concerns scepticism about induction. We can imagine a sequence of steadily stronger challenges. It might be pointed out that I rely upon particular inductive strategies that are highly unreliable: for example, I am insufficiently sensitive to the size of my sample when I draw conclusions about the distribution of a property among a population. Such a challenge is not deep, and requires me only to revise that feature of my practice. A slightly stronger challenge could hold that whereas induction is reliable as a method of establishing whether theories are true, it is far from clear that we can rely upon the verdicts it delivers in the short run. Inductive conclusions so often turn out to be false that I should view the products of inductive reasoning as 'unfalsified so far' rather than accepting them as true. A much stronger challenge would hold that any run of experience provides no defensible basis for prediction. Either the second or the third challenge could put at risk a wide range of opinions and could put into question our ability to carry out a wide range of inquiries. Even the second can thus have a sceptical impact although the third cuts deepest of all.

To serve our purpose, the challenge must insinuate the suspicion that the reliability of our cognitive instrument cannot be explained. Again it is easy to see that familiar sceptical arguments work in this way. Once we come to treat exceedingly general or fundamental aspects of our methods of acquiring beliefs as instruments whose accuracy could, in principle, be explained, then the possibility of providing such explanations can be questioned in several ways. In each case, we question the legitimacy of using, in such explanations, the only materials that seem to be available for providing them. For example, when we explain the reliability of a thermometer, clock or other instrument, we appeal to theoretical explanations of its functioning and to evidence of its successful operation. It is clear that if we treat our reliance upon ordinary observational reports as such an instrument, it would be unsatisfactory to rely upon observation (or anything which depends upon observation) in order to assess the reliability of our observations. To do so would be comparable to assessing the reliability of aneroid barometers to serve as altimeters by comparing the results obtained with those given by other altimeters which rely upon the same mechanisms. Similarly, once we treat our inductive habits as instruments, it is hard to see how we can rely upon inductively acquired information in order to demonstrate their reliability. The extent to which all of our knowledge rests upon the 'instrument' in question plants the suspicion that there may not be the materials available to explain its reliability in the way in which we demonstrate the reliability of more familiar instruments. If we do just take its reliability for granted, then the basis of our assurance cannot be the same as when we trust to the reliability of the clock or thermometer.

The Pyrrhonist modes exhibit this pattern. Juxtaposing contrasting appearances reveals to us our unthinking or habitual ways of preferring one appearance to another. The ease with which such confrontations of opposing appearances are set up illustrates that if we cannot respond to *this* challenge, an endless series of similarly insoluble problems faces us. And the appeal to the modes of Agrippa – the threat of infinite regress or circularity – together with the problem of the criterion suggest that we will be unable to meet the challenge. We cannot put it aside as a boring challenge which we lack time to bother with for the challenge suggests the problem is insoluble rather than trivial: we cannot responsibly continue our practice.

As a final illustration of this, we can turn to a recent attempt to explain the structure of sceptical arguments by Crispin Wright (1985 pp.434–8). Compare two arguments:

    I Five hours ago Jones swallowed twenty deadly nightshade berries.
    II Jones has absorbed into his system a fatal quantity of belladonna.
so III Jones will shortly die.

    I' Jones has written 'X' on a piece of paper.
    II' Jones has just voted.
so III' An election is taking place.

In each case, the first line provides defeasible evidence for the second which entails the third; but only in the first case is the evidence provided by I transmitted into evidence for III. I' provides defeasible evidence for II' only conditional upon the *prior* reasonableness of III'.

Wright is specifically concerned with someone who defends the belief that there are external objects by claiming that the character of his experience provides defeasible evidence of his possessing a hand, which entails that there are external objects. He insists that this resembles the second of these two arguments: the statement about experience supports the belief about hands only on condition that belief in external objects is reasonable. The latter provides part of the 'scaffolding'. Establishing the reliability of an *ordinary* instrument involves an argument from experience more like the belladonna example: the conclusion we seek is supported by the observations that are adduced in its favour. Once again the force of the sceptical arguments involves simultaneously treating our cognitive responses as 'instruments' and recognizing that an attempt to ground our use of them as seems appropriate in the case of instruments seems destined to misfire.

It seems clear that the only prospect for blocking scepticism, for avoiding seeing our fundamental epistemic commitments as arbitrary, and as determined in ways that we cannot control, is to find a way of seeing our refusal to take challenges seriously as legitimate. This must involve denying that we can always look upon our cognitive responses as instruments whose reliability can be assessed. In other words we must understand how a responsible inquirer, anxious to exercise rational self-control over his investigations, can accept such principles as forming the scaffolding or framework which sets the terms for his investigations without limiting his freedom to exercise sovereignty in his reasonings.

6. Conclusion

This description of our appreciation of the force of sceptical challenges might suggest that the sceptical dilemma involves possessing a clear sense of the goals of inquiry while unable to understand the legitimacy of any methods that might be used to pursue those aims. It need not take that form. Sceptical reasoning confronts the lack of defensible criteria for explaining our right to rely upon our fundamental epistemic commitments. This might involve finding it impossible to show that they meet our cognitive goals: the problem of induction faces the difficulty of explaining why inductive reasoning can satisfy intelligible goals such as making predictions that will not be surprised by experience. But confrontation with our lack of criteria for establishing the adequacy of our methods of inquiry can also bring home to us the fact that we have no clearly formulated cognitive goals: we respond to particular problems in ways that are recommended by our teachers or fellow inquirers but we are unable to take responsibility for formulating cognitive goals which are clear enough to provide criteria for evaluating methods. Or even if we know what our cognitive goals are, sceptical challenges could lead us to confront the problem of why those goals are good ones. If our cognitive goals are arbitrarily adopted, and we are unable to explain why a rational agent should have those goals, we again encounter the kind of estrangement from our practice of inquiry which, I have suggested, is constitutive of the sceptical position. We find ourselves adopting a variety of methods to achieve goals which we find ourselves endorsing, or we find ourselves carrying out particular investigations without being able to explain the goals which make us judge these activities worthwhile.

Avoiding these problems requires an understanding of the process of rational reflection, and the activity of inquiry, which reconciles a sense of being in control of what one is doing with a resistance to pursuing all of these demands for critical assessment. Rational autonomy must not require the possibility of reflecting on each feature of our practice and saying why it provides a reasonable way of conducting inquiries. And resisting these challenges must not depend upon holding a reflective theoretical view of the nature of critical reflection which can itself be subjected to sceptical attack. We find ourselves carrying out our inquiries in various specific ways. We can agree that our doing so reflects the physiology of our brains and sensory systems, the training we have received from our parents and teachers, and myriad other influences. Yet this does not threaten our sense that we are sovereign, that we can take responsibility for how our inquiries proceed. We can come to terms with scepticism only by understanding how these demands can be reconciled.

CHAPTER IX

Comparisons and Consequences

1. Introduction

This chapter discusses a variety of topics which will help to clarify the perspective on sceptical arguments defended in the previous two chapters. Sections 2–4 examine three alternative ways of explaining the force of sceptical arguments, investigating their similarities with our preferred way of understanding them and using the latter to reveal their inadequacies. The remaining sections discuss some topics in the theory of justification in the light of the position defended here. Picking up unfinished business from the beginning of chapter VII, it is explained that arguments directed against the possibility of certainty and justified belief do have sceptical implications; and we consider the source of the demand for an 'internalist' theory of justification as well as the role of 'foundationalist' metaphors in accounting for the ways in which we order our inquiries.

2. Universalizability

Many sceptical arguments attempt to weaken our confidence in our opinions by pointing to cases in which we (or other people) have previously succumbed to error. We now consider a diagnosis of how such arguments work. According to Jonathan Adler (1981) and Jonathan Dancy (1985), they rest upon principles of universalizability analogous to those proposed in Ethics. Although this suggestion fails, it will help us to understand how the arguments do work. Ethical principles of universalizability vary, but they generally exploit the intuition 'that the same act cannot be right for one agent and not for another, unless there is a morally relevant difference between them' (Adler 1981 p.144): 'A judgment that an action is morally good is universalizable in the sense that by making such a judgment one commits oneself to holding that any relevantly similar action is morally good' (Dancy 1985 p.12). As well as differing in choice of moral term ('right', 'good', etc.), such principles will have a different impact according to the author's view of the sorts of factors which are 'morally relevant'.

Comparable principles in epistemology would hold that contrasting epistemic valuations can be made of different cases only if there are epistemically relevant differences between them. To assess this, we must consider some specific proposals: although they involve values which have not been central to our discussion, we shall consider versions cast in terms of 'knowledge' and 'justified belief'.

1. If A and B are in *epistemically indistinguishable circumstances* and A *does* not know that p, then B *cannot* know that p.

(Adler p.144)

The kind of case we are supposed to think of is one where A and B hold the same background beliefs, have similar experiences and use the same method to arrive at the belief that they can see a house. But while B genuinely perceived a house, A was on a film set and saw only a painted screen. Since A lacks knowledge, and B's situation is epistemically similar, B's true belief does not count as knowledge either. If permitted, such arguments might undermine all of our claims to knowledge – especially if we expand (1) to allow that it only be plausible, or possible, for there to be someone in A's position for B's knowledge to be undermined.

As Adler sees, this formulation is unsatisfactory: since its sceptical force could be resisted by insisting that the epistemically relevant circumstances include the truth of p, it is necessary explicitly to restrict the 'epistemically relevant' to what is, in some sense, available to the cognitive agent. However, making such a restriction is likely to destroy the principle's plausibility. Unless we think that there is an effective procedure for deciding whether we know a given proposition, so that we can always tell whether we have knowledge of it, we have to allow that a belief can be sufficently *justified* to count as knowledge yet not be true, and hence not be known. We should retreat to a universalizability principle concerning justified belief (or concerning *claims* to knowledge (Hale 1988)):

2. If *A* and *B* are in *epistemically indistinguishable states* and *A* is not justified in believing that *p*, then *B* cannot be justified in believing that *p*.
3. If *A* and *B* are in *epistemically indistinguishable states* and *A* was not justified in claiming to know that *p* then *B* is not justified in claiming to know that *p*.

Maintaining the same interpretation of 'epistemically indistinguishable', we must ignore the fact that some causal or reliability theories of justification would deny (2) and (3): if we are attracted by such theories we might amend (2) so that it concerns the circumstances in which we are justified in *claiming* to be justified in believing *p*. The fundamental weakness of (2) and (3) is that they yield no sceptical conclusions because the existence of error need not make the antecedents true. Unless I can never be justified in believing, or in claiming to know, propositions which are not true, we can simply allow that the person in the case described *was* justified in believing (and claiming to know) that he saw a house (Hale 1988, and Brueckner 1984, 1985 discuss these issues much more fully).

We could express the intuition underlying these arguments in the terminology I have preferred by saying that if a method of inquiry has let us down in the past, we are irresponsible to rely upon it in a present inquiry unless we can be confident that the situation is now different. It seems only a small step from this to the claim that if we learn that the method let us down in the past because of undermining factor *F*, we should establish that *F* does not apply in the present case *before* employing the method: to do otherwise would be irresponsible – this is suggested by Adler's principle (II) (p.145). Since we are highly fallible in arriving at our beliefs, reflection on the past shortcomings of our methods would then burden us with an enormous number of prior investigations before adopting a method of inquiry.

This 'small step' should be resisted. Consider an example. I make a regular habit of consulting the library catalogue to discover the location of the books I need. This method is pretty reliable: the catalogue has few errors and it has let me down once in a hundred times. I have no idea what went wrong on that occasion, and although I am aware that the method is fallible, I am now confident that relying upon it will almost certainly provide the information I require. While awareness of the possibility of error may make me suspicious of the method if avoiding error is a matter of life or death, it seems clear that my confidence is sufficient to enable me to escape the charge of irresponsibility. To require more of me is unreasonable: awareness that the method was fallible on one occasion (or on a few occasions) does not threaten my assurance that it is highly trustworthy. Responsible inquiry, and rational self-control, require no more.

So does the existence of error have no role in developing sceptical arguments? Actual cases of error can have a dual role. First, suppose that we notice that a method we employ in our inquiries is fallible. This can provide the occasion for reflection on that method as an instrument. We can become interested in explaining the error, in evaluating how often the method will lead us to error, and in explaining how the method secures its successes. So awareness of error can have a role in pushing us towards more abstract reflection, towards seeing our methods of inquiry as instruments for achieving our cognitive purposes. At the same time, we become aware of the methods we employ to correct the errors of our fallible method, and we can be forced to confront the question of why these methods possess authority over the others. Error can provide the stimulus to epistemological reflection which attempts to understand what is typically taken for granted.

Second, actual cases of error can provide a model which is used to construct more threatening hypothetical cases of error. In other words, understanding how our method is occasionally fallible can introduce the possibility that it is often or always fallible. Or observing how we actually do respond to the fallibility of our everyday methods of inquiry can rebound to sceptical effect when we turn to the evaluation of fundamental epistemic commitments. In order to understand this, we must examine the diagnosis of sceptical arguments offered by Cavell and Stroud.

In concluding this section, we can note a further source of attachment to universalizability principles. If we hold to the mistaken idea that 'sovereignty' requires us to have the power to render our lives free of risk, to allow no role at all for luck in the success of our projects, then fallibility may be experienced as limiting our self-control. But there is no reason to accept this requirement for autonomous self-control: we can be fully in control of our inquiries without being able to guarantee their success. The desire to eliminate risk is a manifestation of the desire for absolute security in a threatening environment which John Dewey has seen as the source of the philosophical quest for certainty (Dewey 1929).

3. *Claims and challenges*

The arguments considered here will again be cast in terms of 'knowledge': more accurately, they arise out of our attempts to *claim* knowledge and thus assume that such self-evaluations are epistemically important. Thus the first chapter of Barry Stroud's *The Significance of Philosophical Scepticism* (1984) expounds a version of Descartes' dream argument which, he urges, provides sceptical challenge to the most favourable kind of knowledge claim. If Descartes cannot know that he is in a warm room by the fire, then, it seems, he can know nothing at all; if we can establish a sceptical suspicion about the most elementary kind of sensory knowledge, we should hold a sceptical attitude towards sensory knowledge as a whole.

Stroud attempts to ground the dream argument in 'a simple and obvious fact about knowledge'(pp.27 ff.). Suppose that I claim to know that a bird is a goldfinch. I am then challenged: how do I know that it is not a canary? The challenge introduces a possibility which is inconsistent with what I claim to know. We naturally feel that unless I can meet the challenge by showing that I do know that the bird is not a canary, I ought to withdraw my initial claim to knowledge:

> I must be able to rule out the possibility that it is a canary if I am to know that it is a goldfinch. Anyone who speaks about knowledge and understands what others say about it will recognize this fact or condition in particular cases.
>
> (1984 pp.24–5)

Stroud offers several examples of this 'fact or condition'. Some differ from the goldfinch example in a crucial respect. Whereas in that case the possibility I have to exclude is incompatible with the *truth* of what I claim to know, there are others where I must exclude possibilities which are consistent with the truth of what I claim to know but inconsistent with my claim to *know* it. If a juror cannot eliminate the possibility that the testimony suggesting that the accused was in Cleveland at the time of the crime was all invented, he must withdraw his claim to know that the man was in Cleveland although it is possible that the witnesses were lying but, for all that, the man was in Cleveland (p.25).

Another example of Stroud's takes us neatly to the dream argument:

> A hallucinogenic drug might cause me to see my bed covered with a huge pile of leaves, for example. Having taken the drug, I will

know the actual state of my bed only if I know that what I see is not just the effect of the drug; I must be able to rule out the possibility that I am hallucinating the bed and the leaves.

(p.25)

The possibility that I am dreaming seems parallel to this. If I were dreaming that I saw a bed and leaves, I would not possess knowledge; so I must be able to rule out this possibility if I am to claim perceptual knowledge.

Stroud's position is that although we do not normally see the need to exclude the dream possibility, the pressure to do so comes not from arcane philosophical doctrines but from our ordinary use or understanding of the word 'know'. If somebody makes a *claim*, saying:

There is a goldfinch in the garden

or

I know that that is a goldfinch

an auditor can challenge the claim, asking *how* he knows that it is goldfinch. He might reply that its red head distinguishes it from canaries; but this can invite a further challenge to the 'basis' offered for the claim:

But that is not enough: woodpeckers also have red heads.

(Cavell 1979 p.132)

The appropriateness of making such challenges is implicit in our ordinary practice of claiming knowledge and making claims. And, the argument goes, the structure of the sceptical argument is exactly parallel. Having claimed that a table is nearby, a speaker is challenged to provide a basis for the claim. The reply that he *sees* that it is a table meets the further challenge: you could have *that* experience if you were dreaming. The sceptical challenges are introduced on the coat tails of our ordinary practice of making and criticizing claims.

As Stroud sees, the principle being exploited appears to have the consequence that I cannot know some proposition unless I know all of the logical consequences both of what I claim to know and of my claim to know it. This is because the negation of each of these logical consequences is incompatible with my claim to knowledge and so can be used to challenge my claim. This does not *seem* to be part of our ordinary concept of knowledge; and most people would agree that these

174

claims and challenges *seem* unnatural. We should also be surprised if we met someone who regularly made claims to knowledge of facts which were open to view; and we should be surprised if other people demanded to know the basis of everyday claims about our immediate surroundings. But of course this may simply be because we expect everyone to know these things so that such claims have no communicative role, and we expect everyone to agree upon the appropriate basis. If that were so, the observations would carry no philosophical weight.

Cavell tries to present a sceptic with a dilemma. I might intelligibly claim that a bird is in front of me if it is in shadow or if a companion suspects it is a model bird, or if I am speaking to someone else on the telephone. A 'concrete claim' requires a special context to be intelligible. But such cases do not represent the 'most favourable' situation where a lack of knowledge in the particular case threatens the legitimacy of all of our claims. The 'traditional epistemologist' considers cases which lack the context required to make these claims intelligible: '*no concrete claim is ever entered as part of the traditional investigation*' (p.217); the traditional epistemologist merely *imagines* a claim to be made and ignores the need to explain the context in which it makes sense (p.218). Hence the dilemma of 'the traditional investigation of knowledge' is:

It must be the investigation of a concrete claim if its procedure is to be coherent; it cannot be the investigation of a concrete claim if its conclusion is to be general. Without that coherence it would not have the obviousness it has seemed to have; without that generality its conclusion would not be sceptical.

(p.220)

The attraction of this as an anti-sceptical strategy is that it exploits the odd unconvincing character of sceptical challenges to beliefs in order to explain both why they *seem* unanswerable, and why the opponent of scepticism has already made a fatal error when he allows the 'traditional epistemologist' to formulate his arguments. Once we agree to play the sceptic's game, all is lost. We should refuse to recognize these everyday examples as *claims* to knowledge at all, and so we should refuse to see the force of the demand that a basis be provided for them.

However as Barry Stroud and Marie McGinn have explained, this argument fails. Although the 'context' in which these claims are made is not an everyday practical one in which information is being transferred to someone who lacks it, only an essentialist prejudice would suggest that *all* contexts in which knowledge claims are made must have this character. McGinn explains that the 'traditional epistemologist' takes up a 'reflective stance' towards our everyday practice of making and defending knowledge claims. This is grounded in noticing that our practice rests upon a 'framework of judgments' which we 'implicitly claim to know'; and the attempt to justify the judgments making up this frame shows that they rest upon 'unproved assumption' (McGinn 1989 p.95). If this project is intelligible, then it provides a context which suffices to give sense to the claims that the epistemologist considers. Cavell's strategy would be intelligible if philosophical concern with scepticism simply grew out of an ordinary claim and an ordinary challenge which just happened to be directed towards a claim simple and obvious enough for sceptical consequences to follow from the discovery that it is indefensible. But so long as trial by scepticism is initiated – as it is for Descartes – by a recognition that a general assessment of our ways of arriving at opinions is required in order to tease out sources of error, we cannot deny that real claims are made (see Stroud 1984 conclusion, McGinn 1989 ch.V).

Cavell sees his work as Wittgensteinian in spirit but this criticism shows, I think, that his critique of sceptical reasoning does not go deep enough. It is necessary to question the attractiveness or intelligibility of this philosophical project. McGinn would claim, with Wittgenstein that the damage is done when, in setting up the epistemological project, the sceptic 'discovers' that the framework is composed of things which we 'implicitly claim to know' and describes them as 'unproved assumptions'. Such terms introduce the kinds of evaluations that are considered appropriate within the project, and they pre-empt the Wittgensteinian complaint that it is a mistake to think of the hinge propositions or the scaffolding as objects of *knowledge*. In *On Certainty* (481–2), Wittgenstein remarks that on hearing Moore claim to know that an observed object is a tree, 'one suddenly understands those who think that that has by no means been settled'. Having suggested that by this choice of words Moore has put things in the wrong light, he comments (in 482): 'It is as if "I know" did not tolerate a metaphysical emphasis.' The 'traditional epistemologist's' project is precisely an attempt to use this phrase to conduct an investigation into the metaphysics of experience.

In chapter VII I argued that treating 'knows' as our fundamental term of epistemic evaluation was a mistake. In particular, it distorts our understanding of scepticism and the attempt to escape it if we see the debate as solely concerned with what we can know. 'Know' is one evaluative term among others, and we must understand its role as part of a system of concepts employed to achieve rational control over our inquiries (see chapter X). If scepticism challenges the possibility of self-control, it is far from obvious that its success in doing so stands or falls with our ability to describe our fundamental commitments as objects of knowledge. Parallel remarks could be made about the effect of thinking of fundamental commitments as 'assumptions' or as 'claims'. Using such terms smuggles in a commitment to a deliberative model of self-control: we assume that we are in control of our inquiries only if we can articulate and defend all of the commitments which ground our practice. Treating situations where we explicitly reflect upon the grounds of our beliefs – or situations where we critically assess the assertions of others in order to decide whether we should accept their testimony – as paradigms of rational control over cognitive processes can lead to a highly distorted perspective upon these matters. Indeed, if criticizing and defending claims is possible only if those involved have a shared understanding of the propositions concerned and the standards employed in making the criticisms, it seems inevitable that they should share a scaffolding of uncriticized commitments which are not challenged or defended.

4. Realism and the structure of reflection

It is sometimes argued that the appeal of scepticism rests upon a distinctive metaphysical doctrine: 'realism'. Traces of this view have emerged in our discussion of Kant and Carnap: each holds that we legitimate our methods of inquiry by recognizing that some methods or principles are not correctly seen as 'answerable to reality'. Kant's principles and the rules that make up a Carnapian linguistic framework create the possibility of raising questions with determinate answers but the legitimacy of using them does not depend upon their being true of reality 'as it is in itself '. Carnap would probably follow Kant in holding that scepticism is unavoidable if we defend 'realism'; and in claiming that 'realism' is indefensible. Others, less impressed by our assurance that we have knowledge, might defend scepticism by suggesting that the appeal of the familiar challenges shows that they answer to the implicit 'realism' of common sense.

'Realism' is a term of philosophical art with a variety of meanings. It can express the view that we have knowledge of objects external to ourselves and not just of our own ideas. Another 'realist' thesis holds that we are part of a wider natural world which is the object of our knowledge rather than being, in some sense, implicated in the construction of the world we claim to know. Some philosophers tie it to the view that meaning is to be explained in terms of truth conditions rather than epistemic concepts such as assertability or use, or to the claim that there can be facts which, in principle or in practice, will not be discoverable by us. It is far from clear that these doctrines are equivalent or that they capture what some philosophers call 'metaphysical' or 'external' realism. It is the latter doctrine which is connected with scepticism, but it is not at all clear what it involves. It would be too great a digression to try to clarify it here; it will serve our purposes to identify it through some familiar slogans and to understand the use to which it is put.

The central tenet of realism is that our conception of reality or truth is wholly 'non-epistemic': we can make sense of the possibility that reality may be seriously distorted by our ways of describing and classifying it; and we can understand that our methods of inquiry may be wholly inadequate for revealing the character of this reality to us. An echo of this conception was noted in Descartes' motivations in his epistemological investigations. He was concerned to develop a scientific theory which displayed the underlying nature of things to be very different from the way they appear to ordinary perceptual experience or from the descriptions offered by the prevailing science. The view we are currently considering takes the fact that the Cartesian arguments seem to undermine all of our knowledge as indicating that all of our dealings with the world reflect a conception of reality which is analogous to the Cartesian one: the conception of reality is not fixed by our current beliefs or tied to our current methods of inquiry. We shall first examine, briefly, the suggestion that 'realism' encourages scepticism; and we shall then consider the view that our readiness to follow sceptical arguments and to see their force, reflects our implicit 'realism'.

We shall begin with a characterization of one of the goals of our activities as inquirers:

1. We desire to arrive at an accurate representation of reality.

Then, we characterize this 'realist' conception:

2. The character of reality is *wholly independent* of our dispositions to draw inferences, or form beliefs.

In other words:

3. For any method of inquiry upon which we rely, it is a *contingent* matter that it contributes to the success of activities governed by the goal specified in (1).

If the reliability of any aspect of our approach to inquiry is thus a contingent matter, it seems that any such aspect can be regarded as an *instrument* of inquiry. Once it is considered as an instrument, then, as we have seen, an evaluation of its effectiveness and an explanation of its successes are (in principle) required. So there is a route from this conception of reality as wholly non-epistemic to the need for the developing process of reflection which seems to lead to scepticism. If we accept this form of realism, then it seems that sceptical challenges can intelligibly be mounted. Rational self-control of the attempt to carry out such an inquiry should at least recognize that all aspects of our methods of inquiry can be regarded as instruments and assessed as such; and failure to investigate the reliability of these 'instruments' can only be justified when it rests upon an assurance that the instruments are, in fact, reliable.

Realism and the picture of our methods of inquiry as instruments appear closely linked to the idea that our ways of approaching our inquiries are answerable to something independent of ourselves – the nature of reality. And realism motivates an ideal of responsible autonomous rational self-control over our inquiries which is potentially exceedingly burdensome. The fact that we respond to sceptical arguments, appreciating the realist possibility that we may be brains-in-vats or deceived by an evil demon so that our knowledge of 'reality' is minimal, can be taken as showing that common sense is (implicitly) realist. If this were so, then sceptical challenges would indeed provide a threat to our everyday knowledge of the world. Furthermore, if this were so, then scepticism could be avoided by abandoning this part of our common sense metaphysics. By endorsing some form of anti-realism, we could avoid having to engage with the sceptical arguments.

However we should resist the suggestion that this kind of realism is implicit in common sense. Justifying these claims will help to illustrate the merits of the approach to scepticism which I have adopted. In exploring the effects of sceptical arguments, we have noticed a kind of sceptical progress: we begin with instruments of inquiry like thermometers and grant that it is proper to expect evaluation of their reliability and explanations of their successes. It is plain that at least some aspects of our reliance upon our own spontaneous judgments or our adoption of methods of inquiry can similarly be seen as analogous to employing instruments. Hence these too can become an object for reflection and evaluation. We are then, apparently, forced to acknowledge that ever more abstract, general and deeply embedded features of our practice should be regarded as instruments in this way, and hence evaluated. We seem to be driven to adopt the practice of evaluation and explanation which, we suggested, realism requires of us.

If common sense is 'realist', we should expect this progress to flow naturally from our practice of evaluating methods and results of inquiries: worries about induction or about the reliability of perception could occur in a natural way in the course of ordinary epistemic reflection. We should also expect such sceptical worries to be perceived as a threat: if they cannot be answered we cannot view our methods of inquiry as good means to our cognitive ends. If, on the other hand, common sense is 'anti-realist', then we should expect a cut off point; at the very least, there would come a point where such reflection was perceived as inappropriate. There would be an assured, grounded, resistance to this progression of challenges. If we share Wittgenstein's view that 'the common-sense man ... is as far from realism as from idealism' (1958 p.48), we might expect a more complex and confused response. I shall suggest that this is what we do find.

We want to explain the observation that we are generally ready to see the force of the demand that we establish the reliability of our methods of inquiry and explain their successes. If we were 'realists', the observation would be explained. But it can also be explained as the product of two other tendencies. As Reid, Wittgenstein and others have insisted, our fundamental epistemic commitments are manifested in habits of action and inference rather than in propositions actively assented to, in the grammatical structure of our language rather than in the particular choices of sentences to accept. Our normal experience is that a commitment only emerges reflectively as a proposition to be evaluated or debated when some positive reason has emerged for wondering whether it serves our needs in inquiry. In other words, our practices become objects of reflection only when it has become appropriate to evaluate them as instruments. If Wittgenstein is correct in his claims about 'hinge' propositions and scaffolding, this is not manifested in our having some positive reason for rejecting the demand to evaluate such claims; it is reflected, rather, in our having no tendency to formulate these 'propositions' or to try to evaluate them at all. This is the first of the two tendencies involved in our response to sceptical arguments.

The second is that the tendency of philosophical reflection is to *articulate* what is implicit: we attempt to arrive at principles which rationalize our practice, and to become reflectively aware of how our unreflective practice is possible. We formulate what is not formulated in our ordinary practice of inquiry. If, in accordance with the first tendency, we are inclined to treat something as an epistemic instrument as soon as it is formulated, philosophical reflection encourages us to treat as a cognitive instrument what is properly part of the scaffolding. The source of this is not any implicit realism; it is, rather, the fact that the special role of scaffolding depends upon its implicit unquestioned character. We do not normally have to *recognize* propositions as 'not expressing cognitive instruments'; and our lack of means for doing so prompts philosophical reflection to set excessive demands for the rational control of inquiry.

There is a second contribution from the nature of philosophical reflection. As well as making us reflective about what is normally implicit, it can introduce classifications of methods of inquiry which are exceedingly general. Someone might question the reliability of my eyesight in poor light or of human colour vision under fluorescent lighting, but philosophical reflection can encourage us to identify 'perception' as one of our methods of obtaining knowledge. It can then seem a small step from evaluating one person's perceptual capacities in particular circumstances while taking our shared perceptual knowledge of the world for granted to recognizing the demand to evaluate 'perception' as such. 'Perception' is classified as *one* instrument or one method. Together with the first tendency, this can encourage an especially destructive kind of sceptical challenge: we are asked to justify our reliance upon perception in general rather than particular uses of perception; we are asked to justify induction as such rather than particular inductive techniques or uses of induction.

This process is encouraged by a view of self-control as essentially reflective. Since philosophical analysis makes us reflective about induction or perception as sources of knowledge, we see it as revealing to us the requirements for proper cognitive self-control. Our willingness to take sceptical arguments seriously, then, results not from an implicit commitment to 'realism' but rather from the interaction of a number of disparate tendencies which are operative when we seek a philosophical understanding of our ability to control our inquiries. Our search for a justification of induction (for example) exploits our ordinary tendency to seek justifications for what is articulated in the course of our inquiries; and we fail to notice that this tendency has acquired a target which results from the 'unnatural' activity of philosophical reflection.

Consider sceptical worries about induction. Common sense reflection does not instigate reflective concern about induction: we do not find ourselves wondering whether it is a good means to our purposes in inquiries. Thus far, we accord with a kind of anti-realism. However, when we are presented with such challenges, we can easily be struck by their similarities with more familiar acceptable challenges and we are aware of no basis for simply rejecting them: an apparently realist prejudice intrudes. It cannot be denied that we perceive such challenges as, in some way, unserious: we are not prevented from continuing our inquiries. However, our inability to say anything to ground this failure to take them seriously can be experienced as an embarrassing failure fully to master our cognitive activities. This confusion of contrasting intuitions renders it highly unlikely that we are under the influence of a deep, although unstated, metaphysical prejudice.

If there is an implicit 'metaphysical' picture behind our response to sceptical arguments it is best seen not as realism but as an ideal of autonomous self-control which is closely related to realism. This is the picture of the self as able to stand back from all of its practices and methods, and to take responsibility for them by evaluating them in accordance with criteria and, so to speak, actively endorsing them. Self-control involves the self taking control over all of its aspects which can be made an object of reflection. If 'realism' is correct, a responsible inquirer may well require such self-control; and if such self-control is impossible, then scepticism about our ability to participate in inquiry in a responsible fashion may be unavoidable. But the argument of this section is that the source of the attraction of sceptical arguments to us is not a prior commitment to realism, but rather the fact that we are naturally attracted to this kind of picture of self-control. It leads to an extraordinarily thin or recessive self: nothing of which the self can become reflectively aware belongs to the self essentially. We are potentially alienated from any of our practices or attitudes, as we can come to see them as (perhaps) practices or attitudes which we cannot abandon, but which the monitoring self cannot endorse.

Of course, some thinkers may have independent grounds for accepting an extreme form of realism and use that to ground a sceptical attitude towards our inquiries. The claim defended here is that we can explain the route taken by our engagement with sceptical arguments without explaining it as the result of an implicit commitment to a distinctive view of reality. Possession of distinctive ideals of self-control is enough to direct us along that route if our comments on the interaction of philosophical reflection and our ordinary practice of evaluating beliefs are roughly accurate. This may illuminate, too, the difficulties facing attempts to explain 'metaphysical realism', the extreme realist view supposed to have sceptical implications. Such attempts often involve strained and unhelpful metaphors, and it is far from obvious that the view is required by the more moderate realist claims mentioned above: we know about external things which would exist even if we did not; inquiry is a matter of discovery rather than invention; we are part of the empirical world which is the object of our investigations. It is conceivable that our sense that we understand the more extreme doctrine derives from thinking of it as the doctrine which calls for such extreme reflective self-control if we are to be able to carry out inquiries in a rational manner. The claims about the structure of rational self-control are the fundamental ones.

5. The appeal of internalism

A distinction is often drawn between *internalist* and *externalist* approaches to epistemology (BonJour 1980, Goldman 1980). Those who defend externalism sometimes allege that sceptical arguments rest crucially upon internalist assumptions. I cannot provide a full discussion of this debate, which is complicated by the fact that there is little settled agreement about what 'internalism' and 'externalism' involve. However, in the light of views presented in earlier sections of this chapter, we can begin to understand the source of the appeal that internalist approaches have. This will subsequently be valuable in helping us to understand how far we can abandon the more extreme internalist approaches.

The key to the distinction is that internalists hold that epistemic evaluation is ultimately grounded in what is 'available' to the knowing subject. Whether beliefs are justified, for example, depends upon the reasons that can be given in support of them; when they are not held on the basis of reasons, then they are justified only if they are self-evident or intrinsically justified. We evaluate beliefs and claims to knowledge in terms of evaluations of them which are available from the believer's perspective. We can best sharpen our understanding of the distinction by offering a caricature of the externalist position. Suppose somebody holds that a belief is justified if it is obtained through a method which is, in fact, reliable. So long as use of this method provides (mostly) true beliefs, any belief obtained through using it is justified. Thus, so long as most of my sensory beliefs are correct, I am justified in relying on my senses; so long as relying on induction does contribute to the accuracy of my view of my surroundings, I am justified in relying upon induction. We can bring out the non-internalist character of such a theory by pointing out that my sensory beliefs would then be justified even if I had no reason to suppose that my senses were, in fact, reliable. The justification of the sensory beliefs depends upon the fact that the method is reliable; and whether it is reliable or not may not be 'available' to me. Consequently, I could find myself admitting that I am in no position to tell whether my sensory beliefs are in fact justified.

This is an extreme externalist view. More plausible and sophisticated versions have been defended, but describing this one helps to fix the terms of the debate for us. The internalist approach accords with the intuition that fundamental questions of epistemological evaluation have a first-person character. With Descartes, we ask: what do *I* know?; which of my beliefs are justified? Externalism at least allows for the possibility that others may be in a better position to assess my cognitive position than I am myself. On the crude version of externalism we described, others may know whether I am justified in believing as I do although I cannot assess this. Externalist approaches have much to commend them. They help to block sceptical arguments: unlike internalist approaches, there is no need to trace back a potentially infinite sequence of reasons which can be blocked only by finding propositions which are self-evident or intrinsically justified. Scepticism is blocked so long as some of our methods of inquiry actually are reliable. Moreover, abandoning the first person perspective seems to accord with the co-operative nature of the ways in which we do develop our knowledge. And it is often argued that our ordinary use of terms like 'justified' and 'knows' accords with the externalist picture better than with the internalist one. As we have several times noted, someone's cognitive integrity is not generally thought to be impugned by the fact that he can give no reason for relying upon the senses.

In spite of this, the appeal of internalist approaches is something of which we are vividly aware. Something *seems* highly unsatisfactory about the crude version of externalism I described, and responses to scepticism which can be described as 'externalist' often read more like impatient dismissals than genuine responses. Before explaining the source of this appeal, we must make some preliminary points. First, although familiar forms of externalism present accounts of knowledge or justified belief, we shall do better to focus on a more abstract thesis. Internalism, as we shall use the term, claims that fundamental forms of epistemic evaluation must depend upon what is available to the cognitive agent. This allows for the possibility that externalist views of knowledge and justification may indeed be correct, but be acceptable only because internalist vindications are available for certain more fundamental evaluations.

The second preliminary point depends on the first. The internalist picture which I described runs together two distinct doctrines: formulating internalism as a claim about justified belief or knowledge is likely to make them seem inseparable. The first is the claim that fundamental forms of epistemic evaluation are fixed by what is available to the cognitive agent. The second is an individualist approach to knowledge. Descartes, recall, starts from the first person question: what can I be certain of ? Modern discussions of scepticism can share this feature: what do I know? This suggests that justification depends crucially upon what I can validate. It gives rise, too, to the suggestion that once we recognize the extent to which our knowledge is a shared possession secured through co-operative inquiry, then we should abandon the internalist perspective.

The co-operative character of inquiry, and with it the view that our knowledge is a joint achievement, brings to our attention several features of our knowledge which, granted internalism, seem to be open to sceptical attack. First, many of our beliefs are accepted from teachers, textbooks, television newsreaders, friends, and acquaintances, and we are often in no position to assess the reliability of the individual concerned before accepting their testimony. Second, as our knowledge grows, we commonly lose track of the sources or grounds of our beliefs. I may, at one time, have had good grounds for accepting a scientific theory, or been guided by a convincing proof in accepting a mathematical result. It is highly probable that I now forget what it was that convinced me, so that the belief will probably survive my hearing that the grounds or proof I relied upon are discredited. I may now have relatively little to offer in defence of even my most confident beliefs and opinions. Internalists would be required to make some delicate philosophical manoeuvres if they are not to conclude that most of these opinions are unjustified.

One might respond to this by viewing the community of inquirers as a single cognitive agent. Internalism would then require that *we* be able to justify the beliefs on which we rely. I can be confident that the proof is available in books and libraries even if I do not know it. But my preferred route here is different: first person epistemic evaluations have a fundamental role even if knowledge is identified as a communal possession and a shared achievement. Unsurprisingly, this involves those evaluations which enable an individual to believe that he is behaving responsibly and exercising autonomous rational self-control in carrying out his activities. In line with my two preliminary observations, I shall take this in two stages.

If I am to participate in inquiries in a self-controlled autonomous fashion, accepting responsibility for the nature of my contribution, then sufficient information must be available to me for monitoring the progress of my inquiries. If it turned out that I lacked the information required for directing my inquiries in the light of my cognitive goals, then something like scepticism would result. In consequence of this, it seems that the possibility of responding to scepticism depends, at least in part, on the information which is available to the knowing subject. At first sight, this is sufficient to warrant an internalist or first-person approach to at least some epistemological issues: since we are interested in *self*-control, evaluation must rely upon information available to the self. This does not yet commit us to an internalist theory of justification or knowledge. This further commitment would arise only if it turned out that being able to decide which of our beliefs were justified or known was necessary for this rational self-control. We could conceive of a position which legitimated the practice of relying upon a practice of evaluating beliefs as justified or unjustified which was externalist in character, so long as the practice of doing so stood firm for the inquirer.

This leads to the second stage. Once we recognize that knowledge is a communal possession and a shared achievement, then the questions which must be answered from an internalist perspective may concern less the justification of particular beliefs than the extent to which our participating in this practice can be the responsible choice of an autonomous rational agent. The following two sections examine some of the complexities which this involves, and the following chapter develops these points through an examination of 'knowledge'.

6. *Foundations and coherence*

Many of the philosophers whose views we have discussed have appealed to the danger of a regress of justification if we insist that a belief is justified only if reason can be given for accepting it. It was employed by the Pyrrhonists as one of the modes of Agrippa; Reid relied upon it in defending his own foundationalist perspective; and in *On Certainty* Wittgenstein emphasized that the giving of grounds comes to an end in 'an ungrounded way of acting' (1977 110). The standard response to the regress of justification is that justification must terminate in judgments or practices that require no further justification.

A standard way of introducing 'coherentist' theories of justification is that they deny that a regress of justification will occur if all justification is inferential. Any proposition can be justified inferentially but ultimately justification can go in a circle, beliefs being justified by reference to a corpus of opinions some of which, in turn, rest upon a body of justificatory support which includes the original proposition. If one defends an internalist theory of justification and thinks that justification is paradigmatically a matter of giving reasons, then this may be the only way of understanding the view that justification is a matter of coherence. Either reason giving comes to an end in what is certain or self-evident, or reason giving can go in a circle, or scepticism is unavoidable: foundationalism or coherentism or scepticism.

If we take account of the ways in which our corpus of beliefs evolves, a wider perspective comes into play. We hold many beliefs which were acquired for (good) reasons which have now been forgotten; or we learned them from the testimony of others whose identity we forget or who have forgotten the reason they had for adopting these beliefs. An internalist foundationalist view might hold that no such beliefs are justified: they are not self-evident, and we cannot reply to a demand that we vindicate our allegiance to them. This conflicts with our ordinary practice: our outlook is *conservative*, beliefs being retained although we have forgotten their original justification and abandoned only when positive reason is given for doing so (Harman 1986 ch.IV). The *giving* of reasons comes to an end in what is uncontroversial, in what we have no reason to doubt; it does not terminate in what a traditional foundationalist would recognize as a self-evident foundational belief. It is in a similar spirit that we often accept the testimony of other people without inquiring into their justification for the testimony that they offer or into their normal reliability as sources of information. There is a presumption in favour of other people's testimony just as there is a presumption in favour of what we have learned and not forgotten.

This 'Coherentist' picture (Harman p.32 ff.) suggests a mixture of internalist and externalist themes. The giving of reasons obviously appeals to information available to the giver: we control our attempts to extend our knowledge and eliminate errors by reference to what is available to us. But we find nothing irrational in acquiescing in a body of beliefs, and practices of belief revision, whose legitimacy we cannot explain. We might defend these practices through common sense slogans: everything counts for then and nothing counts against them. But such slogans do little more than gesture towards our trust in the coherence of our practices, and they do not ground any detailed recommendations to be employed in exercising our self-control. We express an optimistic trust that there is a coherence in our practices and opinions which will prevent further disruptions or dislocations; but we acquiesce in a limitation to self-control. Others may assess our reliability as informants and allow this to guide their decisions about whether to accept our testimony: the judgments they make will rely upon information not available to ourselves. So long as our practices *are* coherent, we conform to them without question; we do not need to satisfy ourselves that the scaffolding is secure.

This perspective fits some of the claims in Wittgenstein's *On Certainty*; it also fits Quine and Neurath's ship metaphor. The position recognizes limitations on our abilities to take responsibility for our own successes and failures in inquiry. Whether this makes it a sceptical position is an issue for subsequent discussion. For the present, it is enough to clarify how a proper attention to the communal character of inquiry and the ways in which our beliefs develop through time make a foundationalist internalist picture of justification much less attractive than it might seem.

7. Certainty and justified belief

In chapter VII, we warned against formulating the issues raised by sceptical challenges in terms of certainty, knowledge or justified belief. The objection to such formulations was they did not do justice to the deep issue raised by philosophical scepticism. Chapter VIII and earlier sections of this chapter, explain how these challenges should be under-stood. In this section, I shall argue that this explanation of the threat of scepticism enables us to understand how certainty and justified belief do indeed matter: if certainty and justified belief are not possible, nor is responsible participation in inquiry as an autonomous agent. A parallel claim about knowledge will be defended in chapter X.

'Traditional' epistemology sometimes grounds a demand for cer-tainty in the regress of justification. If beliefs are to serve as foundations, it is argued, they must have two properties. First we must be certain, or sure, of them; if we are uncertain of them, it seems, we should recognize that they need further justification, in which case they are not suited to serve as foundations. Second, this assurance must be warranted; we cannot ground the whole structure of our knowledge in a psychological compulsion to accept these things. Certainty is characterized in psychological and normative terms: we are assured of these things, and they have a self-intimating character which prevents our psychological assurance being an epistemological embarrassment. In principle, such certainty is compatible with fallibility. Such beliefs can be defeasible: we are warranted in being certain of them unless we encounter positive reason to question them. This acritical (p.153 above) character confers a *prima facie* warrant.

Notice that this characterization has three elements. The first is a kind of psychological indubitability. The second is also phenomenological but introduces a normative dimension: not only can we not doubt these things but we experience them as needing no positive justification. The third element is straightforwardly normative: our phenomenological response is correct or warranted. Our task now is to determine whether such certainties are required for the possibility of pursuing an activity in an autonomous responsible fashion. Whether such certainties are possible and legitimate is a topic for subsequent investigation.

If there are no such certainties, responsible, autonomous participation in inquiry is impossible. Such self-control, too, has three elements. We must be sure that we know what we are doing and that we can evaluate the adequacy of our means and the success of our ventures. In addition, this certainty must not be a mere psychological compulsion; we must feel warranted in our assurance. Finally, our assurance must be correct or warranted. These elements correspond to the three com-ponents of certainty described in the previous paragraph. But why must such self-control be grounded in *certainty*? After all, we do employ methods when we are aware that there is some risk of their leading us to false belief; and we rely, provisionally, upon assumptions whose fallibility is evident to us. Perhaps we could rely upon methods and assumptions which all had this status.

Although I have no conclusive argument showing that this is not possible, several considerations support that view. If all of our beliefs are held tentatively and provisionally, then none of them, in Wittgenstein's phrase, 'stands firm': we are aware in each case of the real epistemic possibility that we are mistaken in holding on to them. This includes the beliefs which are used to set our goals in inquiry and those which are used to formulate our methods for pursuing those goals. In normal circumstances, when I accept a belief tentatively, I have a sense of the risk that I take: I know what I could do to test the belief further, and I can consciously choose not to do those things; I can feel confident that if I do succumb to error, further exposure to relevant experience will lead me, and fellow inquirers, to eradicate the error. If *all* acceptance is tentative, then I cannot be certain of what would be relevant to testing a belief; and I can have no assurance that error will be exposed by further inquiry. For my methods of inquiry may be grounded in false beliefs which distort my investigations in such a way as to conceal their own falsity and the falsity of other beliefs which were obtained through using those methods. A sense of being in control of one's own inquiries requires a *confidence* in one's ability to formulate goals clearly and pursue them responsibly; and however this is related to defeasible certainty, it is not consistent with tentative acceptance (cf. in another area of discussion, B. Williams 1985 pp.170–1). Without this, we can only participate in inquiry in a spirit of ungrounded optimism which conflicts with the aspiration to be in control of our activities.

Much inquiry is co-operative: we accept the testimony of others, often without demanding that its credentials be established; we expect others to share our sense of what questions are worth pursuing, and of how much evidence of what kind is required to warrant accepting an answer to a question; we anticipate that arguments that will satisfy us will also satisfy them, and so on. Such assurances are part of what is involved in our comprising a 'community' of inquirers – alongside accepting the same paradigms of successful inquiries and the same authorities. If these shared attitudes rest upon tentatively accepted beliefs, then the community of inquirers will be highly unstable and our own membership of it will also be provisional and insecure. For if we all know that these commitments are held tentatively by the members of the community, we must admit it likely that other members may abandon them (indeed may have abandoned them) when we wonder whether we can accept their testimony. Hence we cease to function as a cognitive community: before accepting the testimony of another, it would be necessary to establish that their tentatively held epistemic standards correspond to our own. And if *all* such commitments are tentative or provisional, there may be a sceptical obstacle to our arriving at an assessment of their epistemic commitments from what they will say about them.

So it appears that self-controlled inquiry and co-operative inquiry rationally pursued require a foundation of confident certainty: commitments tentatively held leave us estranged from other inquirers and from our own practice. We arrive at a vindication of the need for certainty which treats it as a derivative epistemic value. The same can be said for justified belief. When others offer their testimony, they present an opinion, we may suppose, as deserving of belief in the light of these shared underlying epistemic commitments. And when we accept a belief, without being certain of it, and treat it as evidence for further inquiries without standing in need of further investigation itself, we similarly evaluate it favourably in the light of these commitments. Unless these evaluations were legitimate, our ability to conduct investigations would be severely limited. Hence some notion of 'justified belief' is required for autonomous participation in inquiries. If neither certainty nor justified belief is possible, then self-controlled inquiry is not possible either.

The aim of this chapter has been to clarify what is required by the approach to scepticism outlined in chapters VII and VIII. We have used this approach to examine some alternative diagnoses of the structure of sceptical challenges; and I hope that it has gained support from its ability to throw into perspective the strengths and weaknesses of these other analyses. Moreover, especially in our discussion of realism (section 4), we have identified one possible route for mounting resistance to scepticism. And throughout the chapter, but especially in sections 5–7, we have distinguished some of the requirements for carrying out inquiries in a self-controlled fashion. Chapter X continues in the same vein: we shall investigate the role of knowledge ascriptions in controlling our inquiries and in obtaining justified beliefs; and we shall arrive at an understanding of this central term of cognitive evaluation which will enable us to explain (in chapter XI) how scepticism can be avoided.

CHAPTER X

Why Knowledge Matters

1. Introduction

In chapter VII, I warned against formulating the challenge of scepticism in terms of knowledge, suggesting that it was possible that we could be deprived of knowledge yet not feel alienated from our attempts to discover the nature of reality because we were capable of justified belief. It was also suggested that we might possess knowledge yet feel alienated from our cognitive endeavours because we were unable to recognize which of our beliefs count as knowledge. In spite of these observations, it is natural to view scepticism as challenging our ability to know anything. In this chapter, I am ready to explain why, after all, knowledge does matter. Once we understand the role of knowledge ascriptions in our cognitive economy we shall be in a position to see how far scepticism can be kept at bay. I shall argue that knowledge is required for our beliefs to be justified, and for us to participate in inquiry as responsible autonomous individuals.

As is well known, philosophical discussion of knowledge has, since the early 1960s, focused on some puzzles of a kind introduced by Edmund Gettier (1963). These confront attempts to provide reductive definitions of 'knows', sets of necessary and sufficient conditions for the truth of statements of the form:

X knows that *p*.

Gettier challenged analyses which equated knowledge with justified true belief. Given that acceptance of a false belief can be justified by appropriate evidence and that we are justified in believing deductive consequences of our justified beliefs, counter-intuitive results can be obtained. Believing, with reason, that Jones will obtain a particular job,

192

and also justified in believing that Jones comes from Boston, I am justified in concluding that the successful candidate will be a Bostonian. This justified belief is true; but only because Smith – a stranger to me who actually gets the job in question – is also a Bostonian. Since my justification rests upon a falsehood – that Jones will be appointed – my justified true belief does not count as knowledge: I have arrived at the truth through an accident.

The last twenty-five years have witnessed a progression of more sophisticated analyses of knowledge succumbing in turn to ever more ingenious counterexamples. It is easy to despair of a successful analysis. Although it would be too great a digression to discuss this history here, it will be helpful to describe some of the approaches used in providing analyses.

An early suggestion was the belief that *p* would count as knowledge only if it was caused by the fact that *p* (Goldman 1967). Since Smith was causally irrelevant to my belief about the appointee's place of origin, my belief does not count as knowledge. But this promising suggestion fails. It would rule out knowledge of mathematics if, as seems likely, numbers, sets, and mathematical structures are causally inert. Moreover it too faces counterexamples. Suppose a doctor selects a thermometer from a box to take the temperature of a patient. By chance, he selects the only instrument which is not faulty. Hence he forms a true belief about the patient's temperature and his belief is caused by the state that it describes. However, because his method is generally unreliable, we judge that because he arrived at the truth through luck, he has not obtained knowledge. A similar example was introduced in Goldman 1976 pp.121 ff.

Connecting possession of knowledge with use of a reliable method of belief formation is a plausible development; but this too faces difficulties (see Goldman 1986 pp.42 ff.). How are we to describe a 'method'? The method of using *that* thermometer is very reliable, while if we describe the method as simply 'selecting an instrument from the box and using it' we shall find that he used an unreliable method. Once we have agreed upon a method, how reliable must it be? Must it be reliable in all circumstances, or only in circumstances close to those which concern us. Suppose that the thermometers are reliable but only when the ambient temperature is maintained within narrow limits. The temperature of the hospital ward is restricted in this way. If the doctor is not aware of these limitations on the instrument's use, does he know the patient's temperature?

Related difficulties face the most influential recent analysis of knowledge, due to Robert Nozick (1981 pp.172–8). Nozick claims that a true belief counts as knowledge if, in forming it, the believer *tracks* the truth. If the doctor knows the patient's temperature is 37°C, then:

1. If the patient's temperature had not been 37°C, then the doctor would not have believed that it was.
2. If (in slightly altered circumstances) the patient's temperature had been 37°C, then the doctor would have believed that it was.

The second clause is intended to explain why the doctor who uses the only reliable thermometer in the box lacks knowledge. We cannot hold that the doctor would have believed the temperature was 37°C so long as this was the temperature since he might easily have picked up a different instrument.

Although the relevance of tracking to the analysis of knowledge is clear, it faces difficulties. The conditional statements built into the analysis of tracking concern what would have been the case in situations other than the actual one. We consider a range of alternative possibilities where the patient's temperature is different, and we ask what the doctor would then have believed. How large a range of alternatives should this be? If we consider all possible situations in which the patient's temperature is not 37°C, then we run into those where the thermometer was interfered with the previous day, or someone inserts a heat source in the patient's mouth which the doctor does not notice, etc. Knowledge would then be too difficult. If we restrict attention to those alternative possibilities which differ from the actual case only in that the patient's temperature is different, then knowledge becomes too easy: the fact that the doctor might easily have selected a different thermometer from the box becomes irrelevant to whether he possesses knowledge.

As Alvin Goldman has remarked, possession of knowledge requires the ability to discriminate the actual case from a range of other 'relevant' possibilities. Someone does not know that he sees Judy across the street unless he can distinguish her from her identical twin Trudy (1976 pp.128–9). However, even if he lacks this ability, Nozick's account may ascribe knowledge to him. Unless we know that if Judy were not across the street, Trudy would be there, Nozick's analysis does not assign this discriminatory capacity any role. Although Nozick's conditionals are relevant to the understanding of knowledge, they do not provide a complete account. One test of a philosophical account of knowledge is how well it captures the source of our intuition that tracking is part of our concept of knowledge. Another is whether it helps us to understand these puzzles about the range of alternative situations that a putative knower must be able to distinguish from the actual state of affairs.

In concluding this introductory section, we should note some intuitions which are often ignored when analyses of knowledge are proposed. Return to the doctor who has fortunately picked the one good thermometer in the box. Our earlier discussion exploited the natural intuition that he does not know that the patient's temperature is 37°C. But there is a conflicting intuition. Suppose that *I* know that he has picked a reliable thermometer. If somebody else wishes to know the temperature of that patient, and I have now forgotten what it is, I could reasonably say: ask Doctor X, he knows. Even if we feel that this is low-grade knowledge, it is far from obvious that what I say is literally false. It would speak in favour of a philosophical account of knowledge if it explained, and supported, my saying this.

If we take my claim literally, then the requirements for knowledge would be very thin indeed. Suppose that somebody has arrived at the correct answer to a calculation through committing several errors which cancel each other out. Suppose too that I have noticed that he has the right answer, but I have now forgotten what the correct answer actually is. When a third party asks for the answer, it would not be a misuse of language for me to say: ask so and so, he knows. All that 'knowledge' would then consist in is true belief. I shall offer an elucidation of knowledge which supports my saying what I do in this case but also explains why we naturally feel that this knowledge is not the real thing.

Section 2 notes some logical and grammatical features of knowledge sentences which will subsequently provide a clue to understanding the concept of knowledge. This will lead to a discussion of the importance of knowledge for our cognitive autonomy and the contribution that our analysis can make to our attempt to respond to scepticism.

2. *'Knows'*

Most philosophical discussions of knowledge focus on sentences of the form

X knows that *p*.

For example:

The doctor knows that the patient's temperature is 37°C.

Such sentences parallel the logical and grammatical form of those typically used to ascribe beliefs to people:

The student believes that the answer to the arithmetical problem is 59.

This encourages the belief that knowledge is so to speak, a species of belief: both are relations between individuals and propositions; and philosophical analysis has to explain which subset of beliefs counts as knowledge.

It supports this view that while beliefs are invoked in order to explain people's behaviour, knowledge has no independent explanatory role. If the doctor's knowledge of the patient's temperature explains his treating the patient as he does, this is only because the belief that the patient has a temperature of 37°C appropriately causes his actions. The fact that the patient has knowledge, rather than mere belief, may explain why his treatment was successful. But whether he knows or merely believes makes no difference to his choice of treatment. To avoid confusion here: if the doctor believes he knows the temperature, he may act with greater confidence than if he believes without being sure whether he knows. But this is a difference between two beliefs, not between believing and knowing. He will act in the same way on his belief that he knows whether he actually knows or not. Although this does encourage the view that belief and knowledge are logically or grammatically analogous, it also reminds us that the conceptual roles of the two notions are rather different. *Belief* has a role within an explanatory framework: if we lacked the concept of belief we would be unable to explain people's behaviour as we do. If *knowledge* is not an explanatory concept, it is natural to ask what we need it for. Why does it matter whether we possess knowledge? In some sense, it is a term whose use is primarily evaluative; this is why it might be relevant to our attempts to control our inquiries. But how are we to understand this evaluative use?

Many knowledge sentences do not have the form described above. Some, like the following take an indirect question complement:

X knows who committed the murder
X knows why water expands on freezing
X knows when the train leaves for London
X knows whether the atomic weight of sodium is 29
X knows how the prisoner escaped.

Their form can be expressed:

X knows *Q*.

I shall speak of *Q*-claims and *P*-claims to distinguish these sorts of knowledge sentence.

Concentrating analytical efforts upon describing the truth conditions of *P*-claims must rest upon the belief that *Q*-claims can always be paraphrased by sentences of this favoured form. In fact it is trivial to paraphrase *P*-claims in terms of *Q*-claims.

> John knows that the bus has just left

is equivalent to:

> John knows whether the bus has just left and it is true that the bus has just left.

If we attend solely to locutions like 'knows whether', or other cases where a question has a determinate and finite number of answers, the reverse paraphrase seems trivial too.

> John knows whether the bus has just left

is equivalent to:

> Either John knows that the bus has just left or John knows that the bus has not just left.

It may be less easy to find paraphrases where questions have infinitely many possible answers: unless the analysans is allowed to be an infinite disjunction, it must quantify into the scope of 'knows':

> X knows how many trees there are in Canada

would be paraphrased:

> (E*n*) X knows that there are *n* trees in Canada.

Another problem arises for 'how' and 'why' questions which appear not to have definite sets of possible answers associated with them at all. Perhaps

> John knows why water expands on freezing

is equivalent to:

> (E*p*) John knows that water expands on freezing because *p*.

But such a programme of analysis would face many problems.

Fortunately, the view I wish to defend does not require me to establish whether *Q*-claims are reducible to *P*-claims. It is enough that 'knows' takes an indirect question complement as well as a propositional complement while 'believes' admits only of the latter. 'Believes why', 'Believes when', 'Believes who' simply make no sense. I suspect that in ordinary discourse, *Q*-claims to knowledge are far more common than *P*-claims. Hence my strategy is to see what we learn about knowledge from focusing on *Q*-claims. Why do we have a concept of knowledge which receives such expression? Once we understand what we do with *Q*-claims, we can ask what properties knowledge must have if these claims are to receive their customary use. We hope for philosophical insight from assigning primacy to *Q*-claims.

In order to guard against misunderstanding, note that the distinction I have drawn does not correspond to the familiar one between 'knowing how' and 'knowing that'. 'Knowing how' refers to the possession of a practical capacity and philosophical use of the notion is commonly invoked to combat an excessively intellectual conception of mind. Knowing, we are reminded, need involve no more than possession of a skill. I hope it is clear that the *Q*-claims I have used as illustrations all involve straightforward theoretical knowledge, the possession of truths. The question complements have been factual questions rather than practical ones. 'Knowing how' might be given a role in my discussion however. The focus on *Q*-claims could enable us to distinguish practical and theoretical knowledge relying upon a distinction between practical and theoretical questions. Since the irreducibility of 'knowing how' to 'knowing that' seems to be well established, this could demonstrate that, in general, *Q*-claims cannot be reduced to *P*-claims and hence justify our attaching primary philosophical importance to the former.

3. The knowledge inference

The remainder of this chapter is an attempt to derive philosophical illumination from examining the logic of *Q*-claims. Consider the following argument form:

I The doctor knows whether the patient's temperature is 37°C.
The doctor believes that the patient's temperature if 37°C.
so The patient's temperature is 37°C.

The argument is valid, and it could easily be informative: we could establish the truth of the premisses while agnostic about the patient's temperature and use them as grounds for accepting the conclusion. This 'knowledge inference' exemplifies the form:

II X knows Q
X believes that p
p is an answer to Q
so p.

We can try to understand knowledge by examining the role that such arguments have in our practice as inquirers, and then investigating what properties knowledge must have if the knowledge inference is to occupy this role.

A fundamental role for this pattern of argument lies in learning from the testimony of others. If I am aware that somebody has consulted the railway timetable I may believe that whatever view they have about the time of the train is correct: if they believe it leaves at 3 p.m., then it leaves at 3 p.m. and so on. In other words, whichever answer they give to 'When does the train leave?' will be correct. If this licenses me in saying that they know when the train leaves, I can acknowledge the truth of the first premiss of an argument that fits our schema without myself knowing when the train leaves. This enables me to learn from the knower's testimony: I believe myself to be justified in accepting any answer which they sincerely offer. When I assert that someone knows something, I commit myself to the claim that their sincerely expressed answer to the question is the correct one.

I shall subsequently argue that this suggestion offers much insight into the concept of knowledge. Another attempt to elucidate the concept of knowledge by reference to the role of knowledge ascriptions in learning from testimony is Craig 1986–7: although he deals primarily with *P*-claims, his paper complements the present discussion. At first sight, it may seem unpromising for two reasons. The first is that it suggests that knowledge is important only for facilitating learning from the testimony of others. We use the concept so that we can be saved the effort of finding things out for ourselves. If we believe that relying upon testimony is a secondary form of inquiry, we might suppose that the concept of knowledge is of little importance for the 'primary' activity of finding things out for ourselves. In that case, this approach confirms the view that demonstrating the possibility of knowledge is not of fundamental importance if we wish to avoid scepticism. The next two sections will attempt to refute this criticism.

The second reason for doubting that this approach will provide much insight is that it threatens to lead to the view that there is little of a systematic nature to be said about knowledge. In particular, the view that true belief is sufficient for knowledge is close at hand. Recall the example of a student who has reached the correct answer to a calculation because the various errors he has made have cancelled out. If I remember only that he has the correct answer but can no longer recall what it was, I seem to be in a position to assert that whatever answer he gives will be correct, and thus to remind myself of the correct answer through his testimony. In other words, if I assert that he knows the answer to the calculation, I will be able to exploit the knowledge-inference in order to expand my knowledge. Whenever somebody has the correct answer to a question, however he has obtained it, if I am persuaded that whatever answer he gives will be correct, then I am warranted in ascribing knowledge to him.

I shall subsequently claim this as a strength of the position I wish to defend; we noted in section 1 that we do not find it counter-intuitive. The challenge is to explain why we refuse to ascribe knowledge to people in the many cases when we are emphatic that although they have the right answer they do not know. The following two sections will offer such an explanation. In concluding the previous section, I referred to practical knowledge (knowing-how). Reliance upon this obviously cannot exploit the knowledge inference, but it should be straightforward to construct a parallel explanation of how our assurance that someone knows how to do something warrants us in relying upon the results of their attempts to do it.

4. Testimony: the third person case

We face two difficulties. First, our argument has suggested that knowledge is just true belief; indeed, any case of true belief might non-metaphorically be described as knowledge if an appropriate context is provided. Although this engages with some of our intuitive judgments it conflicts with most of those which have guided attempts to provide reductive definitions of *P*-claims. We must either explain the conflict away or show how to avoid the conclusion that any case of true belief can count as knowledge. Second, by apparently linking *knows* to our practice of learning through testimony, the argument seems to view it as a secondary term of epistemic evaluation.

Consider some cases where someone is ascribed 'knowledge' although their possession of this truth is epistemically flawed. As well as the example of the pupil who reaches the correct answer to a calculation because several errors have cancelled each other out, we could consider someone who infers the true belief that there is a vase in the room in which he is standing from the false belief that he is now seeing one – he is really looking at a hologram or picture. As I argued above, once we were told that these people possessed knowledge, we could learn from their testimony. If use of the knowledge-inference is the clue to the concept of knowledge, there seems to be no reason to deny that they know. How can we accommodate the intuition that use of unreliable methods, reliance upon false premises and the absence of appropriate causal connections between what is known and the knowledge of it, mean that the knowledge ascribed here is not 'real knowledge'?

These are odd cases of testimony. Typically, relying upon testimony involves accepting the authority of our informant, taking his word for the truth of what he says. In these odd cases, our acceptance of one person's testimony rests upon the authority of a third party who attests to the truth of what is said. We are to accept what *A* says because *B* tells us that what *A* says will be true. If we accept the testimony and are misled, the focus of our complaints should be *B* rather than *A*. Learning from testimony is typically a two-party transaction; these cases require the connivance of a third person.

If I am aware that my informant employed a reliable method, for example, that will put me into a position to accept the first premiss of the knowledge-inference: I accept that whatever answer he gives to the question at issue will be the correct one. If my knowledge of his capacities and his position enables me to affirm that if the answer is *p* then he will accept *p*, while if it is not-*p* he will not accept *p*, then, once again, I am in a position to accept his testimony. Information about methods and capacities enables me to be sure that the informant knows whether *p* (for example) without relying upon anyone else's knowledge of the matter. In many such cases, we can be in a position to decide whether X knows *Q* before anyone has discovered which answer to *Q* he will offer.

This has a bearing on a question raised in the first section. How is it determined which 'relevant alternatives' a knower must be able to discriminate from the state of affairs of which he claims knowledge?

The perspective I am offering makes this highly context relative. Recall the example of somebody who claims that he sees Judy across the street, but who was unable to distinguish Judy from her identical twin Trudy. Does he know whether Judy is across the street? If I am confident that Trudy is away on holiday or sick in bed, then I am justified in affirming that whatever answer the informant gives will be correct. If I am not confident of this, I am not so justified. Whether it is correct to say that he possesses knowledge depends upon the background knowledge of the person who makes the ascription. There need be no difference in the informant's state of mind which distinguishes these cases. In most cases, I am warranted in ascribing knowledge to someone and exploiting their testimony if they employ methods which are locally reliable.

One way to understand this is to identify a question with a set of possible answers. A knower must be able to discriminate which of these answers is the correct one. The ascriber's background knowledge influences which answers are regarded as possible: if I already know that Trudy is not across the street, it does not matter that my informant would not be able to discern the truth of *that* answer. All that is required for the correctness of the knowledge ascription is that he be able to evaluate the answers which I deem possible (or even plausible). Hence context is a determinant of which question is expressed by an interrogative clause.

Although these remarks account for some of the intuitions which philosophers have allowed to guide their reflections about knowledge, there are others which have not been accommodated. Some would insist that, in the case described, the informant does not *really* know that Judy is across the street. For present purposes, what is important is not whether this is correct. Rather, in so far as we can sense the force of this intuition, it is important to understand its source. Does it point towards a role for the concept of knowledge in ordering our inquiries which has not been accounted for here? There are two sets of considerations which are relevant to answering this question. The second will be discussed in the following section. The first also responds to the charge that our reliance upon the knowledge-inference and its role in testimony has tied 'knows' to a secondary or peripheral aspect of inquiry.

Since inquiry is a public communal activity, reliance upon the testimony of others is essential to the ways in which our knowledge grows (cf. chapter IX sections 5 and 7). I inevitably rely upon other people and upon information stored in books and other records. If the concept of knowledge is involved in the ways in which we learn by testimony, it is required for the conduct of almost all investigations. I participate in inquiry responsibly only if the members of the community aspire to be – and interpret each other as – reliable informants. As well as refuting the suggestion that the focus on testimony directs attention towards what is epistemologically of secondary importance, this suggests a way of explaining those intuitions about knowledge which conflict with the context-relative claims made above.

Knowledge has a contagious character. If I inform others that our subject knows whether Judy was across the road, they will retain this information and use it themselves if her location should become important to them. And the information may pass through many hands. It is carried by the sentence 'X knows whether Judy was across the road', and is not accompanied by information about the background assumptions which guided my attribution. This exposes us to two kinds of risks. Suppose I learned that Trudy had undergone a sudden recovery (or suddenly returned from holiday). Within the original context, that provides reason for withdrawing the assertion that the agent knows whether Judy is across the road. A piece of background information on which the assertion depended has been discredited. Those who have learned from me about the agent's knowledge but who are not party to the original context will be unaware that this information defeats the knowledge claim. A knowledge claim which thus depends upon specific features of context of that sort is not suited for transmission to others outside the original context.

For certain purposes, we want our knowledge acriptions to be 'impersonal' (see chapter XI section 5). Those who repeat the knowledge claim in other contexts still make the same assertion; it does not reflect idiosyncratic features of particular sets of background assumptions. Within particular practices of inquiry, there will be shared assumptions about which possibilities must be discriminable for a knowledge claim to be warranted, or about the general acceptability of the methods of inquiry employed. Unless these shared assumptions are adhered to, those who learn about who knows what may form false expectations about what else the subject of knowledge knows or about when the claim should be abandoned in the face of new information.

This does not refute the claims about context relativity (see section 6). Rather it reminds us that if we expect our assertions to be available to a wider community of inquirers, we must be aware of the implications this has for responsible claims to knowledge. We address the wider community of investigators and should make our utterances sensitive to the expectations which others in the community would bring to interpreting our utterance. Of course, we do not always have to do this. The general point about context relativity stands. But the fact that, in some of our assertions, we defer to a wider community explains the presence of intuitions about knowledge which suggest we should not describe someone as possessing knowledge unless we can show that they employed methods of inquiry which would be reliable over a range of cases much wider than that which is relevant to our immediate concerns with learning from someone's testimony.

In concluding this section we can relate the apparently unsatisfactory character of the 'knowledge' which consists in no more than true belief to our concern with cognitive autonomy. We noted above how our reliance upon testimony in such cases can require the assurance of a third party that our informant possesses truths. This may prompt the suspicion that it is not our *informant's* knowledge that we are exploiting, since it is not his authority on which we rely. In many such cases, we shall not take the informant at his own estimation, and the suggestion that we deny his autonomy by using him simply as a means to our cognitive ends, denying him the status of one member of a community of rational inquirers, has much appeal. In other words, perhaps our reluctance to speak of knowledge here is linked to the fact that we transform the knower from a fellow inquirer into a mere instrument of our own inquiries: we deny his autonomy as a cognitive agent.

5. The first person case

Rather than stress the importance of testimony for inquiry, we could argue for the epistemological importance of *knowledge* by claiming that first-person knowledge ascriptions are implicated in our evaluations of our own epistemic position. How important is it that I should be able to establish whether I know things? I shall offer three reasons for thinking that *knowledge* does have such a role. I am least confident of the first but its close parallel with the topic of the previous section makes it a useful starting point.

Consider a first-person version of the knowledge inference schema:

> I know Q
> I believe that p
> p answers Q
> so p.

For example:

> I know whether that bird is a goldfinch
> I believe that it is a goldfinch

so

> That bird is a goldfinch

It seems obvious that such an inference can have no role in the ways in which I acquire beliefs. If I accept the conclusion as a result of such an inference, my beliefs are unchanged, for, if the second premiss is true, I already believe the conclusion. I cannot learn from my own testimony.

This may be correct. However a minimal revision to these formulations may permit us to learn from our own testimony. As it stands, the second premiss may be too strong even for the third-person cases. Consider somebody who learned his multiplication tables by rote at school. They are no longer sure whether they remember them correctly. So when the question

What is 7 times 9?

is fired at them, they find themselves inclined to answer '63' although they are not confident that they should endorse this answer. Before acting on this result they would carry out a more careful computation. It is the answer they would offer if prompted, although it is not an answer that they believe with any confidence.

If informed by a third party that this person had not forgotten the multiplication table in question, then I could learn from their testimony: in an appropriate context I could say, quite unmetaphorically, that they know what 7 times 9 is. A 'willingness to say', falling short of full belief, would thus suffice for the second premiss of the inference. A similar story could be told for the first-person case. If I am the person we have been discussing, I could affirm that I find myself disposed to say that 7 times 9 is 63 while uneasy about assenting to this claim. Once I am informed by someone that I know this multiplication table, I accept my own testimony on the matter: the tentative willingness to say is transformed into a belief. This is at least analogous to learning from my own testimony. It also accords with earlier discussions of our ability to regard our own responses to phenomena as instruments to be evaluated and used in pursuing our cognitive purposes. A concern with how far my own responses can be trusted is very much like a concern with how far another person's testimony is reliable.

Here is another example: I perform a complex calculation, tentatively accepting the result. Since I am aware of how easy it is to commit errors in carrying out such calculations, I am reluctant to endorse my conclusion with any confidence. If I can assure myself that I know what the answer to the problem is, then I can endorse the answer which I have arrived at. We can envisage different ways in which I could arrive at that assurance. Least interesting is being told by somebody else that I know. Or, over time, I may come to appreciate through induction that I am less prone to mistake than others, so I believe that, with a high probability, whatever answer I offer will be correct. Or studying my methods for doing the calculation may reveal to me that they are less likely to lead to error than more widely adopted ones. Although my claim to know the solution to the calculation is fallible, it can receive a grounding which enables it to reinforce my tendency to accept the answer I have arrived at. I accept my own testimony and arrive at full belief.

The second reason for assigning importance to first-person knowledge claims relates to remarks about testimony made in the previous section. Because of the public character of inquiry, belief is contagious: there is generally a presumption that others' assertions can be accepted without inquiring into the grounds for their claims or the methods they used to arrive at them. Of course, there are kinds of beliefs for which this does not hold, and there are many circumstances which alert us to be cautious in accepting testimony. But the point holds for the most part. When I assert that p, I indicate that an auditor can justifiably conclude that p on the basis of the knowledge-inference. It is an implicature of my assertion that the auditor's presumptions about what grounds the first premiss of the inference in such cases, and in such contexts, are in fact justified: there are the appropriate sorts of grounds for claiming that I know whether p. It follows from this that I can view it as a desideratum that my beliefs can be represented as conclusions of instances of the knowledge-inference the first premisses of which can be justified in contextually appropriate ways. Thus the knowledge-inference has a role in determining the kind of justification required for any belief which I am to look upon as assertable (cf. chapter IX section 7).

Third, we can claim that it is an independently desirable constraint upon the coherence of a corpus of opinions that I hold a belief only if I am sure that I would hold it only if it were true. This could be expressed thus:

If I believe that *p* with justification, then I must be assured of the premisses of an instance of the knowledge-inference which has *p* as conclusion. (Where acceptance of the first premiss, the *Q*-claim, does not depend upon acceptance of the conclusion.)

In other words, being justified in believing *p* requires an assurance that whatever opinion I have concerning whether *p* is correct. An explanatory theory of perception which explains our reliability at making certain sensory discriminations could ground this assurance, as could experience of making successful judgments of this sort in the past.

It is not part of this claim that our beliefs are inferred according to the knowledge-inference, although I suggested above that this might sometimes be the case. Rather, it is desirable that we can view our beliefs as knowledge for this involves moving towards a kind of coherence and completeness in our system of opinions. Viewing a belief as knowledge rests upon being able to view it as the product of a well calibrated instrument. We have noted several times that one of our cognitive aspirations is towards being able to evaluate the methods (instruments) of belief formation.

6. Knowledge and scepticism

These arguments suggest that sceptical challenges threatening the possibility of knowledge put into question our ability to exercise self-control in our inquiries. Unless I am confident that I am capable of knowledge, I cannot participate in co-operative inquiries in which others depend upon my testimony. When I attempt to inform others of the results of my investigations, I represent myself as possessing 'knowledge'. If I cannot responsibly so represent myself, then I am irresponsible in offering my testimony; if I suspect that no one can correctly represent themselves as possessing knowledge, then I am in bad faith if I believe that we can undertake co-operative inquiries as responsible autonomous cognitive agents. Moreover, if my claims about the first-person role of knowledge claims in learning from my own 'testimony' and in evaluating the coherence of my own opinions are correct, then I can only carry out investigations in a responsible autonomous fashion if I am warranted in ascribing knowledge to myself.

As well explaining why a threat to the possibility of our knowing anything actually matters, these arguments suggest that it is actually useful to formulate sceptical issues in terms of knowledge. The previous chapters have suggested that seeing our cognitive armoury as open to sceptical attack is linked to being able to regard our sensory responses and inferential habits as instruments for achieving our epistemic goals. If, through reflection, we regard these responses and habits as instruments, then, it was argued, it is appropriate to recognize a demand for an evaluation or explanation of the efficacy of these instruments. Although we may not bother to carry out such evaluations or seek such explanations, this is because we take it for granted that favourable results would be obtained. In the previous section, I conjectured that once we regard our habits or responses as *instruments* of inquiry, then we should describe our use of them as, so to speak, learning from our own testimony, relying upon the knowledge-inference. Furthermore, once we interpret these as instruments, then it becomes plausible that we require that form of coherence in our beliefs which involves thinking of these habits and responses as yielding knowledge.

If this is correct, then raising the question of what we know and pursuing the issue of how we can obtain autonomous self control in our inquiries come to the same thing. Moreover, if our best means of avoiding sceptical embarrassment requires us to see that it is inappropriate to regard various aspects of our practice simply as instruments for securing our cognitive goals, then this should be accompanied by a refusal to admit that there is any point in talking of our knowledge (or lack of it) of their reliability (cf. chapter VI section 6). If our spontaneous sensory judgments are not an instrument whose usefulness for our cognitive goals must be evaluated, then the role for Q-claims about the reliability of the senses must be highly restricted. Our sense that there is something odd about asking for a proof that the senses reveal the real world to us is the obverse of the sense that there is something slightly strained about saying that I know whether the senses are reliable.

Concentrating upon the role of Q-claims and the knowledge-inference helps us to keep these issues in focus. First, it reminds us that the question whether someone knows something always arises within a specific context which fixes the range of answers to the question from which the knower must discriminate the correct one. When we use the inference to learn from the testimony of others, this context is determined by the background assumptions and expectations of the person hoping to learn from the testimony and by the expectations common to a wider community of inquirers who may subsequently acquire beliefs which depend upon that testimony. In the first-person case, it is determined by the goals which govern the individual's investigations and the ways in which they see themselves as contributing to wider communal inquiries.

If philosophical discussion of knowledge is primarily concerned with *P*-claims, confusion is encouraged. The role of the concept of knowledge in our cognitive economy may be obscured and the wrong significance attached to the observation that our readiness to ascribe knowledge to someone can depend upon context. While it is plausible that the question raised by an interrogative clause can vary with context, no such plausibility attaches to the thought that a different proposition is expressed by the complement of a *P*-claim in different contexts. Hence it is natural to conclude that whether one possesses knowledge is an all or nothing context-free matter. Philosophers thus look for analyses of knowledge sentences which make no reference to the inquiries to which knowledge claims are subordinate or to features of the contexts in which they are made. This may lead them to seek for a description of the circumstances in which knowledge would be truly ascribed to someone relative to any context of inquiry at all. It is doubtful that such an account is available.

I have argued that avoidance of scepticism requires a demonstration that we possess knowledge. Does it require that when we know something, we know whether we know it? Since we can rely upon another's testimony, ascribing them knowledge, when they are uncertain whether they have knowledge at all, it is plain that knowing does not entail knowing that one knows. However, if we are to use the concept of knowledge, as described in section 5, in order to evaluate our own cognitive functioning, it might still be the case that responsible participation in inquiry requires us to know which things it is that we know. This appears to be the case. If my assurance that a belief serves as knowledge cannot itself be endorsed as knowledge, then the right with which I take it seriously may be hard to sustain. If I discern in myself a tendency to regard a given belief as knowledge, why should I accept the 'testimony' of that tendency? If I inform others that I know whether *p*, without being prepared to accept *that* as knowledge, why should I expect them to take my word for it? If our analysis of the role of the concept of knowledge in ordering our beliefs and inquiries is correct, then second (and third?) order knowledge is as important as the first order variety (see chapter IX section 5 on the 'appeal of internalism').

7. *Tracking and the avoidance of scepticism*

In the course of this chapter, we have discussed the analysis of know-ledge defended by Nozick. In *Philosophical Explanations*, he argues that scepticism is easily defeated once we accept his analysis of *P*-claims in terms of tracking. I wish now to explain and evaluate his argument, which involves denying an initially plausible closure principle concerning knowledge:

Suppose that
   i) X knows that *p*
  ii) *p* entails *q*
 iii) X knows that *p* entails *q*
 iv) X infers *q* from *p*
then
     X knows that *q*.

If this principle is correct, it provides one warrant for allowing the impact of sceptical challenges to spread through our entire corpus of beliefs. Since

I can now see the clock tower of Birmingham University

entails

I am not now a brain-in-a-vat,

then, if I do not know that I am not a brain-in-a-vat, I do not know that I can now see the Birmingham University clock tower. This supports the view that unless I can rule out the possibility that I am a brain-in-a-vat (or that I am dreaming), I cannot claim experiential knowledge of external things (see chapter IX section 3).

Nozick claims that one consequence of his analysis of *P*-claims is that the principle is false: although I do not know that I am not a brain-in-a-vat, I do know that I can see the clock tower. Consequently we can avoid scepticism without engaging with the more extreme Cartesian sceptical challenges. The suggestion that our right to feel confident of our everyday knowledge claims does not depend upon the possibility of defeating these sceptical arguments may be an attractive one. My present concern is with Nozick's distinctive development of the thought, which rests upon the evaluation of two claims:

1. If I were not now looking at the clock tower of Birmingham University, I would not believe that I was.

2. If I were now a brain-in-a-vat, then I would not now believe that I was not a brain-in-a-vat.

Nozick's analysis of knowledge requires that my true belief that I now see the clock tower would not count as knowledge unless (1) were true; it also requires that unless (2) is true, I do not now know that I am not a brain-in-a-vat. (For simplicity, I am ignoring the second clause in the definition of tracking and I have tidied up the antecedent of (2).

Nozick accepts a version of David Lewis' analysis of counterfactual conditionals (Lewis 1973). To determine whether a counterfactual conditional is true, we consider those possible situations in which the antecedent is true but which are otherwise as much like the actual situation as possible. The conditional is true in the actual state of affairs if the consequent is true throughout these 'close' possible ones. (1) is highly plausible: if we consider situations where I am looking in a different direction, or the blinds are closed, or there is a thick fog over the campus, we can accommodate my believing that I am inspecting the clock tower only by incorporating a lot of other changes to explain my having this strange belief. Throughout *these* possible situations, I am not a brain-in-a-vat. However, they are not the situations which are relevant to evaluating (2). For that purpose, we consider situations where I am a brain-in-a-vat, deceived by evil scientists, and those most like the actual situation are likely to be those in which I am caused to have just those beliefs which I do now have. Hence, if I were a brain-in-a-vat, I would believe that I was not one; so I do not know that I am not a brain-in-a-vat.

Criticism of Nozick's argument could take several forms. We might dispute the details of his argument, challenging the account he offers of the truth conditions of counterfactuals or denying that it has the consequences he alleges. Or we could hold that, even if these details are correct, his argument fails as a response to the threat of scepticism. Before discussing these issues, notice that Nozick's response to scepticism is closely related to his views about which alternative possibilities are relevant to whether someone knows something. When we raise the question whether I see a clock tower, my being a brain-in-a-vat is not an alternative explanation of my experience which is relevant to my cognitive position: when we consider my belief that I am not a brain-in-a-vat, then it is. In section 1, we suggested that Nozick has no satisfactory basis for determining which alternative possibilities are relevant to cognitive evaluation. This supports the sense that Nozick has not satisfactorily responded to scepticism.

Scepticism

Crispin Wright has two objections to Nozick's account, both of which are relevant to our discussion (1985 pp.444–6). The first is that it rests upon the assumption that sceptical challenges exploit the facts about closure described above. None of the sceptical arguments we have examined have proceeded:

> If I know that that is a clock tower, then I know that I am not a brain-in-a-vat.

> I do not know that I am not a brain-in-a-vat

> So, I do not know that that is a clock tower.

They rather rest upon my finding my reasons for believing that there is a clock tower in front of me inadequate: as we saw, Wright holds that my evidence is adequate only on the assumption that there is an external world. In that case, a demonstration that the first premiss of the above argument is not true may not help me to see what is wrong with the troublesome sceptical arguments.

Wright's second objection is that, even if it shows successfully that we possess knowledge, it fails to engage with sceptical challenges to reasonable belief. Reasonable belief, he alleges, cannot be explained in terms of a notion like tracking: 'I may reasonably believe P because of what I reasonably take to to be symptoms that P even though, in this case, the symptoms would obtain even if it were not the case that P' (Wright 1985 p.446). So another response to Nozick is to accept his conclusion but hold that a deeper form of scepticism, directed against reasonable belief, has not been touched.

It might be supposed that the weight I have placed upon the possession of *knowledge* would prevent my endorsing this objection. This is incorrect. Since I have emphasized the role of knowledge ascriptions in the ordering and evaluation of my own opinions, my participating in inquiries in a responsible and autonomous fashion requires not only that I possess knowledge but that I am well-informed about which things it is that I know. The 'externalist' possibility that I know many things but lack any basis for identifying *which* of my confident beliefs are known would leave me with no basis for planning my inquiries and evaluating my cognitive position. Although my claims to knowledge are fallible, responding to the threat of scepticism requires that I be justified in my claims about what I know, indeed, ideally I should know what I know. Since it is easy to imagine cases where I am justified in believing that I know something when I do not know it, and where I justifiably believe I do not know something which I know, Nozick's argument does not provide assurance that I can take responsible control over my inquiries. At best, it offers me the solace that if I do know anything, this need not be undermined by my failure to know that I am not a brain-in-a-vat, without providing positive reason for accepting the antecedent.

Nozick's analysis focuses upon *P*-claims, and this prevents his appreciating the context-relativity of knowledge ascriptions and the principles we use for determining which set of answers to a question a knower must be able to discriminate between. If we take him to have recognized, without clearly understanding, the fact that different kinds of knowledge claims can arise in different contexts, then something may be learned from his claims. Since his theory does not focus upon internalist notions like justification, we shall examine some third-person examples where knowledge claims are exploited to learn from someone's testimony. Suppose that I wish to know the time and hence wonder whether someone can see the clock tower and hence knows what time it is. Since I take it that neither of us is merely a brain-in-a-vat, the situations I require them to be able to discriminate are limited. Since it is presupposed that they are not brains-in-vats, that is not to be taken into account. It is enough that they can discriminate clock tower appearances from other appearances and that they can read the positions of the hands. Brain-in-vat hypotheses do not interfere with my ability to exploit the knowledge-inference and rely upon their testimony.

Suppose I am genuinely interested in whether someone knows whether they are brains-in-vats. Contrast two cases. First, I am a psychiatrist examining an ex-philosophy student subject to strange delusions: he alternates between believing himself a brain-in-a-vat, a fly in a fly bottle, a prince's brain in a cobbler's body, a disinterested observer, and an undetached rabbit part. Today, he assures me that he is not a brain-in-a-vat. Perhaps he is dissimulating; perhaps he thinks that that is what a brain-in-a-vat should say; perhaps this is not a sign of progress because today he thinks he is a beetle in a box or he is fully occupied trying to escape from the fly bottle. So, does he know he is not a brain-in-a-vat? If I believe that his sanity has returned, it is natural to conclude that he knows whether he is a brain-in-a-vat. His opinion on the matter can be trusted; he tracks the truth. (Interestingly, I may not believe that if he were a brain-in-a-vat, then he would not believe he wasn't: this counterfactual possibility seems too remote to have a bearing upon my evaluation of his cognitive state – and indeed, too remote to be seriously entertained. This may point to a deeper difficulty with Nozick's analysis of knowing.) Within this context of investigation, where the fact that we are not brains-in-vats is taken for granted, ascribing to someone knowledge that they are not brains-in-vats seems unproblematic. As a corollary of this, within the context in which I ascribe to someone knowledge of the time according to the clock tower, it is obvious that they know whether they are brains-in-vats.

A second case: a colleague has devised a proof of the existence of the external world and I wonder whether he *knows* whether he is a brain-in-a-vat. In this context, his proof fails, we might suppose, unless the brain-in-a-vat possibility can be excluded. It becomes relevant. We shall discuss below whether talk of 'knowledge' is to the point here and whether the colleague's enterprise even makes sense. Nozick's discussion points to the fact (which it does not clearly identify), that raising this philosophical question occurs in a different context. The background knowledge and goals of the inquiry are different, and possibilities become relevant which do not appear relevant to everyday inquiries.

We have developed a picture of some of the evaluations that we make in planning and controlling our contributions to inquiries of different kinds. We have also explored how scepticism can emerge from our attempts to exercise such autonomous self-control, hinting that it may result from a natural tendency to extend the search for such self-control further than is really appropriate. We naturally regard some features of our practice as *instruments* of inquiry which ought not to be so regarded, so that we ask how we *know* that they are reliable, when the question should be resisted. The final chapter extends our examination of the structure of rational self-control in order to understand better the possibilities for avoiding scepticism.

CHAPTER XI

Naturalism and Autonomy

1. Naturalistic epistemology

Sceptical challenges question our ability to participate in inquiries while retaining the sense that we are autonomous, responsible agents (chapters VII, VIII). We can understand the importance of concepts like 'knowledge' and 'certainty' by reference to their role in our search for cognitive self-control (chapter IX section 7, chapter X). In that case, a sensible strategy for responding to scepticism is to suggest that these challenges employ a distorted conception of what intellectual freedom requires. Does the demand that we exercise autonomous self-control over our investigations and inquiries really require us to have answers to the challenges familiar from the sceptical canon?

At several points, I have argued that the challenge of scepticism can be viewed as a special case of the free will problem. We could present the current state of debate over the latter issue as posing a dilemma: either compatibilism (or soft determinism) is true or we are not really free. The compatibilist view, that all that is important in the concept of freedom can be reconciled with admitting that many of our fundamental commitments are beyond our control, explains much of our normal practice of claiming responsibility for actions or blaming others for their deeds. But it *appears* to omit the crucial core of our sense of being free self-controlled agents. If no more can be secured than compatibilism offers, it is difficult to establish whether our claim to be free autonomous agents is thereby vindicated or whether we have an explanation of how we are reconciled to our unfree state. It is difficult to formulate any further aspiration which compatibilism fails to secure. Is it a reasonable but unobtainable ideal? Or is it simply unreasonable? It is natural to see sceptical arguments as the source of a similar dilemma: although we can live with our ordinary practice of forming and criticizing beliefs, our readiness to admit the force of these arguments suggests that a recognizable cognitive aspiration cannot be achieved. If we can sustain our optimism that our inquiries will be successful without answering sceptical arguments, does this provide a way of recognizing that sceptical concerns are unreasonable, or does it reconcile us to the correctness of scepticism?

We shall approach these issues by examining a particular 'epistemological' project. Quine has argued that psychology or cognitive science can carry out the tasks traditionally associated with epistemology (see chapter VI section 5). Epistemological questions can be answered by an account which 'has a good deal to do with the learning of language and with the neurology of perception.' Evolution, natural selection, even physics could feature in the account: epistemology 'or something like it, simply falls into place as a chapter of psychology and hence of natural science.'(1981 p.72). The details of such a theory are not relevant to my current concerns – as well as Quine's writings, Goldman 1986, Millikan 1984 and Papineau 1987 provide examples of such investigations. Humean in spirit, it avoids the theory of ideas, and hopes, by viewing humans as physical objects which are part of the physical world which is the object of their investigations, to avoid scepticism and explain our successes in carrying out inquiries.

Our concern is not with whether these naturalistic explanations are interesting, but with challenges, mounted by Barry Stroud among others, to its right to regard itself as inheriting the mantle of 'epistemology'. They argue that it simply 'changes the subject', turning its back on questions of traditional, and legitimate, concern. As Quine himself acknowledges, 'the surrender of the epistemological burden to psychology ... was disallowed in earlier times as circular reasoning'. If our goal is 'validation of the grounds of empirical science', we 'defeat our purpose' by employing scientific results in our reasoning (1969 pp.75–6). Suppose we adopt the sceptical worry that, in spite of the coherence of our scientific beliefs and our ability to make useful predictions, these beliefs might all result from the manipulations of a demon or wicked scientist and be largely false. The demon might ensure that we would develop a coherent cognitive psychology which 'explains' our 'success' in arriving at true beliefs about our surroundings. So relying upon scientific psychology appears to have no power to exorcize demon scepticism. It cannot 'validate' science as a whole; so it has no relevance to our epistemological concerns if these arise out of a concern with 'Cartesian' scepticism.

This charge of circularity can be met by denying that concern with 'validation' is central to epistemology. Philosophical theory of knowledge must explain the possibility of science: it explains how we make scientific progress on the basis of experiment and observation. Unless we are suspicious of the credentials of science to begin with, it is hard to see why we should not use our hard-won scientific discoveries in providing such explanations. If our cognitive psychology suggested that the evidential basis of science was so feeble that it would be a miracle were any of our theories even approximately true, then concern with 'validation' might emerge. Until this occurs, it is needless self-denial (or unwarranted 'neutralism' (chapter VI section 3) to refuse the help of the numerous scientific discoveries of which we are confident. In view of its record, science is innocent until proved guilty. Unfounded speculations about demons and brains-in-vats cannot shake this presumption of innocence.

Questions about the demands of the 'epistemological tradition' are hard to answer because the very idea of 'traditional epistemology' is questionable. Different philosophers have had different reasons for investigating epistemological issues, and any characterisation of the 'tradition' will distort the philosophical ambitions of many with claims to belong to it. Mindful of such risks of over-simplification, we can describe 'traditional' epistemology in two different ways: as a response to issues typified by the sceptical arguments of the first *Meditation*; and as a search for a framework within which we can describe, evaluate, control and generally make sense of of our methods of inquiry. One characterization of 'traditional epistemology' connects these themes: we cannot respond to sceptical challenges without providing a framework of the sort described; and unless a framework does this, it will be inadequate to the demands of evaluation, control and explanation.

If we suppose that engagement with sceptical doubts is unnecessary, that the importance 'traditionally' attached to them results from philosophical illusion, we can retain the project of seeking a theoretical framework which could be used to evaluate, control and explain our cognitive practice. A scientific or naturalistic framework, used for this purpose, would exhibit continuity with our fictional 'tradition'. However, merely providing this framework and working within it provides no satisfaction for someone for whom the need to respond to sceptical challenges is real and pressing. If we characterize the 'tradition' in the first of our two ways, then the continuity has vanished. We simply turn our backs upon sceptical arguments. A 'naturalistic epistemology' does not itself explain why we need not take these arguments seriously; it must be accompanied by a commentary which encourages us to seek no more than it can provide. If this commentary, which offers philosophical therapy or attempts to dissolve the problems, is not itself provided by the naturalistic epistemology, then, if we identify the problems of epistemology in the first fashion, a naturalistic epistemology cannot adopt the *whole* mantle of 'traditional epistemology'.

Another challenge to naturalistic epistemology alleges that epistemology is a normative discipline while cognitive psychology, like all science, is descriptive. If we raise questions about how we ought to conduct our inquiries, or about whether we are correct to conduct them as we do, a scientific explanation of our current practice is not enough. Quine's talk of 'validation' may already suggest that a normative concern of the older tradition is being displaced. And our stress upon the importance of freedom and self-control suggests that normative questions are central to responding to scepticism: we need standards for evaluating our inquiries which can enable us to take responsibility for the way they are carried out. The fundamental issue concerns the possibility of epistemic norms: sceptics suggest that we cannot satisfy ourselves of the correctness of those which we employ; and naturalistic epistemology is accused of a version of the naturalistic fallacy. Psychological explanations of how we do form our beliefs cannot provide defensible accounts of how we *ought* to conduct our inquiries.

I shall suggest that naturalistic approaches to epistemology are analogous to compatibilist approaches to other questions of freedom. We shall see how they can contribute to our ability to answer many normative issues; and that they have a role in cognitive self-control. Just as philosophical debates about freedom focus on *deep* evaluative issues which compatibilist approaches to questions of responsibility make poor sense of, so the present issue concerns whether sceptical challenges introduce deep evaluative issues which must be settled for us to have *real* control over our inquiries.

2. Normativity

Epistemology typically grows out of methodological reflection: it asks which criteria should be employed in evaluating theories and opinions, and which methods we should use in carrying out inquiries. The current objection is that while psychology can describe mechanisms whereby theories are produced, it cannot explain why our favoured criteria for evaluating theories are the best available (Siegel 1980 pp.318–19). Quine is charged with the naturalistic fallacy: the 'is' of cognitive psychology fails to deliver the 'ought' of normative epistemology (see Brown 1988; Gibson 1988 pp.67–9, for further discussion).

Stated bluntly, the objection is obviously ineffective. Quine responds: 'normative epistemology is a branch of engineering. It is the technology of truth-seeking ... It makes use of whatever scientific findings may suit its purpose.' Thus mathematics helps us to avoid, for example, the gambler's fallacy; psychology exposes perceptual illusion; neurology may help us to discount 'testimony from occult or para-psychological sources'.

> There is no question here of ultimate value, as in morals; it is a matter of efficacy for an ulterior end, truth or prediction. The normative here, as elsewhere in engineering, becomes descriptive when the terminal parameter is expressed.
>
> (Quine 1986 pp.664–5)

'Applied' epistemologists use information about the effects of using different methods to justify hypothetical 'ought's: anyone interested in making reliable predictions of a certain kind *ought* to use method *m*. In particular, such applied epistemology can ground knowledge ascriptions, including self-ascriptions, which guide our control of our reliance upon others' testimony and our evaluation of our own responses to specific questions (see chapter X sections 4–5).

Critics of naturalistic epistemology will protest that all of Quine's examples involve 'local' evaluations which are made against the background of a large body of beliefs which are taken for granted. Not only is Quine's focus on 'making reliable predictions' controversial, but we can express anxieties such as the following. Suppose we accept:

1. We frequently continue to hold beliefs long after their original evidential basis has been discredited.
2. For the most part, the evidential support a belief has is long forgotten. We retain beliefs with little specific to say in their favour; they have kind of *prima facie* recommendation from the fact that we hold them.

Accepting (1) on the basis of an empirical psychology to which (2) applies may suggest that, for all that we know, the evidential basis of most of our epistemological beliefs has been discredited. Could we not be in the grip of a mistaken empirical epistemology which has *ad hoc* means for explaining away all apparent counter-evidence? The fact that there is no longer anything to say in its favour may be concealed from us.

The charge is that once we move beyond local challenges and consider global ones, we can respond to them naturalistically only by making the gratuitous assumption that most beliefs which are a matter of general consensus are true: we test our methods according to whether they come up with (what we take to be) truths (Putnam 1982 p.20). But surely the role of the methods is to provide a basis for evaluating those very beliefs. Although the move from local challenges to more general ones lies at the heart of the difficulties that some have with naturalistic epistemology, it is difficult to respond to the argument when formulated in this fashion: it invites too readily the charge that we are being invited to take seriously an unnatural and hypothetical doubt; and makes it easy for the naturalistic epistemologist to respond smugly that the merit of his approach is that it deals with real rather than invented problems. While I am ultimately sympathetic to this response, it is of no value unless accompanied by an understanding of the strengths of the opposing view.

To that end, I shall now reformulate the normativity objection in order to confront a naturalistic epistemologist with what appears to be a paradox. 'Traditional epistemology' has a distinctively first-person character. It asks:

What do *I* know?

Quinean epistemology lacks this first-person character. We could use it to describe the methods of belief formation used by other people, and, relying upon our better understanding of the matter they are investigating, we might discover that many of their conclusions are false, or that much of their probabilistic reasoning is invalid. Such empirical investigations rely upon a body of beliefs which hold firm. Criticism of the beliefs and methods of another person need not threaten my own beliefs: unless they are fellow investigators whose testimony has grounded some of my own opinions, I can treat them as objects of investigation while remaining confident of the certainties I use to question their views.

A consequence of this is that nothing in what has been said so far limits the error we might find: someone may turn out to be prey to errors in probabilistic reasoning; or they may succumb to wide ranging errors, perhaps being susceptible to fashionable and indefensible systems of belief. Or the error could be very extensive: suppose we are taken to the laboratory where the scientist shows us the wired up brain or body of our friend, and explains how he is stimulating our friend's brain to have a view of the world which is wholly illusory. Sentences issue from the brain (never mind how) which seem to report upon this illusory view of the world. Secure within our view of the world, we can decide that nearly all of our friend's beliefs are mistaken. Since threatening his beliefs does not threaten our own, the amount of error that we could uncover does not appear to be limited.

When we begin to evaluate our own beliefs, the position is different. I might uncover a tendency to make errors of a localized kind: I keep forming beliefs which subsequent experience forces me to revise. I might discover that I too have previously been susceptible to fashionable but silly beliefs – even that I will continue to be so if I am not alert. Already there is a difference from the third-person case: when I criticize my own beliefs, the set of opinions from which I mount the criticism is affected. Doubts about my cognitive reliability offer a potential threat to the standpoint from which the criticisms are made. Once the criticisms acquire a wide target, I lose the basis upon which to mount criticisms. Given the principle that we should not rely upon beliefs which are threatened by a criticism in responding to it, the materials available for responding to criticism directed (by myself or others) at myself will always be more restricted than the resources available for evaluating criticisms directed at someone else. In that case, while a naturalistic epistemology can be used to evaluate criticisms of someone else's beliefs which challenge wide ranges of his beliefs, it is powerless to do so when the target of the criticisms is my own beliefs.

So, it is argued, a range of deep normative issues can be raised about the cognitive powers of other people against the background of our own view of the world. When our attention turns to our own ways of evaluating hypotheses, there are limits to the criticisms that a naturalistic epistemology can make. There is a range of global normative questions with the following two properties:

1. We take them to be intelligible: indeed, we can formulate them and answer them in connection with other people.

2. A naturalistic epistemology does not permit us to formulate them, or answer them, about *ourselves.*

The conclusion is: the deep first-person normative issues which prompt epistemological investigations cannot be answered within a naturalistic epistemology. It does not help us to see how we can realize autonomous self-control in carrying out our inquiries.

3. Neurath's ship

Quine likes to cite Otto Neurath's metaphor: our cognitive position is not that of a shipowner who, aware that his ship is leaky, removes it into a drydock, strips it down, and attempts to rebuild it from the keel up. Rather we resemble the sailor who rebuilds his raft or ship at sea: individual timbers are replaced while the remainder of the structure keeps the ship afloat. Hence we rely upon our physical and psychological theories while adjusting our views about how science works and so on. We inhabit an evolving corpus of beliefs: we cannot step back to a 'first philosophy' from which we can rebuild our science according to a better blueprint.

The metaphor emphasizes the piecemeal character of both scientific inquiry and epistemic evaluation. Particular scientific questions can be investigated against a background of theories and assumptions which, for the time being at least, hold firm. And particular features of our methods of inquiry may be evaluated, this too occurring against a background of accepted scientific theory and of other methods which are not being questioned. Such investigations always arise in a context which is partly constituted by the mass of scientific and methodological opinions which it does not occur to us to challenge. It accords with this that we can test methods of investigation by establishing whether their results accord with entrenched scientific opinion; and we can critically evaluate our beliefs and theories by applying our methodological standards to the investigations which led to their acceptance. Beliefs about contingent states of affairs, scientific theories and methods of inquiry can be classified according to their degree of entrenchment in our framework of knowledge as a whole: the division into the controversial and the unquestioned cuts across the distinction between methodological and substantive scientific opinions (see chapter VI section 5).

Such an interpretation only sharpens our sense of the problem about normativity. Is Quine claiming merely that this is how we generally do proceed in revising our scientific beliefs and our methods of investigation? Or is he recommending that we should allow our corpus of opinions to evolve in this piecemeal fashion, tackling problems as they arise but not disturbing the entrenched consensus unless forced to do so? The naturalistic fallacy objection suggests that he moves illicitly from the first descriptive claim to the second recommendation. Why should we accept that this is how we *ought* to proceed? Indeed, this would be a poor strategy for a brain-in-a-vat to adopt. Moreover the previous paragraph reveals the circularity involved in any normative use of naturalistic epistemology: methods are accepted if they vindicate entrenched theoretical assumptions; and we decide which theories to accept in accordance with accepted methodological standards. Perhaps Quine is making the third claim that we *cannot* adopt any other strategy, so that it is empty to suggest that we ought to do so. But at the present stage of our discussion it is difficult to see how that can help. Rather than helping us to see how a naturalistic epistemology can yield a constructive response to scepticism, it offers the pessimistic prospect that since full self-control over our methods of inquiry cannot be achieved, we must rest content with a policy of piecemeal tinkering whose legitimacy as a way of approaching truth cannot be established. If this is all that can be said, naturalistic epistemology appears to acquiesce in scepticism rather than try to overcome it.

The remainder of this chapter explores some responses to this challenge. Some are suggested by elements in Quine's own discussion, but I am more interested in using this problem as a means of bringing together a variety of themes from twentieth century discussions of scepticism. In concluding this section, I shall make some preparatory remarks. Quine, as we saw, sees methodological evaluations as instrumental: does adopting a particular method of inquiry, method of calculation, or experimental technique serve as a means of arriving at the truth about the questions that concern us? Such means-ends evaluations take for granted a specification of the goal of the inquiry. When our concern is with how best to measure the temperature of a liquid, or with the evidence required to confirm an hypothesis about the behaviour of a species of bird, it is easy to identify the cognitive goal against which methods should be measured. When we ask whether piecemeal tinkering is a legitimate epistemological strategy, what end or ends do we have in mind? It seems clear that such evaluation requires an exceedingly general cognitive goal – 'making reliable predictions', 'revealing the true nature of reality', 'discovering the non-evident natures of things'. Unless such general goals are available, the question whether Neurathian tinkering is legitimate is not well posed.

One moral to draw from the Neurathian metaphor might be that such general cognitive goals are not available. We have no overarching cognitive goal which the Cartesian and Neurathian recipes provide competing means towards. Rather, our cognitive goals emerge piecemeal from our evolving body of beliefs and methods. All of the normative questions that arise are 'local' ones which take for granted a body of entrenched methods and opinions. We do not need to vindicate 'induction' in general or 'perception' in general because we have no cognitive end by reference to which they can be evaluated. Against the background of a corpus of beliefs in whose formation induction and perception have had a fundamental role, we can question particular inductive strategies or particular kinds of perceptual judgment (cf. chapter IX section 4). If such a moral can indeed be drawn, a constructive response to scepticism may be available: rather than finding limits to rational self-control, we find a better understanding of what rational self-control requires.

So far we have only a metaphor and a moral which we should like to draw from it. Since the apparent force of sceptical arguments of both Sextus and Descartes suggests that we feel the power of the contrasting picture, we cannot rest without some further argument in support of this perspective. Moreover, once again, our consideration of the position of our friend the brain-in-a-vat provides an obstacle too: we are inclined to judge that there are some global issues of justification which he *ought* to confront even if he does not do so.

4. *Charity and the brain-in-a-vat*

If we knew most of our beliefs are (at least approximately) true (indeed, that most of everybody's beliefs are true) we should have a basis for agreeing that substantive normative issues are all 'local'. We would also have further justification for adopting piecemeal strategies in revising our corpus of opinions. There are several routes to such a view, and two of them are examined in this section.

What is 'reality'? What is involved in wanting to know the character of reality? One answer is: I want to know more about the earth, about other people, about sticks, stones, animals, buildings and the like. If I possess no general abstract concept of reality which can be set against this empirical conception of the nature of 'reality', then this may be the only sensible answer I can give. In that case, there must be a sense in which my understanding of 'reality' is determined by the remainder of the ship, by my general conception of reality. When I step back and ask: what reason have I to think that any of this is *true*, I use a form of words rather than a substantive conception. The truth predicate, it will be argued, serves only as a predicate of disquotation: '"Grass is green" is true' says no more or less than 'Grass is green'. In particular, it does not introduce any conception of correspondence with an independent reality which can be used to mount a general challenge against the adequacy of our beliefs. A naturalistic conception of reality provides our metaphysics: no more abstract conception is available against which our shared view of the world can be measured and found wanting.

Once again, this is an attractive picture which points towards the possibility of an anti-sceptical stance. But we need a reason to believe that this is true. The fact that we are disturbed by the possibility that we are brains-in-vats suggests that we *do* have the concepts required to formulate the more general challenges: if a brain-in-a-vat was convinced by these arguments, we are tempted to claim, it would be wrong.

In an influential series of papers, Donald Davidson has offered a different, albeit related, argument for the conclusion that most of everyone's beliefs are true (1986). Lacking the space to examine this argument in detail, I shall sketch its underlying strategy and make some general remarks about its cogency and relevance. Davidson relies upon an account of how we go about interpreting the beliefs, desires and utterances of another person. Very roughly, we identify the contents of an agent's beliefs on the basis of information about the inferential relations that obtain among them and the causal relations holding between the belief states and the world. In doing this, we employ what is often called 'charity': systems of beliefs are assumed to be largely coherent, and (especially perceptual) beliefs are interpreted so as to be largely true. It is thus a product of our understanding of the concepts of belief and meaning that an agent's corpus of beliefs can be neither substantially incoherent nor massively in error. We interpret people as holding largely coherent, broadly correct beliefs about 'our world': and since an omniscient interpreter would do that for our beliefs, it follows that our beliefs are largely true.

These views have not lacked critics (see Williams 1988b, McGinn 1986, Klein 1986). My concern here is to question their application to our paradox involving the brain-in-a-vat example. Davidson admits that there are limits to the degree of true belief that we would expect to find. We expect explicable error: if the only other person in a room is concealed behind a pillar, we would be surprised if an observer did not falsely believe that the room was unoccupied; if an inconsistency would only be detected through complex and subtle reasoning, we are more surprised when someone avoids it than when they do not. But this need not allow for the possibility of extensive error: it is only against a background of substantial agreement, it is argued, that such intelligible error can be uncovered.

Our interest is in whether this argument can undermine the asymmetry that prompted our sceptical paradox in section 2. If we can establish that nobody can have substantially erroneous beliefs, this must hold for our friend whose brain has been placed in the vat of nutrients. In that case, only local normative issues can arise even when evaluating the inquiries of a third-person, as well as when we reflect upon our own methods of inquiry. If we are convinced that the example of the brain-in-a-vat shows that somebody could have largely false opinions, an argument of the sort Davidson employs would be unlikely to convince us that we were mistaken. We can see this by considering a dilemma. Either the Davidsonian theory of interpretation employs a kind of *a priori* transcendental argument or it is an attempt to provide a naturalistic explanation of our ordinary practice of interpretation. The former is likely to be unsatisfactory as a response to scepticism: not only is it unacceptable to somebody who wishes to endorse a naturalistic approach to epistemology, but the philosophical reasoning which supported the conclusion would itself be subject to sceptical challenge.

More interesting for us is the second possibility, that it exploits a naturalistic explanation of our practice of interpretation. It invites the following response: let us admit that, in normal cases, we do not tolerate finding massive error or incoherence in the beliefs of another person; but when we confront a brain suspended in a vat, the situation is highly abnormal. The 'beliefs' we wish to interpret largely result from the interference of the scientist rather than ordinary perceptual processes. Far more of the brain's beliefs have histories which are abnormal or deviant than is normally the case. If confronting such a case, we might rely upon our knowledge of the causes of these belief states rather than charitably expecting the beliefs to be largely true. Why shouldn't we allow the contents of these beliefs to be fixed by the intentions of the scientist? This accords with our reaction when we carry out familiar thought-experiments involving the brain-in-a-vat hypothesis. At the very least, we cannot insist that our understanding of how interpretation proceeds in normal cases has authority to override independently plausible guesses at how we would interpret somebody who had undergone the misfortune of being manipulated in this fashion.

But our reliance upon the intelligibility of pervasive error on the part of a brain-in-a-vat should be treated with caution. Our suspicion that it is an intelligibile possibility accompanies a doubt that it is appropriate to think of a disembodied brain as a person, possessing beliefs and desires, at all. Such doubts rest, in part, upon suggestions, due to Wittgenstein, that we can apply psychological predicates only to creatures whose modes of expression and behaviour resemble those of a human being. Identification of beliefs, emotions and other psychological states exploits features of behaviour and nuances of facial expression of which we are hardly reflectively aware. We only think of the brain as possessing a mind, in spite of its lacking the capacity to act or look like a human being, because it is the 'residue' of an embodied human being. Although such arguments have force, they are probably insufficient to shake our assurance that since such disembodiment could occur in the history of a creature which, at other times, is undeniably human, we can ascribe psychological states to the brain-in-a-vat. The argument I shall now offer yields a conclusion slightly weaker than that which can be obtained from the Wittgensteinian argument.

We can distinguish two roles for interpreting the beliefs of other agents. First, we can treat the other as a source of testimony, as a source of reliable information which otherwise would not be available to us. If this is our only interest in the other person's beliefs and utterances then, in effect, we treat him as a measuring instrument. His utterances are interpreted, typically, as signs of his internal states which are, in turn, interpreted as signs of other states of affairs. If we do interpret somebody as a measuring instrument in this fashion, then, as with other measuring instruments, it is appropriate to calibrate it, and to assess its reliability.

Consider some alternative interpretations of the 'utterances' issuing from the brain. We could interpret them homophonically, taking them to provide information about external states of affairs. So understood, we may suppose, 'his' testimony is a highly unreliable source of information about our surroundings. We could also interpret his utterances as signs of the 'experiences' which he undergoes, of the intentions of the manipulating scientists, or of the states of the computer apparatus which controls 'his' 'thoughts' and 'experiences'. Let us suppose that such interpretations will yield much reliable information. If I view my 'friend's brain' simply as a measuring instrument, then there is little sense to be attached to the question which of these interpretations is correct: since I am interested in obtaining truths rather than falsehoods, I should be ill-advised to employ the homophonic interpretation; but the other interpretations may prove to be useful for adding to my information about the world. If this is all that is going on, it is misleading to describe the brain as substantially in error.

Moreover, and more important, the normative issue raised by the brain-in-a-vat possibility then becomes a local rather than a global one; and a first-person rather than a third-person one. The question is simply: given *my* cognitive goals and my beliefs about my surroundings, is reliance upon the 'testimony' of the brain a good means of acquiring true beliefs about the world, the computer, the scientist's intentions, and so on? But in that case, my own beliefs about the world are not touched by the discovery of my friend's fate unless they rest specifically upon an unsatisfactory interpretation of his 'testimony'. The question of the reliability of this 'instrument' arises against the background of a substantive view of the world which is not, yet, threatened.

We retain a sense that one interpretation of the brain's 'utterances' ought to be the correct one; we judge that the brain is deceived; and we have not yet exorcized the feeling that awareness of what has happened to our friend ought to insinuate a doubt about our own beliefs. This unease can be expressed in a Kantian fashion which relates it to our concern with freedom and autonomy. We seem to be treating our friend as a mere measuring instrument, using him as a means to our own cognitive ends (cf. chapter X section 4). We do not recognize his rational autonomy, and we fail to acknowledge him as a fellow inquirer investigating the same questions as ourselves.

This introduces the second role for interpreting the utterances and beliefs of another person: as we saw in chapter X, we understand them as fellow inquirers, able to co-operate with us in collaborative investigations or to carry out investigations whose results can be applied to our own purposes. Someone can fill this role only if they 'share our world'. They are open to argument, seeing the critical force of challenges to opinions which we find worrying; their testimony has a *prima facie* claim upon our credence without it being necessary for us to assess their reliability; we can expect them to share our understanding of which questions are worth pursuing and which responses to them are sufficiently plausible as to be worth attention. In other words, the

Davidsonian position that we must interpret other people as sharing our beliefs, concerns and standards of rationality, seems plausible as a claim about what is required for interpreting someone as a fellow inquirer, as a possible collaborator. An investigation of how co-operative inquiry is possible, of the respects in which co-operators must inhabit a shared world, could fall into place as part of a naturalistic account of inquiry.

Interpreting the brain-in-a-vat as a potential collaborator is simply out of the question. An argument for this need not rest upon the problems of finding enough agreement to constitute a shared world. It is enough to point out that the autonomy of the brain is compromised by the fact that he is the tool of the manipulating scientists. If his 'utterances' have a role in my inquiries, it is the scientists that are my collaborators, not the brain. This is sufficient to introduce an asymmetry in my evaluative attitudes towards my unfortunate friend and towards myself or my collaborators; and it is sufficient to put into question the sceptical impact of the brain-in-a-vat hypothesis.

We are now in a position to resist the paradox of section 2, and to argue that the apparent possibility of raising global normative questions about a third-person does not threaten the adequacy of a naturalistic epistemology to address the important normative issues that arise when we attempt to control our participation in inquiry. We saw, in chapter X, that we sometimes exploit our own testimony in order to arrive at warranted opinions which can be employed in further inquiries. When I do this, I must evaluate myself as a source of such testimony: how good a method of arriving at truth *is* relying upon my own testimony: how good am I at mental arithmetic, judging the worth of students at interview, identifying warblers on the basis of their song? But such evaluations occur within specific cognitive projects: I evaluate such reliance as a means to arriving at truths, just as I evaluate my friend's 'testimony' as a means to my cognitive ends. Whereas I can view another person simply as a means to my cognitive ends, I cannot so view myself. To do so would be, simply, not to have any cognitive ends at all. The first-person/third-person asymmetry reflects the fact that when I am engaged in means/ends reasoning, the ends in question are mine.

But this argument does not even establish the possibility of a naturalistic epistemology which answers to our normative needs. It suggests a way of containing the doubts which issue from speculations about brains-in-vats, but it does not establish that the containment can actually be achieved. The sceptical force of the worry that we might be brains-in-vats appears to remain; and it will continue to do unless we can establish that all of our cognitive goals can be understood as local or particular ones which arise against the background of our established view of the world. Moreover, even if we could establish that all of our cognitive goals are local or restricted in this way, sceptical arguments may still have force. Our argument appears to have rested upon the assumption that all cognitive evaluation concerns means to ends: our cognitive goals are taken as given and are the products of our current cognitive position. One could imagine the brain-in-a-vat speculation suggesting to somebody that their cognitive *ends* do not have the value they take them to have, that the whole activity of inquiry is worthless. With this reflection, the charge that a naturalistic epistemology cannot tackle substantive questions of cognitive evaluation resurfaces as the complaint that it reduces all such evaluation to means/ ends evaluation.

5. *Restricted inquiries and self-control*

We shall begin with inquiries which are subordinate to particular practical projects: we collect information which is required if we are to achieve our practical aims. For example, I may check the larder to establish whether I have all of the ingredients for a dish I wish to cook; or I read the map in order to decide upon the best route to my destination; or I judge the likely trajectory of a tennis ball in order to decide whether to try to hit it. In normal cases, we obtain the required information against the background of a body of presuppositions about our surroundings and about our cognitive capacities. The goal we set ourselves already takes a good deal for granted. For example, in the third case, my aim takes for granted that there is such a game as tennis, that tennis balls behave in regular ways, that I am able to estimate the location, direction and velocity of the balls with a fair degree of success. Unless I took these things for granted, I would not play tennis: they provide the context in which my search for information emerges.

To allow sceptical worries to intrude in such investigations would be absurd – neurotic or obsessive. My right to be confident in what I am doing does not require that I be able to respond to sceptical worries; and deliberate, criterial self-control is usually out of place. If it were put to me that my experience might all be a dream, this would not shake my confidence in checking the 'larder' or 'observing' the ball; if all is a dream, then so are the tennis match and kitchen, so I do not require observations of reality beyond the dream. The 'observation' is understood as part of the wider practical activity. If I am reaching for a ball in the corner, it is irrelevant that I may be dreaming that I am playing tennis. The tennis match (real or dreamed) provides the context for the inquiry.

In general we are *certain* of the background view of things which guide such inquiries and we are certain of the methods we employ in carrying them out. These are things which it does not occur to us to question. If we were not certain of (at least a sizable proportion of) these things, we could not carry out these restricted inquiries with confidence and with assurance that we know what we are doing. Moreover many of these presumptions are things we have no specific justification for. We do not know why we believe them: we were trained to accept them; we accepted them along with the rest of the world view we acquired as we grew up; or they represent information acquired from books, other people, or experience over a long period.

The background assumptions fall (very crudely) into three classes. Some comprise our general understanding of what the world is like: assumptions about physical objects, persons, space, time, numbers and so on. Others are specific to the kind of inquiry with which we are concerned: beliefs about tennis or about the court on which we are playing; views about cooking ingredients and the geography of the kitchen. And finally, there is a body of information we have acquired about the particular case: a particular movement of the shadow of the ball today suggests that the ball will be in even if I would otherwise expect it to be out; memories of what was bought at the supermarket yesterday are a poor indication of what is in the larder because I lost a bag of shopping on the way home.

The key point is this: the value of the inquiries lies wholly in the contribution they make to particular practical projects. Suppose that my regular victories confirm that I am good at playing tennis, and that my attempts to cook meals are rarely thwarted by a lack of ingredients. The success of the practical projects vindicates each component of my technique in carrying out the project: nothing more is wanted of my methods of checking the larder or estimating the trajectory of the ball than that I am successful at tennis and at cooking meals. To describe these 'methods of inquiry' as 'ways of acting' usefully reminds us how limited is the role of reflection in carrying them out. The idea that self-control demands a reflective awareness of the methods we employ, the criteria employed in evaluating them and the processes involved in executing them seems out of place.

An example will illustrate some consequences of this. A tennis player's possession of a good eye for the trajectory of the ball, like a golfer's possession of a good swing, does not involve reflective deliberation: a sportsman 'finds himself' possessing such a skill. The attempt to insert deliberation or self-control into its operation is likely to be destructive: a confident trust in one's possession of the skill may be required if the skill is not to be lost. The inability to take responsibility for the ways in which individual movements or observations contribute to possession of the skill does not lead to sceptical alienation from possession of it: it is embraced as a gift rather than perceived as evidence of lack of self-control. But it retains a fragility or contingency: confidence in one's skill can be accompanied by the sense that it can go – players who are out of form are conscious of loss of a gift.

With such inquiries, the success of the overarching practical projects is sufficient to vindicate the methods used to obtain the information; I am certain of their adequacy without having a clear understanding of their precise character or being able to justify my reliance upon them. In many cases, successful pursuit of these practical goals can require me to be unreflective about the methods of inquiry used. And an inability to understand or control how one achieves one's success is a reminder of the contingency of human confidence and attainment rather than a stimulus to scepticism. Practical success breeds confidence which can extend to the inquiries which are subordinate to the practical concern. Refusal or failure to justify my methods need not produce any sense of alienation or any sense of not being in control. My unreflective mastery of practical techniques, including techniques of information gathering, is a means of control over practical concerns. A sense that I function as an autonomous individual grows out of the fact that my various capacities and aptitudes are in harmony, that they contribute to the achievement of my goals and prevent me being constantly subject to disconcerting and unpleasant surprises. If all inquiries were restricted, and if unpleasant surprises were few, scepticism would not be a problem: sceptical arguments would not flow out of my practice.

We might argue that sceptical challenges retain their bite because they can be mounted against the claim that tennis, or golf, or cooking is a desirable activity. But for those who take pleasure in such activities, the challenges would be hard to take seriously. In order to see how sceptical arguments may still have force, we must look at less restricted inquiries. Our discussion oversimplified the structure even of restricted inquiries. The tennis player's information about the position and trajectory of the ball is used at a crucial point in the game and then forgotten: it is no longer of value (see chapter X section 4). The larder checking example is more complex. Suppose that for all *my* culinary purposes, it does not matter if I confuse fennel seeds and dill. The recipes still work, and my discriminations are not fine enough for the resulting difference in taste to matter. The practice of inquiry is vindicated by the success of the culinary project, and my confusion does not threaten this success. However, in this case, the practical impact of my information gathering may not be restricted to the immediate practical application. I continue to believe that there is dill in the larder, and, without further investigation, I shall use this information for other purposes or pass it on to other people. Although it seems unlikely in this particular case, we can see that I might retain and use this information while forgetting where it has come from. The success of the practical ventures which provide the original context in which the information was obtained does not vindicate the retention of this information or its use for different purposes.

Even if practical success vindicates our certainty in our information as we acquire it and employ it for restricted purposes, subsequent reflection upon retained information can provide a focus for critical reflection. Can we store it as part of a general theory of our surroundings which can be exploited for a wide variety of purposes? Notice the parallel with Descartes' strategy: retained knowledge (memory) requires a kind of epistemic underwriting not required for spontaneous certainties employed for restricted practical purposes. We can distinguish two aspects of this 'generality' of our knowledge: we retain the results of inquiries and employ them for a wide variety of purposes. And we adopt purely cognitive goals: we seek a scientific understanding of ourselves and our surroundings. Although such understanding contributes to technological advance, we find it valuable for its own sake, providing a body of laws and theories which explain why things behave as they do. Once this stage is reached, the role of practical success in grounding confidence that we know what we are doing is more limited. We have to reflect about the nature of our goals and the means available for achieving them.

6. Levels of confidence

Although we cannot investigate the structure of the more impersonal inquiries in detail, we should distinguish the different kinds of confidence they require. The first can be called 'local confidence': when a particular question arises, against the background of a body of theoretical and methodological certainties that stand firm, we are confident in our ability to answer it. Our trust in measuring techniques, in methods of calculation, in experimental practices all contribute to local confidence. Local confidence can be grounded in 'practical success': our confidence in it results from our success in answering particular questions in satisfactory ways in the past. A tradition of experience and success ensures that they stand firm for us.

Second comes 'explanatory confidence': we are confident of our ability to explain why these techniques have the successes that they do. We can arrive at a theoretical understanding of our techniques of measurement, calculation, experiment and so on which suggests that they track the truth: if we employ them, we shall normally arrive at the correct answers to our questions. Such confidence can rest upon our already possessing the desired explanations, but it need not do so. So long as the techniques are successful, and we have a good record of explaining the successes of other methodological tools, we may trust that such an explanation will be forthcoming. Just as we trust that cognitive psychology will eventually explain how tennis players judge the trajectory of the ball, so we trust that methods employed in more reflective inquiries will be explained.

Third is 'prospective confidence': we are confident that scientific progress will continue. We shall continue to find interesting questions to investigate; we shall continue to be reasonably good at thinking up plausible hypotheses and thus settling questions before despair sets in; we shall not find that our environment is so unrepresentative of the universe as a whole that the laws we arrive at are often discovered to be very special cases of the general laws that we aspire to. Unless we ground such optimism in faith in a benevolent God, it is unlikely that we would arrive at a theoretical framework which explains why this trust is bound to be fulfilled. Confidence in continued progress has the status of a regulative hope: it can be accompanied by a sense of the fragility or contingency of our assurance that further progress will be secured – just as the golfer's trust in his swing can be accompanied by a sense that it is a gift which might be taken away. The suggestion that our cognitive skills are the product of natural selection and are thus likely to serve our needs has only a limited role. It may provide explanatory confidence in connection with our ways of forming beliefs serving our vital needs for food, sex and the like; there is little reason to suppose that an ability to solve arcane problems of theoretical physics ever had much selective advantage.

Prospective confidence was defined in terms of our trust that new questions will arise that we can answer. It did not involve confidence that we shall achieve some overarching goal which is distinctive of scientific activity: uncovering the true natures of things; or maximizing predictive control. A further level of confidence could hold that the methods we use for settling questions are in harmony with some such overarching goal: discovering the truth, or arriving at opinions which will be the object of a stable unforced consensus among all reasonable inquirers. And a further level of confidence still could have as its object the claim that the kind of cognitive activity we are engaged with has the best cognitive goal, that we are right to attempt to contribute to the steady progress towards the truth of the scientific tradition.

The first three kinds of confidence cannot be guaranteed, but our sense of their fragility or contingency need not lead to the kind of alienation from our cognitive achievements that is characteristic of scepticism. Continuities with practices of restricted inquiry, together with a tradition of success provides us with a scaffolding of acritical certainties of the sort that Wittgenstein and Reid describe. This scaffolding can ensure that these confidences stand firm for us. Our sense that this standing firm may be illegitimate may be quelled by thinking of them as rational *hopes*. Peirce often draws an analogy between the hopes which guide our inquiries and hopes that may rationally be adopted by a card player: if, at a certain stage of play, only one distribution of cards will give any chance of winning, it is reasonable to plan strategy on the hope that the cards are so distributed. So long as we find scientific activity rewarding and worthwhile, it is reasonable to plan our contributions in the hope that this trust will not be misplaced; for only if this hope is fulfilled will our contributions have any value. The hope gives a veneer of legitimacy to the certainty which grounds our confidence.

The need for these first three kinds of confidence in inquiry does not threaten naturalistic epistemology: it can meet the demands of explanatory confidence; and the other kinds of confidence need no kind of grounding which it cannot provide. The description I have offered suggests that the search for defensible criteria to vindicate our choice of methods is not required for us to feel in control of our activities. Yet our trust in our ability to contribute to inquiries is accompanied by a sense of the contingency or fragility of the abilities on which it rests: so to speak, we trust to luck. It can be argued that admitting this contingency opens the door to scepticism: it shows that we cannot take full responsibility for the ways in which we seek our epistemic objectives. Answering scepticism requires us to have a response to this charge.

There are two circumstances under which the charge could be unanswerable. First, suppose that our scientific activity is motivated by a general overarching goal: discovering the true nature of things, or contributing to the discovery of a stable unforced universal consensus. If these characterizations are understood as so general and abstract that we have no established tradition of success in achieving them, but just a history of failed attempts, then it is hard to see how our attachment to them can stand firm. Participation in such activities requires reflection upon the precise character of the goal, and about how far the methods we have available will put us into a position to achieve this goal. Reflection of a highly general kind is required. Since we have no firm confidence in our ability to do these things, appeal to rational hopes will not help us either. *Tentative* hopes can only prompt anxiety about the value of devoting extensive effort to achieving goals which may be beyond our reach. If the last two kinds of confidence mentioned above are required for scientific inquiry, then recognizing the fragility of our confidence can have sceptical implications.

Second, the same conclusion may follow from a highly reflective or criterial model of self-control. If we think that self-control requires us to reflect upon the standards we employ, and to be able to defend the criteria we make use of in order to defend those standards, then the sense that we are determined to operate with standards which we find compelling but which cannot be defended in a reflective or deliberative manner may be a cause for concern. Our discussion of restricted inquiries was intended to shake the grip of such a conception of self-control, as was the section on realism and the structure of reflection in chapter IX (section 4). Still, the awareness that we cannot take control of the processes determining which standards and practices will stand firm for us can prompt the thought that the degree of control over our inquiries that we can achieve falls short of what is required for the autonomous self-control required for truly responsible inquiry.

7. How to avoid scepticism

Naturalistic epistemology attempts to provide answers to the normative questions that arise in the course of our inquiries without having to respond to the global challenges prompting sceptical doubts about our abilities to conduct inquiries successfully. When it is asked whether this displays sufficient continuity with 'the tradition' to be a successor to earlier epistemological projects, the question concerns whether a naturalistic epistemology can genuinely avoid confronting these global challenges or whether it simply evades the responsibility to answer them. Are we offered a perspective from which we can continue with our inquiries while quite legitimately ignoring sceptical challenges? Or are we shown how to live with the impossibility of legitimating our use of familiar techniques of inquiry? And if it is proposed that we can avoid sceptical challenges, how is this to be expressed within the framework of naturalistic epistemology?

What is required for us to feel that our inquiries are subject to rational self-control, that they are things that we can take responsibility for? What justifies us in claiming to *discover* the answer to questions that concern us rather than, with the Pyrrhonists, merely *finding ourselves* disposed to accept certain appearances? We have suggested that responding to scepticism requires a secure *confidence* that our means are adequate for our cognitive needs; and sceptical arguments obtain a bridgehead from the fact that much of this confidence (especially prospective confidence) has a contingent and fragile basis. We are sure that cognitive progress will continue. But this may be attributed more to the fact that we have never doubted that it will do so than to the fact that we can say anything to quell such doubts when they arise.

The difficulty we face in deciding whether the control we achieve over our inquiries is all we should require, and thus enables us to avoid scepticism is that we have no clear conception of what is required for rational self-control. Highly reflective criterial models of self-control are clearly out of place for our attempts to plan ordinary practical activities; but the character of philosophical analysis, which brings what is implicit to reflective consciousness, can easily suggest that anything that falls short of full reflective self-consciousness means that we travel hopefully rather than taking full responsibility for our actions and inquiries. There may be no uncontroversial answer to the question what is required for responsible self-control and thus no straightforward answer to the question whether sceptical doubts are avoided or evaded.

As we have seen, naturalistic epistemology may prove adequate to our needs if the only normative issues that need to be solved are local ones: they concern particular methods of inquiry against a firm background of theoretical and methodological certainty. We do not stand back to ask global questions about the reliability of perception, or about the adequacy of our methods to abstractly formulated goals of inquiry. It is hard to see how a naturalistic account of inquiry could justify the claim that we ought only to consider such local questions. However three strategies are available for vindicating such a recommendation without advancing a more ambitious epistemological *theory* than would accord with naturalistic principles.

The first of these involves philosophical therapy. Investigations in the history of philosophy can suggest that philosophical concern with scepticism first emerged in the work of thinkers who employed views of the aims of inquiry or the constitution of the human mind which no longer carry conviction. Alternatively, it can be suggested that our sense that sceptical challenges are unavoidable arises from philosophical mistakes about the structure of reflection or about the kind of security we require in order to feel that we are able to participate in inquiry in a responsible manner. Earlier chapters of this book have contained a number of arguments of both of these kinds which were intended to shake the belief that global sceptical challenges demand a response.

A second strategy bears an analogy with the sceptical practices of the Pyrrhonists. We saw in chapter I that the latter simply refuse to adopt a range of projects which give rise to unanswerable normative questions; and that Pyrrhonist scepticism pointed to the tranquil and satisfying life which this provided as vindicating this refusal. The desirability of the sceptical outlook, in other words, is not defended by philosophical argument but is manifested in the life of individual Pyrrhonists: it cannot be stated, but it can be shown. If a naturalistic epistemology can be developed which enables us to explain the successes of our inquiries, provides the local evaluations that we need, answers the questions that emerge from our investigations, and does not undermine our prospective confidence, then those using the theory may feel that their successes vindicate the decision not to seek a deeper kind of self-control or to worry about traditional sceptical challenges. The best defence of the claims that the only questions of evaluation that arise are local ones and that deep criterial self-control is unnecessary would be a successful naturalistic epistemology: that no more is required would be shown although it could not be defended with arguments that would convince somebody of a different view.

Some philosophers see a role for decision in responding to scepticism. In chapter VI, we noted that Carnap supported the non-factual character of external questions by claiming that adoption of a framework was a matter for conventional decision based upon 'pragmatic considerations'. Crispin Wright has recently made a related use of the idea of conventional decision: we can decide to adopt a principle determining what it is for a proposition to be fact-stating, and then use it to question the fact-stating character of the propositions attacked by fundamental sceptical challenges (1985 p.461). The third strategy for avoiding scepticism makes a different use of decision.

Neurath's ship metaphor suggested that our proper role as inquirers was to engage in piecemeal tinkering against a background of settled certainty: we were to focus on local questions. If that is our perspective, a naturalistic epistemology might answer to all of our needs; our sense that it will not serve our purposes grows out of the belief that a wider perspective is needed in order to underwrite our prospective confidence. However it is difficult to formulate the wider perspective required and it is natural to characterize the position in the following terms: we have no positive reason for mistrust of our hope that progress in inquiry can continue; but we also have no conclusive or positive grounds which support it. There is nothing to weaken its authority apart from the fact that there is nothing to guarantee it. In that case, we might *decide* to orientate our inquiries towards local questions against the background of the ship which, so to speak, floats firm. We may doubt whether this is the best or most noble goal for inquiry, but we cannot dispute that it is a possible goal for inquiry which can prove rewarding and which, we are confident, will continue to progress. So doing involves embracing our cognitive position: accepting the risks attendant on the fragility of our confidence; viewing them as risks which it is appropriate to take for the sake of avoiding a profitless sense of estrangement from our cognitive position.

In so far as this involves actively accepting the risks resulting from the fragility of our confidence and affirming that our confidence is an appropriate response to our position, it is plausible to see it as avoidance of scepticism rather than evasion. Failure can be viewed ironically as an indication of the contingent basis of our engagement with our inquiries without occasioning the despair that a project in which we have invested ourselves has proved impossible. Although the position appears to recognize the truth in Pyrrhonism – and ironic resignation in the face of failure must be a component of Pyrrhonist tranquillity – it retains a view of inquiry as active discovery because of its overall naturalistic perspective. The confidence that what is sought is all that it is reasonable to want appears to contrast with the Pyrrhonist attempt to transform the aspirations which guide our inquiries. According to the view I have outlined, the *decision* to focus on local inquiries does not transform our goals: it merely positively endorses what is present in our practice in a negative way. We proceed against the background of a rationally adopted hope informed by an understanding of the fragility of our grounds for success (section 6).

This provides for the *possibility* of a defensible response to scepticism. Only a worked out naturalistic account of our ways of acquiring knowledge of the world would answer somebody who thought that our explanatory confidence was unfounded and that consequential scepticism was warranted. However it is reasonable to resist such pessimism. Moreover it cannot be taken as a defence of the claims of *naturalistic* epistemologies to answer *all* of our epistemological needs. Quinean epistemologies were used as an example in order to show how it can be reasonable to hold that only local normative questions require answering. Somebody who believes that inquiry in ethics (for example) involves a different ship, settling questions against a distinct framework of beliefs, and methods which stand firm, would find nothing in this argument to shake that view. However they should find a description of an anti-sceptical strategy, involving the recommendation that we should focus on local questions, which could be applied quite generally (but see Hookway forthcoming).

My aim has been to understand our ambivalent reaction to sceptical arguments. They possess a phenomenological force through challenging our sense that we can participate in inquiry in a responsible way that manifests our rational autonomy: we cannot be sovereign in our inquiries. Yet a perspective is available which warrants our impatient dismissal of attempts actually to answer the challenges. Like Sextus, we turn aside from epistemological projects which demand answers to these challenges; and like Descartes we seek a perspective upon our inquiries which leaves us with a response to his first sceptical challenge – we no longer have reason to undertake trial through scepticism. We can agree with Reid that once we adopt Descartes' project of making scepticism give birth to certainty, we are lost. A philosophical response to scepticism, which recognizes the contingency of our confidence without denying its legitimacy, must undermine the attractiveness of that project.

Bibliography

Adler, Jonathan. 1981. 'Skepticism and universalizability', *Journal of Philosophy*, 78, pp.143–56.

Annas, Julia and Barnes, Jonathan (eds). 1985. *The Modes of Scepticism: Ancient Texts and Modern Interpretations*. Cambridge: Cambridge University Press.

Ayer, A.J. (ed.) 1959. *Logical Positivism*. London: Allen & Unwin.

Barker, Stephen and Beauchamp, Thomas (eds). 1976. *Thomas Reid: Critical Interpretations*. Philadelphia: Philosophical Monographs.

Barnes, Jonathan. 1982. 'The beliefs of a pyrrhonist', *Proceedings of the Cambridge Philological Society*, 29, pp.1–29.

Barnes, Jonathan. 1983. 'Ancient scepticism and causation', in Burnyeat (ed.) 1983, pp.149–203.

BonJour, L. 1980. 'Externalist theories of empirical knowledge', *Midwest Studies in Philosophy*, v, pp.53–73.

Brown, Harold. 1988. 'Normative epistemology and naturalized epistemology', in *Inquiry*, 31, pp.53–78.

Brueckner, Anthony. 1984. 'Epistemic universalizability principles', *Philosophical Studies*, 46, pp.297–305.

Brueckner, Anthony. 1985. 'Losing track of the sceptic', *Analysis*, 45, pp.103–4.

Burnyeat, Myles. 1979. 'Conflicting appearances', *Proceedings of the British Academy*, LXV, pp.69–111.

Burnyeat, Myles. 1980. 'Can the sceptic live his scepticism?', in Schofield *et al.* (eds) 1980, pp.20–53, reprinted in Burnyeat (ed.) 1983, pp.117–48. References to 1983 reprint.

Burnyeat, Myles. 1982. 'Idealism and Greek Philosophy. What Descartes saw and Berkeley missed', *Philosophical Review*, 90, pp.3–40.

Burnyeat, Myles (ed). 1983. *The Skeptical Tradition*. Berkeley and Los Angeles: University of California Press.

Burnyeat, Myles. 1984. 'The sceptic in his place and time', in Rorty *et al.* (eds) 1984, pp.225–54.

Capaldi, Nicholas. 1975. *David Hume*. Boston: Twayne.

Carnap, Rudolf. 1937. *The Logical Syntax of Language*. London: Routledge & Kegan Paul.

Carnap, Rudolf. 1956. *Meaning and Necessity* (2nd edition). Chicago: University of Chicago Press.

Carnap, Rudolf. 1967. *The Logical Structure of the World and Pseudo-Problems in Philosophy.* Berkeley and Los Angeles: University of California Press.

Cavell, Stanley. 1979. *The Claim of Reason.* Oxford: Oxford University Press.

Chappell, V.C. (ed.). 1966. *Hume.* London: Macmillan.

Clarke, Thompson. 1972. 'The legacy of skepticism', in *Journal of Philosophy*, 69, pp.754–69.

Code, Lorraine. 1983. *'Father and Son:* A case study in epistemic responsibility'. *Monist,* 66, pp.268–82.

Craig, E.J. 1986–7. 'The practical explication of knowledge', *Proceedings of the Aristotelian Society*, 87, pp.211–26.

Craig, E.J. 1987. *The Mind of God and the Works of Man.* Oxford: Oxford University Press.

Curley, E.M. 1978. *Descartes Against the Skeptics.* Oxford: Blackwell.

Dancy, Jonathan. 1985. *Introduction to Contemporary Epistemology.* Oxford: Blackwell.

Davidson, Donald. 1986. 'A coherence theory of truth and knowledge', Lepore (ed.) 1986, pp.307–19.

Descartes, René. c1628. *Rules for the Direction of the Mind,* trans. in Descartes 1985, vol.1, pp.7–78.

Descartes, René. 1637. *Discourse on the Method,* trans. in Descartes 1985, vol.1, pp.111–51.

Descartes, René. 1637. *Optics,* trans. in Descartes 1985, vol.1, pp.152–75.

Descartes, René. 1641. *Meditations on First Philosophy,* trans. with *Objections and Replies* in Descartes 1985, volume 2, pp.1–397.

Descartes, René. 1648. *Descartes' Conversation with Burman,* trans. by John Cottingham. Oxford: Clarendon Press, 1976.

Descartes, René. 1970. *Descartes: Philosophical Letters,* trans. by Anthony Kenny. Oxford: Clarendon Press.

Descartes, René. 1985. *The Philosophical Writings of Descartes,* trans. by John Cottingham *et al.* (2 volumes). Cambridge: Cambridge University Press.

Dewey, John. 1929. *The Quest for Certainty: a Study of the Relation of Knowledge and Action.* New York: Minton, Balch.

Doyle, James F. (ed.) 1973. *Educational Judgements.* London: Routledge & Kegan Paul.

Duggan, Timothy. 1984. 'Thomas Reid on memory, prescience and freedom', in Hope (ed.) 1984, pp.32–46.

Dworkin, Gerald. 1988. *The Theory and Practice of Autonomy.* Cambridge: Cambridge University Press.

Ferreira, M. Jaime. 1986. *Scepticism and Reasonable Doubt.* Oxford: Clarendon Press.

Finley, M.I. (ed.). 1981. *The Legacy of Greece.* Oxford: Oxford University Press.

Fogelin, Robert J. 1985. *Hume's Skepticism in the Treatise of Human Nature.* London: Routledge & Kegan Paul.

Frede, Michael. 1987. *Essays in Ancient Philosophy.* Oxford: Clarendon Press.

Bibliography

Gettier, E.L. 1963. 'Is justified true belief knowledge?', *Analysis*, 23, pp.121–3.
Gibson, Roger F. 1988. *Enlightened Empiricism*. Tampa: University of South Florida Press.
Goldman, Alvin. 1967. 'A causal theory of knowing', in *Journal of Philosophy*, 64, pp.355–72.
Goldman, Alvin. 1976. 'Discrimination and perceptual knowledge', *Journal of Philosophy*', 64, pp.771–99. Reprinted in Pappas and Swain (eds) 1978, pp.120–45.
Goldman, Alvin. 1980. 'The internalist conception of justification', *Midwest Studies in Philosophy*, v, pp.27–51.
Goldman, Alvin. 1986. *Epistemology and Cognition*. Cambridge Mass.: Harvard University Press.
Grayling, A.C. 1985. *The Refutation of Scepticism*. London: Duckworth.
Hahn, L. and Schilpp, Paul (eds). 1986. *The Philosophy of W.V. Quine*. La Salle Ill.: Open Court.
Hale, Bob. 1988. 'Epistemic universalizability', *Analysis*, 48, pp.78–84.
Harman, Gilbert. 1986. *Change in View*. Cambridge Mass.: MIT Press.
Hiley, David. 1988. *Philosophy in Question*. Chicago: Chicago University Press.
Honderich, Ted. 1988. *A Theory of Determinism*. Oxford: Clarendon Press.
Hookway, Christopher. 1985. *Peirce*. London: Routledge & Kegan Paul.
Hookway, Christopher. 1988. *Quine: Language Experience and Reality*. Cambridge: Polity Press.
Hookway, Christopher. 1989. 'The epicurean argument: determinism and scepticism', *Inquiry*, 32, pp.79–94.
Hookway, Christopher. 1990. 'Critical common-sensism and rational self-control'. *Nous*.
Hookway, Christopher. Forthcoming, Cambridge University Press. 'Fallibilism and objectivity: science and ethics', in *World, Mind and Value: Essays on the Moral Philosophy of Bernard Williams*, (eds) J. Altham and T.R. Harrison.
Hope,V. 1984. *Philosophers of the Scottish Enlightenment*. Edinburgh: Edinburgh University Press.
Hume, David. 1739–40. *A Treatise of Human Nature* (ed.) L.A. Selby-Bigge, 2nd edition. Oxford: Clarendon Press, 1978.
Hume, David. 1748. *An Enquiry concerning Human Understanding*, in *Enquiries concerning the Human Understanding and concerning the Principles of Morals* (ed.) L.A. Selby-Bigge, 2nd edition. Oxford: Clarendon Press, 1902.
Hume, David. 1779. *Dialogues concerning Natural Religion*. Indianapolis: Bobbs-Merrill, 1970.
Kahnman, Daniel, Slovic, Paul and Tversky Amos (eds). 1982. *Judgment under Certainty: Heuristics and Biases*. Cambridge: Cambridge University Press.
Kant, Immanuel. 1781 (1st edition) 1787 (2nd edition). *Immanuel Kant's Critique of Pure Reason* trans. N. Kemp Smith. London: Macmillan, 1961. ('A' indicates reference to first edition, 'B' reference to the second.)
Kant. Immanuel. 1783. *Prolegomena to any Future Metaphysics*, (ed.) Lewis White Beck. Indianapolis: Bobbs-Merrill, 1950.

Bibliography

Kirwan, Christopher. 1983. 'Augustine against the skeptics', in Burnyeat (ed.) 1983, pp.105–23.

Klein, Peter D. 1986. 'Radical interpretation and radical scepticism', in Lepore (ed.) 1986, pp.369–86.

Lehrer, Keith. 1971.'Why not scepticism?'. *The Philosophical Forum*, 2, pp.283–98.

Lepore, Ernest (ed.). 1986. *Truth and Interpretation*. Oxford: Blackwell.

Lewis, David. 1973. *Counterfactuals*. Oxford: Blackwell.

Lucas, J.L. 1966. *Principles of Politics*. Oxford: Oxford University Press.

McGinn, Colin. 1986. 'Radical interpretation and epistemology', in Lepore (ed.) 1986, pp.356–68.

McGinn, Marie. 1989. *Sense and Certainty*. Oxford: Blackwell.

Millikan, Ruth. 1984. *Language, Thought and Other Biological Categories*. Cambridge Mass.: MIT Press.

Montaigne, Michel de. 1935. *The Essays of Michel de Montaigne*, trans. J. Zeitlin. New York: Knopf.

Moore, G.E. 1959. *Philosophical Papers*. London: Allen & Unwin.

Neurath, Otto. 1932–3. 'Protokollsätze', translated as 'Protocol Sentences' in Ayer (ed.) 1959, pp.199–208.

Norton, David Fate. 1982. *David Hume: Common Sense Moralist and Sceptical Metaphysician*. Princeton: Princeton University Press.

Nozick, Robert. 1981. *Philosophical Explanations*. Cambridge Mass.:Belknap Press.

Papineau, David. 1987. *Reality and Representation*. Oxford: Blackwell.

Pappas, George, and Swain, Marshall (eds). 1978. *Essays on Knowledge and Justification*. Ithaca: Cornell University Press.

Pascal, Blaise. 1958. *Pascal's Pensées*. New York: Dutton.

Peirce, Charles S. 1931–58. *Collected Papers of Charles Sanders Peirce*, ed. P. Weiss, C. Hartshorne and A. Burks. Cambridge Mass.: Harvard University Press. Referred to as 'CP': references give volume and paragraph.

Peirce, Charles Sanders. 1982– . *The Writings of Charles S. Peirce: a Chronological Edition*. Bloomington: Indiana University Press. Referred to as 'W'.

Penelhum, Terence. 1983. 'Skepticism and fideism', in Burnyeat (ed.) 1983, pp.287–318.

Peters, R.S. 1973. 'Freedom and the development of the free man', in Doyle (ed.) 1973, pp.119–42.

Pollock, J. 1987. *Contemporary Theories of Knowledge*. London: Hutchinson.

Popkin, Richard H. 1966. 'David Hume: his pyrrhonism and his critique of pyrrhonism', in Chappell (ed.) 1966, pp.53–98.

Popkin, Richard H. 1979. *The History of Scepticism from Erasmus to Spinoza*. Berkeley and Los Angeles: University of California Press.

Popper, Karl. 1972. *Objective Knowledge*. Oxford: Clarendon Press.

Putnam, Hilary. 1981. *Reason, Truth and History*. Cambridge: Cambridge University Press.

Putnam, Hilary. 1982. 'Why reason can't be naturalized', *Synthese*, 52, pp.3–23.

Quine, W.V.O. 1953. *From a Logical Point of View*. Cambridge Mass.: Harvard University Press.

Bibliography

Quine, W.V.O. 1969. *Ontological Relativity and Other Essays*. New York: Columbia University Press.

Quine, W.V.O. 1975. 'The nature of natural knowledge', in Guttenplan (ed.), 1975, pp.57–81.

Quine, W.V.O. 1981. *Theories and Things*. Cambridge Mass.: Harvard University Press.

Quine, W.V.O. 1986. 'Reply to Morton White', in Hahn and Schilpp (eds) 1986, pp.663–5.

Reid, Thomas. 1764. *An Inquiry into the Human Mind on the Principles of Common Sense*, reprinted in Reid 1872, vol.1, pp.93–211.

Reid, Thomas. 1785. *Essays on the Intellectual Powers of Man*, reprinted in Reid 1872, vol.1, pp.213–508.

Reid, Thomas. 1872. *The Works of Thomas Reid DD*. (ed.) Sir William Hamilton, 7th edition. Edinburgh: McClachlan and Stewart.

Rorty, Amelie (ed.). 1986. *Essays on Descartes' Meditations*. Berkeley: University of California Press.

Rorty, Richard. 1980. *Philosophy and the Mirror of Nature*. Oxford: Blackwell.

Rorty, Richard, Schneewind, J.B. and Skinner, Quentin (eds). 1984. *Philosophy in History*. Cambridge: Cambridge University Press.

Ross, Lee and Anderson, Craig. 1982. 'Shortcomings in the attribution process: On the origins and maintenance of erroneous social assessments,' in Kahnman *et al*. (eds) 1982.

Russell, B.A.W. 1948. *Human Knowledge: its Scope and Limits*. London: Allen & Unwin.

Scanlon, Thomas. 1972. 'A theory of freedom of expression', *Philosophy and Public Affairs*, 6, pp.204–26.

Schmitt, C.B. 1983. 'The rediscovery of ancient skepticism in modern times', in Burnyeat (ed.) 1983, pp.225–51.

Schofield, Malcolm, Burnyeat, Myles and Barnes, Jonathan (eds). 1980. *Doubt and Dogmatism: Studies in Hellenistic Epistemology*. Oxford: Clarendon Press.

Schouls, Peter, 1980. *The Imposition of Method: a Study of Descartes and Locke*. Oxford: Oxford University Press.

Sedley, David. 1983. 'The motivation of Greek scepticism', in Burnyeat (ed.) 1983, pp.9–29.

Sextus Empiricus. 1933–49. *Sextus Empiricus with an English Translation* trans. by R.G. Bury, 4 volumes. Cambridge Mass.: Harvard University Press, London: Heinemann. *Outlines of Pyrrhonism* referred to as 'PH', *Against the Mathematicians* referred to as 'M'. Partial translation of *Outlines of Pyrrhonism* in Annas and Barnes 1985.

Siegel, Harvey. 1980. 'Justification, discovery and the naturalizing of epistemology', *Philosophy of Science*, 51, pp.297–320.

Smith, Norman Kemp. 1905. 'The naturalism of Hume', *Mind*, xiv. pp.149–73, 335–47.

Smith, Norman Kemp. 1941. *The Philosophy of David Hume*. London: Macmillan.

Stough, Charlotte. 1969. *Greek Skepticism: a Study in Epistemology*. Berkeley: University of California Press.

Strawson, Galen. 1986. *Freedom and Belief.* Oxford: Oxford University Press.
Strawson, P.F. 1985. *Skepticism and Naturalism: Some Varieties.* London: Methuen.
Striker, Gisela. 1983. 'The ten tropes of Aenesidemus', in Burnyeat (ed.) 1983, pp.95–115.
Stroud, Barry. 1977. *Hume.* London: Routledge & Kegan Paul.
Stroud, Barry. 1984. *The Significance of Philosophical Scepticism.* Oxford: Oxford University Press.
Tebaldi, David. 1976. 'Thomas Reid's refutation of the argument from illusion', in Barker and Beauchamp (eds) 1976, pp.25–34.
Tillotson, John. 1728. *Works,* 9th edition. London: J. Round.
Unger, Peter. 1971. 'A defense of skepticism', *Philosophical Review,* 80, pp.198–218.
Vernier, Paul. 1976. 'Thomas Reid on the foundations of knowledge and his answer to skepticism', in Barker and Beauchamp (eds) 1976, pp.14–24.
Walker, Ralph. 1983. 'Gassendi and skepticism', in Burnyeat (ed.) 1983, pp.319–36.
Wilkins, John. 1675. *Of the Principles and Duties of Natural Religion.* 7th edition, 1715. London: R. Bonwicke.
Williams, Bernard. 1973. *Problems of the Self.* Cambridge: Cambridge University Press.
Williams, Bernard. 1978. *Descartes: the Project of Pure Enquiry.* Harmondsworth: Penguin.
Williams, Bernard. 1981. 'Philosophy', in Finley (ed.) 1981, pp.202–55.
Williams, Bernard. 1985. *Ethics and the Limits of Philosophy.* London: Fontana Press/Collins.
Williams, Michael. 1986. 'Descartes and the metaphysics of doubt', in Rorty (ed.) 1986, pp.117–39.
Williams, Michael. 1988a. 'Scepticism without theory'. *Review of Metaphysics,* 41, pp.547–88.
Williams, Michael. 1988b. 'Scepticism and charity', in *Ratio (New Series),* 1, pp.176–94.
Wilson, Margaret. 1978. *Descartes.* London: Routledge & Kegan Paul.
Wittgenstein, Ludwig. 1958. *The Blue and Brown Books.* Oxford: Blackwell.
Wittgenstein, Ludwig. 1967. *Zettel.* Oxford: Blackwell.
Wittgenstein, Ludwig. 1977. *On Certainty.* Oxford: Blackwell.
Wolff, Robert Paul. 1970. *In Defense of Anarchism.* New York: Harper and Row.
Woolhouse, R.S. 1988. *The Empiricists* (A History of Western Philosophy, vol.5). Oxford: Oxford University Press.
Wright, Crispin. 1985. 'Facts and certainty'. *Proceedings of the British Academy,* LXXI, pp.429–72.
Yolton, John. 1984. *Perceptual Acquaintance from Descartes to Reid.* Oxford: Blackwell.

Index

247

cognitive community 59, 185–7,
187–8, 190–1, 202–3, 206, 228–9
coherentism 187
common sense 37–40, 41, 44, 47–8,
62, 108–18, 188; critical
commonsensism 112, 129; and
pyrrhonism 32–3
confidence 153, 158–60, 166, 171–2,
190; fragility of 235, 240; and self
control 77, 81, 235–6; varieties of
234–5
constructive scepticism *see* mitigated
scepticism
Craig, E.J. 83, 199
criterion 5, 9–11, 15, 22, 23, 26, 35,
44, 66, 115, 120
Curley, E.M. 42

Dancy, Jonathan 169–70
Davidson, Donald 225–30
decision 238–40
deductive closure 210
Descartes, René 131, 132, 136–7,
144, 173, 184–5, 240;
foundationalism 45–6, 48; Reid's
criticisms of 108, 112–16;
sceptical arguments 45–8, 56–8,
158–9, 178; strategy 41–4, 45–8,
58, 77–8, 80–1; *see also*
Cartesican circle, science:
Cartesian
determinism *see* epicurean argument
Dewey, John 172
Diogenes 16,
dogma 4–5, 6, 11–15, 37, 39
dream argument 48–54, 61–2, 70,
121, 173–8, 231; in the *Discourse
on Method* 50, 52; limits to dream
scepticism 53; in the *Meditations*
49–54; in Sextus Empiricus 49;
and transparency of mind 64–5, 83
Dworkin, Gerald 146–7

empiricism *see* medicine
Epicurean argument 154–8, 159
epochē 5
Erasmus 35
error 172

evil demon 48, 53, 54–7, 57–8, 67,
72–3, 156, 216–17
external world 52, 115, 118, 122,
166–7; and Hume 92–3, 94–9;
and Pyrrhonism 2, 33–4, 45, 62–3;
see also brain-in-a-vat, dream
argument

fallibilism 38, 59–61, 69, 76–7
Ferreira, M. Jaime 37, 114
first-person questions 184, 220–2
Fogelin, Robert 86–7
foundationalism 187; in Descartes
42, 44, 45–6, 58–9, 66, 68, 75–8;
in Reid 108, 111, 114, 119; two
versions of 68–70; in Wittgenstein
126–7; *see also* infinite regress
Frede, Michael 13, 28–30
freedom of the will: parallels with
problem of scepticism 132, 143–5,
215–16, 218; *see also* epicurean
argument

Galileo 37, 60
Gassendi, Pierre 37–8, 41–3, 44, 56,
59
generality of sceptical challenges
56–7, 164–6, 175–6
Gettier, Edmund 192–3
Gibson Roger 125, 219
God 42–3, 52, 54–5, 60, 66–7, 74,
75–6, 83, 116–17
Goldman, Alvin 142, 183, 193, 194,
216
Gosse, Philip 140–2, 150
Grayling, Anthony 119

Hale, Bob 170–1
Harman Gilbert 124, 141–2, 187–8
Hiley, David 23, 34
Hobbes, Thomas 56
Honderich, Ted 148, 154–8
Hume, David 36, 39, 108, 111, 131,
137, 144, 216; on causation 91–2;
criticisms of Pyrrhonism 3, 6, 24;
and the false philosophy 90, 96–9;
naturalism of 86–9, 104, 124; as a
pyrrhonist 86–9, 94, 99–100,

Index

106–7, 144; Reid's criticisms 112–13, 115–16; theory of mind 90–1; and the vulgar philosophy 90, 94–6

imagination 78, 92–3, 95–6, 101, 102
individualist approaches to epistemology 45–6, 48, 59, 185–6; *see also* cognitive community
induction 159, 163, 165, 167, 181–2, 224
infinite regress 10–11, 44, 66, 69, 127, 149; Reid on 108–9
inquiries 22–3, 135–7, 172, 178–83, 199–200, 202; as activities 137–40; practical benefits of 101–4; and responsibility 140–3; restricted 230–2; and target of scepticism 143–7, 163–8; unrestricted 232–3; varieties of 81, 117–18, 151–3
insulation 33, 36, 59, 61–2, 107, 130–1, 144
internal and external questions 123, 238–9
internalist and externalist theories of justification 183–5, 186, 188, 212
irresistibility 105, 108, 110–11, 114, 116, 119–20, 122, 153

justified belief 144, 170–1, 185, 191; as a target for scepticism 135–6

Kant, Immanuel 118–22, 127, 177; criticism of Reid 118
Kemp Smith, Norman 86
Kirwan, Christopher 35
Klein, Peter 225
knowledge 125–6, 144, 170–1, 173–6, 184–5; contagious character of 203; context relativity 202–4, 213–14; recent themes in discussion of 192–5; as target for scepticism 133–5, 207–9; *see also* *P*-claims, *Q*-claims, tracking, knowledge-inference
knowledge-inference 198; role in learning from testimony 199,

201–4, 204–6; role in first person cases, 204–7

Lehrer, Keith 57
Lewis, David 211
local versus global evaluations 219–24, 228, 237–8
Locke, John 91
Lucas, John 146
Luther, Martin 35–6

McGinn, Colin 225
McGinn, Marie 128, 175–6
medicine: Pyrrhonist medicine 28–32; schools of Greek medicine 27–32
Mersenne, Marin 37–8, 42, 55
metaphysical doubt 54–6, 61–2, 72–3; as unreal 59, 61, 112, 130–1
methodism *see* medicine
methodological inquiry 70, 75
Millikan, Ruth 216
mitigated scepticism 37–9, 41; Hume 94, 100–4
modes 5, 7–11, 23, 32, 56, 62; of Aenesidemus 5, 7–11, 166; of Agrippa 10–11, 44–5, 66, 93–4, 166, 187; Hume on modes 90
Montaigne, Michel de 35, 41–2
Moore, G.E. 125, 176

naturalism 39, 131; circularity objection 216–18; Hume's 86–9, 104, 124; normativity objection 124, 218–22, 222–3; Quine's 124, 216–20, 222–4, 236–8, 240
Nazianzen, Gregory 35
Neurath's ship 60, 123, 188, 222–4, 239
neutralism 111–12, 124–5
Newton, Isaac 109, 112, 118, 119
Norton, David Fate 86
Nozick, Robert 194–5, 210–14

Papineau, David 216
Para du Phanjas, L'Abbé François 41
Pascal, Blaise 39
P-claims 195–8, 209, 213

249